The
Butler's Child

The
Butler's Child

An Autobiography

Lewis M. Steel

with Beau Friedlander

Thomas Dunne Books
St. Martin's Press
New York

THOMAS DUNNE BOOKS.
An imprint of St. Martin's Press.

www.thomasdunnebooks.com
www.stmartins.com

Library of Congress Cataloging-in-Publication Data

Names: Steel, Lewis M., 1937– author. | Friedlander, Beau, author.
Title: The butler's child : an autobiography / by Lewis M. Steel
   with Beau Friedlander
Description: New York : Thomas Dunne Books/St. Martin's
   Press, 2016.
Identifiers: LCCN 2015051267| ISBN 9781250073006
   (hardcover) | ISBN 9781466884984 (e-book)
Subjects: LCSH: Steel, Lewis M., 1937– | Civil rights
   lawyers—New York (State)—New York—Biography. | Labor
   lawyers—New York (State)—New York—Biography. | Civil
   rights movement—United States—History—20th century. |
   BISAC: BIOGRAPHY & AUTOBIOGRAPHY / Lawyers &
   Judges. | LAW / Civil Rights.
Classification: LCC KF373.S688 A3 2016 | DDC 340.092—dc23
LC record available at http://lccn.loc.gov/2015051267

Our books may be purchased in bulk for promotional, educational,
or business use. Please contact your local bookseller or the Macmillan
Corporate and Premium Sales Department at 1-800-221-7945,
extension 5442, or by e-mail at MacmillanSpecialMarkets@
macmillan.com.

First Edition: June 2016

10 9 8 7 6 5 4 3 2 1

Dedicated to the memory of

Bill Rutherford
whose caring caused me to see with clearer eyes

and
Robert L. Carter
my teacher, mentor, and lifelong friend

And to
Kitty Muldoon Steel
who has made my life whole
and this book possible

Contents

Introduction

Shortly after Jack Warner, cofounder of Warner Bros. Studios, double-crossed his brothers, Harry and my grandfather Major, in May 1956 by secretly arranging to buy back his Warner Bros. stock and take over as president, Harry had a heart attack and then a stroke, from which he never recovered. Harry died on July 25, 1958, in California. His wife, Rea, bitterly said, "Harry didn't die. Jack killed him." After Harry's funeral in Los Angeles, Major and Jack shared a limo. True to his vow, Major didn't talk to his brother. For me, back in New York, life went on as if nothing had happened. I had seen my granduncle Harry only a few times, once in California when Major and my grandmother Bessie had visited his ranch, where he kept his stable of racehorses, and on another occasion in New York City. I worked that summer as a cub reporter on the weekly newspaper the *Riverdale Press,* and played tennis at Major's Westchester country club.

There was little in my life—almost totally detached from the California Warners—that reminded me I was part of a motion picture family. My dad operated a drive-in theater in suburban Westchester County and owned a theater in Jacksonville, Florida, but that was nothing compared to the Warner empire.

Yes, I remained a beneficiary of the wealth spun off by Grandma Bessie. As a result my wife, Kitty, and I moved into our Central Park West apartment in 1966. But when it came to financial backing I had small change compared with two of Harry's grandchildren, Warner and Linda LeRoy. My cousin Warner married and moved into the fabulous Dakota co-op a few blocks north of us, but in reality a world away. He also purchased an East Side movie house, with the thought that he could turn it into a playhouse where he could produce and direct shows. Instead Warner decided to become a restaurateur and turned the theater into a gorgeous restaurant, Maxwell's Plum, with a spectacular Tiffany-glass ceiling, that became the talk of the town. When Kitty and I wanted a special dinner, we used our connection to get a prime table. But that was all. Warner was a mover and a shaker, and I was becoming a civil rights lawyer, helping those who moved and shook only when their lives became intolerable. We would also see Linda from time to time at Grandma Bessie's with her husband, Mort Janklow, who became one of the city's most-sought-after literary agents. From Linda we would hear a few pieces of gossip, like the time her granduncle Jack, whose eyesight was apparently failing, tried to pick her up at a social event. "Uncle Jack," Linda had to say, "I'm your niece." Jack stories, of course, shocked no one. We had heard that he had disinherited his son, Jack Junior, falsely accusing him of making a play for his fading-actress stepmother. Quite an evil man, that Jack Warner, I thought. Fortunately, however, I had nothing to do with him.

But then I did. My brother, John, who kept up some contacts with the Warner family, was happy to inform me after we moved into our apartment that Jack owned an apartment on Fifth Avenue, right across Central Park from us. High up in the tower of an architectural gem, the Sherry-Netherland Hotel, there he was, his picture windows, sparkling in the evening sun, looking down on us. In my imagination Jack was living like royalty, and I was always in his sights. I was sure Jack—who could not even identify his grandniece who had grown up around him— had no idea who I was and couldn't have cared less if he had. But there he was, in his aerie, looking down on me, reminding me that I was a Warner too, although neither in name nor in family connections. Even when Jack died in 1978, more than ten years after my grandfather Major passed away and eight years after Bessie died, I still saw him there, in my mind's eye, looking down, a ghostlike presence who had rained evil on his own family, reminding me of the two worlds I lived in—a heritage of upper-class privilege and my current life as a civil rights lawyer, putting all my Warner connections behind me.

Fifty-three years ago I made the decision to join the legal staff of the National Association for the Advancement of Colored People, a small band of like-minded lawyers dedicated to the fight for racial equality that was being waged in our nation's courtrooms. Later, in private practice with progressive—and some would say radical—attorneys, I continued the struggle. The cast of characters sometimes changed from decade to decade. There are too many to name here, but they comprise every combination of race, religion, and gender. Many have since passed away. Some have told their stories; others have not. For those who didn't, the loss is ours. The stories about what we lawyers tried to accomplish and what we actually achieved are important. Embedded in our efforts, they go a long way toward telling how we got where we are today in a country that is still racially divided. Because so many of these stories are being lost, it has become increasingly urgent for me to tell them as I seek to unravel that age-old question: How did I get involved in the first place?

To answer that question, this memoir takes me back to my childhood, when I first began to question the glimmers of racism that intruded upon my life. At the same time, under pressure from African Americans coming home from the battlefields of World War II, where they fought against racist ideologies, and supported by a growing cadre of idealistic white as well as black youth, the Movement—led principally by Martin Luther King, Jr., and his organization, the Southern Christian Leadership Conference (SCLC), and the Student Non-Violent Coordinating Committee (SNCC) as well as the National Association for the Advancement of Colored People (NAACP)—confronted the outrages of Jim Crow in the South. Watching on television the killings and assaults they endured pushed the issue of racism into my consciousness. The mix was electric. It led me, right after graduating law school in 1963, straight to the office of the NAACP.

Working under NAACP general counsel Robert L. Carter, who had won twenty-one of twenty-two cases in the Unites States Supreme Court, I learned firsthand what an arduous task it was to use the legal system to enforce the Movement's hardest-won victories and confront the segregation and discrimination that permeated every aspect of American life, in the North as well as the South. Taking on the hardest of cases, I knew the highs of winning and the lows of losing when courts of law turned their backs on racial inequality. Frustrated and angry, I vented my feelings in an article titled "Nine Men in Black Who Think White," which was published in the *New York Times Magazine* in October 1968, after Martin Luther King, Jr., and Robert F. Kennedy were assassinated. Written with Robert Carter's approval, it got me fired. In response Carter and the entire legal staff resigned, deeply disturbed that the NAACP, which was dedicated to fighting racism in all its forms, would come to the defense of a Supreme Court that had been called out for retreating from the opening it had helped to create in Chief Justice Earl Warren's fine 1954 opinion in *Brown v. Board of Education*. The shock I experienced when the NAACP cast me off, and the fallout with the staff resigning despite our large and important caseload, was indescribable. Aware of the continuing need for Movement lawyers, however, I refused to be sidetracked and have practiced my craft in every conceivable forum from the Supreme Court to the state criminal courts, where I have defended innocent African Americans falsely accused of murdering whites.

To make sense of my feelings, which have led to my more than fifty years of civil rights work (which continues to this day), I have thought back to the Warner family from which I came, to the advantages being white conferred on me, and to the death of our family butler, William Rutherford, the year before I was fired.

Bill was black, and had worked for my family since I was a little boy on the gentleman's farm in Hendersonville, North Carolina, that belonged to my grandfather, Albert Warner. Bill was a very special person who had given me love, care, and affection. And while it was not clear back then, that was the relationship that sent me on my path.

My bond to Bob Carter, a relationship that grew and deepened till the day he died in 2012, helped me develop the clarity afforded by distance. He, Kitty, and I spent many hours together, both in New York and on vacation. We talked about everything, and his feelings about race and prejudice were never more than a moment away from any conversation. I learned Bob was angry too. Unlike my anger, however, his sprang from facing the outrages of a hostile white world. As a result Bob felt that very few whites knew anything about the searing pain that racism caused. Our talks helped me better understand how black men often feel in America. I was angry and frustrated that we were not making the progress I'd hoped for when I joined the NAACP. But I was white, fighting an enemy that on a fundamental level included myself. Bob was equally frustrated and angry about how progress in the courts had come to a halt, and about the terrible poverty and lack of educational and job opportunities that afflicted African Americans.

I also saw Bob's caring side, and how he could learn to trust a white man like me. And that experience of our endless conversations helped me to understand how many whites could be blind to their own prejudice, seeing themselves instead as being fair. Also, over the years, in a son-to-a-father way, I came to love Bob, and that helped illuminate my formative relationship with Bill Rutherford, our family butler.

At this point in my life, I am able to tell the story of why a white man who grew up wealthy might choose to spend most of his life working to advance civil rights law, representing clients and handling cases against the rich and the powerful. Another crucial undertaking here is figuring out what my work has meant and continues to mean within the framework of post-Movement civil rights enforcement. The personal conflicts caused by having so much while representing clients who couldn't get a fair trial or sought in vain to get the smallest piece of the pie that was my birthright are always there as considerations, but what drove me to write this book is deeper: I wanted to share my experience so that others could see that they can make a difference, no matter where they're from or what their background.

1
Attica

A flash came across the morning news on September 9, 1971, that a riot had broken out at Attica, an upstate New York penitentiary. The inmates had taken over a part of the prison and were holding some guards as hostages. I immediately thought of my client Tony Maynard, who was incarcerated there. Tony had been convicted of manslaughter, but I was convinced he was innocent and was determined to exonerate him. Almost simultaneously the phone rang. It was Dotty Stoub from the National Lawyers Guild.

A postbreakfast scuffle and a defective bolt in a central gate at Attica had literally opened the doors to a full-spectrum revolt. Buildings were set on fire, and forty-two prison employees were taken hostage.

One guard was in extremely critical condition. About a thousand of the more than two thousand inmates housed in the severely overcrowded prison had seized a central hub called "Times Square" and occupied D yard—one of four large exercise areas at the center of the medieval-looking walled fortress. Inmates waved baseball bats. They turned prison blankets into ponchos, undershirts into do-rags and kaffiyehs. They thrust fists into the air and shouted "Black Power!" while others dug trenches and huddled to prepare for battle. Leaders emerged and began issuing demands to the prison administration. A few prisoners roamed the yard wearing football helmets. It was chaos.

I was sitting in my kitchen when Dotty called. My kids had just finished breakfast. There was a cup of coffee in front of me. I had recent experience with prison uprisings in the New York State system. Dotty told me what she knew about the situation at Attica, which wasn't much. The inmates were asking for observers, and a prison activist, probably someone from Youth Against War and Fascism (YAWF), had called the guild. And I was the right person to go. I had spent my entire career becoming the right person to go. A thirty-four-year-old former NAACP trial lawyer, I had been the protégé of the legendary civil rights attorney Robert L. Carter. In fact I had just started at the NAACP when Carter was working on *Gaynor v. Rockefeller*, an employment-discrimination class-action suit brought against New York's then-governor Nelson Rockefeller, who, it turned out, would be the only person with the authority to end the crisis at Attica. In addition, four months earlier I had helped represent the Auburn Six, a group of prisoners from the Auburn Correctional Facility who were awaiting trial for doing more or less the same thing that was going on at Attica, only in that case no prison employees were harmed.

While Dotty was talking, my double life struck me. I already knew I was going, and I could see it in my mind's eye. The prison yard at Attica would be filled with desperate men who faced consequences from the state that beggared the imagination. And the prisoners' only real hope was that the activists who were summoned to be on the observers' committee might somehow do something to avert bloodshed. Immediately the old familiar conflicts stared back at me. The facts were anything but simple. I had three little kids and my wife, Kitty, and we were concerned that I might be putting myself in harm's way.

With help from my grandmother Bessie Warner, Kitty and I had it pretty good. We enjoyed some distance from the overwrought fears that 1970s New York City conjured for many. Crime was on the rise. There were muggings in Central Park and in the streets and subways late at night. The anger in black and Spanish Harlem was very real, but we lived where the police created islands of safety, and Central Park West was a well-patrolled strip of fine-looking apartment buildings, houses of worship, schools, and the Museum of Natural History. Our building had a doorman and a floor captain. We even had a housekeeper to protect us from the lesser evil of a messy apartment and to help with our children. I was just starting out at the NAACP when we bought the place, and I didn't make much money—nowhere near what it cost to live the way we did. But I had no issue with getting help from my family. My dad had gotten a lot of help over the years from my grandmother, and it just seemed to be the way we did things. Though I made a point of not being as showy as my parents, that's not to say that the highly polished, mostly Jewish 55 Central Park West wasn't a nice place to live. The point for me was that it didn't scream wealth and power. I was a civil rights lawyer, so appearances mattered. Our building was about a block from a giant construction site that was slowly becoming Lincoln Center. To many of the people I grew up with, it was still just around the corner from overcrowded, cut-up brownstones converted into deteriorating tenements and condemned buildings to the north of Hell's Kitchen. To me, however, it was just what I was looking for: lots of room and on the liberal West Side.

New York was in free fall, the decades-long aftermath of blockbusting, white flight, and urban blight writ large everywhere on graffiti-covered subway cars, smut-touting marquees lining Times Square, and block after block in poor minority neighborhoods with boarded-up buildings. Property values guttered. Some landlords set fire to buildings to get the insurance money or opened vacant apartments to a squatter army of heroin addicts and prostitutes to drive renters away, sometimes right down the block from where we lived. The city was on the brink of bankruptcy. So there was something edgy about even our area, but it let me live in a way that resembled what I was used to from childhood on the East Side, where the upper classes lived. It was my Park Avenue.

I made an all-cash offer for the apartment, which was generally considered a green light for co-op board approval. The broker assured me we'd get a rubber stamp, but when that didn't happen there was some back-and-forth until the broker told me that we wouldn't be approved until the co-op board saw a picture of my wife. I was pretty sure it was a race thing. I worked at the NAACP, and my wife could well have been black. I produced a picture of my very Irish Catholic wife, and we got in, but I was painfully aware of the contradiction of being a NAACP lawyer who lived in a building that apparently wouldn't allow blacks to live there. Soon after moving in, I got a confirmation of sorts. The building had rules about which workers for apartment owners could use the passenger elevators and which had to ride the service elevators that were used for deliveries and to take out the trash. Just like in the South, a person's color was the key.

"That's the way it's always been," the manager told me.

The board's misgivings about approving a lawyer from the NAACP were not entirely frivolous. I grew up with a black butler and his wife, who served as our cook and maid, and so I was very aware of the ways racial prerogatives affect domestic workers. Quickly I learned that our housekeeper, Joyce McKenzie, who came from Jamaica, had to take the service elevator to our apartment. I was furious.

"As far as it goes with our housekeeper," I told the manager, "that policy is over right now. As for the rest of the building, I'll give you a week."

The building gave in.

The outcome made me feel better about living there, even though I sensed there could be some resentment among my neighbors. But pretty much every all-white co-op in New York at that time had similar explicit or implicit rules.

Almost immediately after the inmates took control of D yard, leaders emerged. They quickly released a statement larded with the stilted rhetoric of 1960s radicalism, "The incident that has erupted here at Attica is not a result of the dastardly bushwhacking of the two prisoners on Sept. 8, 1971," the demands began, making reference to a brutal disciplinary action the day before, "but of the unmitigated oppression wrought by the racist administration network of the prison, throughout the year. WE are MEN! We are not beasts and do not intend to be beaten or driven as such. The entire prison populace has set forth to change forever the ruthless brutalization and disregard for the lives of the prisoners here and throughout the United States. What has happened here is but the sound before the fury of those who are oppressed."

Five demands were made, and fifteen "practical proposals." Among the demands was turning Attica into a federal prison and assuring that the prison would be rebuilt by inmates at minimum wage—not the slave labor that they were protesting. The demands also included, "complete amnesty, meaning freedom from any physical, mental, and legal reprisals," and also "speedy and safe transportation out of confinement, to a non-imperialistic country," which to mainstream America could only sound like self-parody. The final demand was for an observers' committee. The leadership provided a list of people they wanted there—including the famed radical lawyer Bill Kunstler, Tom Wicker from the *New York Times*, and Bobby Seale of the Black Panther Party. They also invited others who wanted to be there or who could be useful. I was in the latter category.

I left for Attica wearing a tan polyester summer suit, with my banged-up leather briefcase holding some work papers, a change of underwear, and a few basic toiletries. I had mutton-chop sideburns and wore horn-rimmed glasses. My hair was black and bushy. I walked past the doorman and the pretty flower arrangement in our lobby to hail a cab for LaGuardia Airport, where a plane would take me to Buffalo. It was sunny and warm out—almost fall.

Among the prisoners at Attica was my client Tony Maynard. There was also Sam Melville, a young man from the Weather Underground, a radical organization that had split away from the Students for a Democratic Society (SDS) to, it said, bring the Vietnam War home to America. He was a client of my partner, Henry diSuvero. Tony being there was definitely a motivating factor for me, but I'm not sure I knew Sam was there until I saw him in D yard.

Maynard had been wrongfully accused of a 1967 shotgun killing in Greenwich Village, convicted of manslaughter, and sentenced to ten to twenty years. Using a shotgun as the murder weapon was completely out of character for this stylish man with an artist's sensibility. The authors James Baldwin and William Styron, who knew Tony, and the editorial chairman and columnist of the then liberal *New York Post*, James Wechsler, had made a considerable amount of noise about the wrongful conviction, but it didn't matter. As I saw it, the "crime" Tony committed was being black. Making matters worse, Tony had a beautiful white wife, and the two of them had spent enough time making the scene in Greenwich Village to become a target. As Baldwin would later tell me, more than being black, Tony became a target because he was "arrogant and didn't know his place."

I agreed with Baldwin. It certainly didn't help that Tony had what you might call an attitude problem, but fighting the prevailing winds of racial prejudice in the 1960s criminal court system was more often than not impossible.

I had tried Tony's murder case, and I bonded with him during the long days we spent together and the discussions on weekends and after court. When Dotty said "Attica," I heard "Tony Maynard." He was transferred there from the Green Haven Correctional Facility, where I had recently visited him in what was called "the Hole." He was disciplined a lot, and was not what one might call a model prisoner. Well spoken, smart, unbending, and rebellious, Tony had all the qualities a prison guard would be unlikely to tolerate. He would make a tempting target when authorities put down the rebellion, which I assumed would happen—maybe even before I could get there.

Tony was wearing a tattered tailored suit—he refused to wear prison clothes—when I caught sight of him in D yard, which we entered with the state corrections commissioner, Russell B. Oswald, to negotiate with the leadership. Tony looked pretty out of place, more like one of the observers than a participant among the thousand or so black, Latino, and white convicts milling around D yard preparing to defend their revolution.

Tony, whose presence made me feel more secure in the chaos of the yard, said, "Once the hacks are back in control, you can forget racial harmony," adding, "Nothing good can come of this." Surveying his fellow prisoners waving homemade flags and chanting "Black Power!" he added contemptuously: "They're all so blind. Today they're kings. They think the world will listen. The TV cameras and negotiations add to the illusion. But no one really cares what happens to a bunch of convicts and the clock-punchers who run an asylum run amok. We're all less than nothing to the people that matter."

I shared Tony's ambivalence about the sort of canned big-talk-but-often-empty radical rhetoric that had emerged from the heyday of the civil rights movement and migrated into the prisons.

Martin Luther King, Jr., once said, "A riot is the language of the unheard." What happened at Attica came close to King's definition. Before they rampaged through the prison, the inmates were an unheard group of people who now had access to the outside world. No one listened to them or even gave them a name. To the all-white guards who controlled their lives, their skin color denoted them as subhuman beings. Their only strength came from communication. That's why what happened at Attica was different from a riot. It was an uprising. But unlike the few uprisings that have succeeded, there was no way the prisoners would be able to hold on to the territory they had taken, and failure appeared to be a given. To prevent the stranglehold the authorities had on the prisoners who were trapped in the yard they had seized from turning into a bloodbath, only the observers could open a dialogue, but the odds of either side listening were slim. That's where things stood. Blacks were fed up. Jim Crow and other forms of apartheid like school segregation were now against the letter of the law, but still the norm all over the country and held in place by force and more passive forms of economic domination. Whites also were angry about the threat of black demands for a share of what they saw as their jobs, and the right to move into their neighborhoods and go to their schools. There was a lot of fear all around, but almost no willingness— or perhaps better, capacity—to occupy the gray area where race issues could evolve and change. As a not-quite-radical, not-quite-mainstream civil rights lawyer, I sensed how difficult it would be to find that gray area in the Attica yard.

The other prisoner I knew about at Attica was Sam Melville. As a white man, he was definitely in the minority there. Because he was my partner's client, Sam sought me out in D yard. He had been convicted for a string of highly publicized Weather Underground bombings that took place in 1969.

When Melville saw me, he talked his way through the phalanx of prisoners guarding the negotiators.

"They're going to come looking for me," Sam said, in a matter-of-fact way. "And I'll be here. I'm a dead man."

"Is there anything I can do?" I asked.

He shook his head. We exchanged a few words, shook hands, and he disappeared back into the crowd.

After it was all over, there were reports that some of the prisoners who led the rebellion were killed long after authorities regained control of the facility. Sam Melville was one of the people mentioned on that list, though he was not part of the leadership. After retaking the prison, state spin doctors said that Melville got shot while trying to explode a fifty-gallon fuel tank. They said he had four Molotov cocktails.

It made no sense. The uprising was over. It would have been suicide, and I saw no inkling that Melville had that kind of ending in mind. To the contrary, the Weathermen issued warnings and planned their bombings to avoid hurting anyone.

Tony Maynard and Sam Melville were both right. The fact that there was a soon-to-be-dead prison guard, and forty-two correction officers and workers—all of them white—being held hostage by prisoners who were predominantly black and Puerto Rican was the best indicator of how the situation at Attica was going to end. It didn't matter that the only thing most prisoners had to do with the takeover was proximity. It didn't matter that prisoners were often confined to their cells for days on end and were only allowed one shower per week, or that they had to make a roll of toilet paper last for a month and do menial jobs for twenty-five cents a day. It didn't matter that dietary restrictions prescribed by religion were not accommodated, or that their personal letters were censored. They were numbers, not names, subject to whatever brutalities the guards visited upon them, slaves of a system from which there was no appeal.

All this stuff was in the Attica prisoner demands—the list of them growing with every passing day—and while officials agreed to twenty-eight of those demands knowing full well that some would require funding as well as a lengthy legislative process that would go nowhere. The list of demands was one that could expand with the ever-expanding universe. And while the prison administrators were willing to rubber-stamp demands that made no real difference, they were steadfast in their refusal to consider any kind of meaningful amnesty.

As I had represented the Auburn Six, I expected as much. In Auburn the prisoners were promised no reprisals if they surrendered, which they did. Then they were terrorized while awaiting trial for charges racked up during the uprising. Word of their treatment traveled far when a federal judge transferred them to prisons around the state, including Attica.

Forty years after the Attica prison uprising was crushed, tapes were released on a Freedom of Information Act request that recorded conversations between Governor Rockefeller and President Richard Nixon discussing the retaking of Attica. The "silent majority" point of view is unmistakable:

"Tell me," Nixon began one of the conversations. "Are these primarily blacks that you're dealing with?"

"Oh, yes," Rockefeller replied. "The whole thing was led by the blacks."

"I'll be darned," President Nixon replied affably. "Are all the prisoners that were killed blacks? Or are there any white . . ."

"I haven't got that report," the governor replied, "but I'd have to—I would say just off hand, yes. We did [it] though, only when they were in the process of murdering the guards, or when they were attacking our people as they came in to get the guards."

"You had to do it," Nixon said, as if he were reassuring himself.

In reality Rockefeller didn't have to do it. After four days of unrest and disorder, things were starting to fray. The weather was horrible. Conditions in D yard were bad and getting worse. Nixon was wrong. I was there. Rockefeller wasn't. Everyone just needed to be patient. If we couldn't talk it out, we could wait it out. Rockefeller didn't want to wait it out. He wanted to make a point. As New York City's most prominent Puerto Rican politician at the time, Herman Badillo, said, "There's always time to die." The claim that prisoners were "in the process of murdering the guards" was a bald-faced lie. Whether Rockefeller was repeating bad information or made it up out of whole cloth is unclear. After the lie became accepted truth in the public imagination, autopsies showed that troopers—not the prisoners—killed the nine prison guards that Monday morning. As for the racial makeup of the prisoners, Rockefeller was wrong about that too, unless he unconsciously lumped Puerto Ricans and blacks together under the heading of "minority" and never got word of the whites in that ocean of rage.

Either way, you get the picture.

Later in the tapes Rockefeller told the president about the observers' committee that I was on, and the three days we spent trying, and ultimately failing, to negotiate a peaceful end to the rebellion.

"We had a committee of citizens," Governor Rockefeller said, "invited by the prisoners, thirty-two of them. Tom Wicker was one. We had that Kunstler, that lawyer."

"Yeah, yeah, I know of him," President Nixon replied.

"We had the head of the Mau Maus," Rockefeller continued. "A motley crowd. And some good people, some legislators. And Tom Wicker was so emotional in this thing that it was unbelievable."

"Which side?" President Nixon asked.

"Oh, on their side," Rockefeller replied.

"Always, always," Nixon said. "I know, I know."

I was in the room when Tom Wicker; Clarence Jones, the publisher of the *New York Amsterdam News*, who had been one of Martin Luther King, Jr.'s, key lawyers; and State Senator John Dunne made the eleventh-hour call to Governor Rockefeller at his 3,400-acre family estate in Pocantico Hills, begging him to show good faith in the negotiations by coming to the prison. I was there when he said no. In addition to the rain and growing squalor, there were limited amounts of food and water, and Warden Vincent Mancusi controlled both. The prisoners' position on amnesty and going to nonimperialist countries would soften. They would get hungry. They would get more miserable. I had already negotiated a provision that prisoners would not be charged with crimes related to property damage. But even though there was virtually no hope we could expand the concept to limited amnesty, we needed to buy some time. Rockefeller declined.

In the morning on the fourth and final day of the uprising, the sound of helicopters signaled the beginning of the end. I didn't know it then, but according to Tom Wicker's report in the *Times*, the attack began at 9:43:28. New York State Police troopers dropped tear gas into D yard and they as well as prison guards let loose a barrage of gunfire, shooting into the thousand or so inmates huddled there. Some used dum-dum bullets, which killed and maimed as many people as possible—including the hostages—until the firing stopped. In a matter of minutes the smoke cleared to reveal a scene of slaughter. The observers inside the prison were safely away from where the shooting occurred. Guards came into our sanctuary and ushered us out of the prison shortly after the attack. Outside, the assembled townspeople jeered and cursed us. In the anguish of the moment, I have forgotten how we were taken away. Inside the yard the guards forced the inmates to strip naked and run a gauntlet, beating them with clubs.

If the Left called it an "uprising," and to the mainstream it was a "riot," Tom Wicker and I ended up calling it a rebellion because for those of us who were there, that's how it seemed. After the prisoner takeover, they were getting a chance to be heard for the first time in America, but they were misheard, distrusted, and ignored while the administration representatives placed all the blame for what happened on them. In short, the keepers and the kept might as well have been speaking different languages. As much as I liked to think of myself as a person with one foot in each world, I was unable to translate, nor was anyone else able to say what needed to be said. In all likelihood there was no solution other than time, as Herman Badillo had put it. And time meant surrender, with whatever promises of reform had been made, something none of the observers was willing to say face-to-face at the negotiating table while they and the prisoners were together in the yard.

A few hours after troopers retook the prison, I was in the back of a cab heading south on Central Park West feeling defeated, angry, and depressed. I came home wearing the same suit. I stank. Where there had been a toehold to push against what looked like an impending disaster and a sense of mission when I left, there was now a massacre. I feared Maynard was dead. I wondered if any of the inmate leadership had survived. For days afterward my calls to the prison went unanswered.

While we were waiting for the light to change, I remember looking at the Dakota where the rich and famous lived, with its Victorian gas lamps and bathysphere-like guard booth. We rolled to a stop at my building six blocks south, just above Columbus Circle. I don't recall who the doorman was that night, or the floor captain. I noted the difference between the stewards' room at Attica, where the observers' committee was camped out, and the shimmering terrazzo floors of the lobby as I trudged toward the elevator at the far end of the southern hallway. The elevator man deposited me on the semiprivate landing my family shared with one other apartment. I could hear the sounds of daily life on the other side of our door. My three kids and Kitty were in there safe and sound. The door was unlocked. That familiar feeling that I led a double life was strong as I stood there with my hand resting on the doorknob. I turned it and opened the door. In the foyer my four-year-old, Patrick, came shooting past with a quick hello. I went to our bedroom to change, gathered all the clothes I'd been wearing, and threw them in the garbage.

There was a message waiting for me on the table from *The David Frost Show*, a big television program at the time. They wanted me to be a guest that night. Frost was hosting a special panel on what had happened that morning. I would join Senator John Dunne, Leo Zeferetti, the head of the Correction Officers' Benevolent Association, and Clarence Jones. Although I was on the show, you won't find my name in the online listing of who appeared that night. David Frost turned to me early for comment, which is the one and only reason I'm not listed as one of the guests. I was exhausted and angry, and to this day I don't regret a thing about what I said. I don't remember what Frost asked me. I do remember attacking Rockefeller: "He only cares about his class prerogatives. The white guards didn't matter any more than the black prisoners to him. They were all expendable."

Cutting me off, Frost turned to cooler, safer voices for the rest of the discussion.

The news was filled with misinformation. Prison officials said the hostages were killed by the prisoners: "I saw slit throats" was repeated over and over. What actually happened took a while to get sorted out, which gave the lies time to settle into the popular imagination. By the time autopsies revealed the truth, Attica was fixed in the public imagination—slit throats and all.

The first of many funerals had been held the same day the story broke about the way the guards had really died. There were two. One was for William Quinn, the corrections officer who was injured on the first day of the uprising and—contrary to official reports—the only prison employee actually killed by the inmates. The other funeral was for the first of nine hostages killed when Governor Rockefeller gave Commissioner Oswald the green light to crush the uprising.

On the day of those funerals, the op-ed section of the *New York Times* published the transcript of a Panglossian speech about prison reform by Commissioner Oswald. It had been recorded and played over the public-address system at Attica a week before the uprising. The decision to play that tape belied the profound disconnect between the prison administration and the prisoners not just in New York State, but around the country.

There was nothing radical about the need for change. About two weeks before Commissioner Oswald's tape got its chilly reception from the inmates at Attica, George Jackson was shot in San Quentin Prison, and the news spread fast. No ordinary prisoner, Jackson had been a symbol of black resistance. Imprisoned for ten years at California's Soledad prison for a seventy-dollar gas station robbery, his letters had been published in an acclaimed book, *Soledad Brother*, the year before. Acquitted of killing a guard, he had been transferred to San Quentin and killed in what the authorities claimed was an escape attempt. Fearing a national movement, prison officials around the country were trying, and failing, to stop the flow of information between prisoner activists. Mail was read, censorship increased, and little if any effort was made to conceal it. The goal was to squelch news about conditions at other prisons. But not all information traveled by mail. Visitors and newly arrived prisoners, like the members of the Auburn Six, brought news too.

Even if the flow of information could have been stopped, prison authorities were working under a false assumption. There was no organized movement, nothing orchestrated in any meaningful way—not by the Black Panthers, YAWF, or anyone else. A limit had been reached. The appalling conditions and human rights abuses that were commonplace around the nation's prisons didn't square with two decades of civil rights upheaval. A few prisoners became readers of historical and political works that sought to explain why they and so many who looked like them found themselves imprisoned. As a result some inmates began to see themselves as a by-product of an inherently biased system. Their crimes, in their eyes, were a form of revolt, with the resulting incarceration making them political prisoners. As for me, I straddled the political fence. On the one hand I saw many of their crimes as the inevitable result of the failure of the War on Poverty. On the other I was afraid of violent crime, and wanted those who would attack me on the streets sent to prison.

As for prison reform, prisoner activists had a good ear for pandering and propaganda, but as Bob Dylan put it, you didn't need a weatherman to know which way the wind blew. Playing the Oswald tape and then doing nothing was a bad idea. Worse, Oswald had been the commissioner while the Auburn Six were being tortured at one of his supposedly reform-minded prisons. The inmates at Attica took it for what it was—lip service. Even more insulting, it must have seemed as if prison officials weren't even trying particularly hard. The *Times* editorial board called the transcript of Commissioner Oswald's speech "New Directions," and with the majority of Attica's dead still unburied when the transcript was published, the irony was clear. Commissioner Oswald, relatively new to the post he occupied, was definitely premature in touting progress in state correctional facilities when he said: "The main impact of the new direction of the department is the recognition of the individual as a human being and the need for basic fairness throughout our day-to-day relationships with each other." The sad thing was that compared to his predecessor, Commissioner Oswald actually was a reformer.

But Rockefeller had turned Oswald into a bagman. It was his job to shut down the uprising: The governor had to remain untouchable.

At around seven thirty in the evening, four days after the uprising was crushed, a bomb ripped through the offices of the New York Department of Corrections in the usually quiet state capital of Albany. The offices were on the outskirts of town; it was a Friday night; they were deserted. The Weather Underground immediately claimed responsibility for the bomb, placed a couple of hundred feet from Commissioner Oswald's office.

It seemed like a lot more than four days had passed. Time had slowed to a crawl. Prison officials kept reporters and lawyers seeking to represent the prisoners outside the walls. News was tough to come by, and I could find out nothing about Tony. The feverish activity of the observers' committee trying to broker a deal among Governor Nelson Rockefeller, prison officials, and the inmates had been talked to death. I could not get the smell of tear gas and gunpowder as we had been escorted through the heavy steel doors to the outside world out of my mind. During the intervening days I'd thought incessantly about the bloodbath hidden behind Attica's thirty-foot walls, and the more than eighty men who were wounded and the thirty-three prisoners and nine hostages who were inside, dead or dying. Repeating in my head, over and over, the final death toll, which was forty-three, I felt as if the forward motion of my life had come to a stop. I was paralyzed. Then the Weather Underground bomb shook me out of it.

Before they set off the bomb, the Weather Underground contacted two newspapers and Pacifica Radio's WBAI in New York City. That was their thing: They made a very public point of being careful not to hurt anyone. Meanwhile the idiocy of setting off bombs remained, and the timbre of the messages attached to these attacks was so overpowered by the Weather Underground's unique blend of overeager, ill-considered radicalism that they might have done better sending no message at all. At least that's how I saw it, but then I suppose from a more radical perch that simply meant I favored the tepid sort of advocacy lampooned in Phil Ochs's 1966 song "Love Me, I'm a Liberal." Ironically, I loved that song. The communiqué that accompanied this particular bombing cited the "white supremacy" of the corrections system, explaining that it was "how a society run by white racists maintains its control." The dispatch went on: "We only wish we could do more to show the courageous prisoners at Attica, San Quentin and the other 20th-century slave ships that they are not alone in their fight for the right to live." It wasn't news-friendly language, like my outburst on *The David Frost Show*. That said, there was an ocean separating my position from the overheated radical groups that were operating in the late 1960s and early '70s. I did not at all identify with the brand of radicalism that marked their communiqués or their bombing attacks. Perhaps it was the way I lived. I had a house in the Hamptons, we had a housekeeper, and I liked to go to the opera. I was not one of them.

Unlike today, when the goal of political bombings here and around the world is to kill and to terrorize the public, the self-described militants of the late '60s and early '70s exploded bombs to publicize their message. Like Sam Melville, at least in America, they sent out communiqués warning of the impending action to make sure no one got hurt. Discussions about the war, racism, and other societal wrongs were forced into America's living rooms after each Weather Underground bomb exploded. Without the spectacle, mainstream media paid little attention to fringe points of view. The Weathermen's Oswald office bombing, however, achieved nothing, because while the kind of actual and figurative noise produced by the bombing got attention, it was virtually all negative, and the underlying message was lost in the haze of mild hysteria and disapproval.

By contrast, compared with what the Weathermen did, I thought that perhaps my legal work had some value. The cases I worked on could open doors. I could trudge the more meaningful road of incremental progress. Maybe I could even help stem the Supreme Court's legal retreat from the promise of equality, something I had written about in "Nine Men in Black Who Think White," the *New York Times Magazine* article that got me fired from the NAACP in 1968.

Commissioner Oswald got the Weather Underground's attention because he was Rockefeller's front man. The order to attack on September 13, 1971, was given by him, but he didn't act alone. Governor Rockefeller wanted the situation to be resolved, and he wanted it done at arm's length. The sort of voter Rockefeller had in mind as he unleashed the force of repression at Attica, or pushed for the infamously anti-black-and-Latino Rockefeller drug laws, was an archetype like Archie Bunker from the sitcom *All in the Family*—which premiered nine months before the Attica rebellion—actually around the time I was at Auburn. It was all conveying to whites that he would hold the line on their prerogatives and keep blacks at a distance to protect their way of life.

Whatever happened to Sam Melville, the bomb that went off in Albany was a response at least in part to his death. I remember a few things: I was unhappy to hear that the Weather Underground did it; I thought the bombing made no sense, and also that the underground was trying to co-opt something that it had very little (if anything) to do with; I was relieved to hear that no one was hurt, and I thought the action would be easy to dismiss, but I could also hear President Nixon's silent majority saying that the Attica slaughter was unavoidable with such lunatics taking over the prison. Having fought against deeply ingrained institutional racism as an NAACP lawyer, I had learned that the way you talked mattered a lot, and if you spun something like an argument about racism even slightly askew, like using the phrase "white supremacy" even if that was exactly what you were facing, there was a cost: You risked losing in the court of public opinion. And perhaps that is what I did on *The David Frost Show*. But what I said was on the mark. If given another chance, I would probably say the same thing again.

If you listen to the Nixon tapes, you will hear Rockefeller's lack of concern, his contempt for the prisoners, the observers, and even his failure to recognize the sacrifice of the guards' lives. It's impossible to miss. It was a class thing as well as a race thing, and I was in a unique position to know. I had deep class roots in my family and plenty of pre-rogatives, and I know how that shaped me. So there was irony in my attack on Rockefeller's prerogatives.

The wealth I was born into exposed me to the social reality of racism from the opposite side of the issue. Growing up, we always had servants, they were always black, and at some point that started becoming emotionally freighted for me. Eventually there was a disconnect in my life when it came to race, which I have spent many years trying to piece together. What happened at Attica, however, was clear. It exposed me to more than the social reality of racism: There I saw all of its absolute ugliness.

2

Childhood

My grandfather Jonas Siegel died in 1924 of influenza, leaving behind my father and uncle—both still boys—and my grandmother Bessie. One of my grandfather's best friends was married to a woman named Bessie, too, who had died not long after my grandfather passed away—also of influenza. It seemed natural that Grandma Bessie and my grandfather's friend gravitated toward each other as they navigated parallel experiences of loss, and when they got married in 1925 everyone thought it was a good match.

Born Abraham Wonskolaser, or Wonsal, my grandfather's new anglicized name was Aaron Warner, which became Albert at some point. Most people called him Abe. Among friends and family he was Major, a nickname that had something to do with his rank in the U.S. Army Reserves. He was big on family. In fact my grandfather went into business with his three brothers Harry, Sam, and Jack, who together formed a film studio they called Warner Bros. Major managed the distribution and finances of the company from New York, while the other brothers took care of the production side of things on Sunset Boulevard and later on in the Burbank studios.

When Grandma Bessie and Major got married, the studio was well established and holding its own during a period of nonstop change and innovation, but while the company was doing all right and had solid prospects, it wasn't until 1927 that Warner Brothers hit it big with *The Jazz Singer*. Featuring Al Jolson in the blackface makeup that was a symbol of mainstream racism in America, *The Jazz Singer* held the distinction of making history as the first "talking picture." Not only did it mark the beginning of the end of the silent era, it made Warner Bros. a lot of money. Overnight the Warner name became synonymous with "Hollywood," and three of the four founding brothers were industry kingpins. Tragically the fourth brother died on the eve of all that. Sam worked tirelessly to figure out the technical aspects of *The Jazz Singer*, only to die from an untreated sinus infection the day before the film's premiere in New York City. The three surviving Warners did not attend that screening. They were burying their brother.

After the wild success of *The Jazz Singer*, Major and his two brothers were wealthy beyond anything Grandma Bessie—who had been fairly well off before she married him—could have dreamed possible.

A child of an immigrant family that fled the pogroms of Middle Europe, Major was known publicly as a person of few airs. That said, by the time Major died in 1967 he had in fact picked up some of the habits associated with great wealth, prime among them, by the time I was old enough to see his routines, that he never seemed to work. Horseracing, "the sport of kings," was his passion. Mostly I remember him quietly reading the racing forms. Family lore had it that he once turned down a chance to buy the Yankees because it would have distracted him too much from the ponies. I don't know if that story is true, but Major certainly spent a lot of time at racetracks in New York and Miami Beach, riding back and forth in the front seat of his chauffeured car. Maybe he had retired or conducted business only between post times. I never asked. Something that did interest me as I grew older, however, was a particular man among Major's racetrack acquaintances. He was famous for many reasons, prime among them being his job as the first director of the Federal Bureau of Investigation.

J. Edgar Hoover and Major saw the world though a similar lens. They shared a deep hatred of communism and the Soviet Union. Certainly Stalin's anti-Semitism fed into Major's antipathy. The Warners veered hard to the right after World War II. I remember Major buying cases of Hoover's *Masters of Deceit*. He would inscribe copies of his distinguished friend's book to friends and family. The inscription in my copy says: "Fight for USA. A great country. To Lewis Steel. Fondly, A Warner"

When I was ten our family took a trip to see the sights in Washington,

DC, and Hoover assigned a special agent to take us around. In the FBI Building my brother and I were brought down to the basement firing range, where we were allowed the rare treat of firing Thompson submachine guns at paper humans—not in evidence then was even a glimmer of the allegedly radical lawyer who would help rebellious inmates striking out at centuries of racism through uprisings like the one at Attica. Filled with wonder, I was trotted around the FBI headquarters, and it would have been a stretch to guess that I would one day number among the enemies described in Hoover's book, with special agents prowling around my apartment building, going through my garbage, looking for dirt because I represented the Weathermen who were willing to blow things up. That I would spend the majority of my life trying to translate into case law the language of moral outrage directed against nationwide school, housing, and employment segregation, the Vietnam War, and a jurisprudence system stanchioned in the status quo racism of America even after the historic Supreme Court *Brown v. Board of Education* decision—none of that would have been easy to spot in me that day my family spent roaming around the nation's capital as the wide-eyed guests of J. Edgar Hoover.

Growing up, I knew nothing of radical politics. I lived in the cool green shade of Major's wealth. A conservative worldview was the only one available to me. But I don't really remember much about that. The main thing I recall about Major was how much he loved my grandmother. He would do anything for her. The full realization that my father and my mother and my uncle (and subsequently my brother and I) were part of a package deal dawned on me only later in life, but even early on there was a sense that while we got to do fun things from time to time through Major's connections, we were still and always the Siegels-turned-Steels (my father changed our last name when I was five), connected to the Warner name by the gossamer of marriage.

With Grandma Bessie as the conduit, Major's money got spread around. She became the matriarch and fairy godmother of her own extended family, the Levys. There was jockeying for position—favored family and outliers. For those within the fold, Bessie's marriage was a very fortuitous bit of good timing, because the Levys were at the beginning of a downward slide from a position of prominence in New York City's garment industry. Bessie's father, Moe, had created a chain of men's stores that pioneered two-pants suits, or what people used to call "Moe Levys." Sadly for the family, Moe's flagship store was located near Canal Street, or maybe on it—I don't remember—which ceased to be a destination for those who wanted to dress like the moneyed classes. Clothing stores were moving operations up to Fifth Avenue. The Levys' fortune suffered because Great-Grandpa Moe and his two sons must have missed the memo.

When he married my mother, my father was a shy, skinny graduate of the University of Pennsylvania with a rich and famous stepfather. Arthur, or "Artie," as his friends called him, must have seemed like a very good catch. He was completely protected from the Depression, and had a managerial job waiting for him in the Warner Bros. movie theater empire. The job was in Milwaukee. After a few years my parents came back to New York. My father left the Warner Brothers office to enter into a partnership to run some Forty-Second Street movie theaters. When that deal didn't work out, he opened two theaters in nearby New Jersey. Again failure. But from what I could tell, the good life went on unabated. My father was a mama's boy, and Grandma Bessie had married about as well as a woman could. Ruthie, as everyone called my mother, quickly attached herself to Bessie, and all was well in a world that was otherwise falling apart right outside their door. My mother liked fine clothes, jewelry, and furs and, although she said otherwise, the parade of Hollywood stars seemed to thrill her. She was always ready to display her insider knowledge: "Clark Gable has bad teeth," she loved to say.

Born in Manhattan's Lenox Hill Hospital in 1937, I was brought home to a luxury apartment building called the Beresford, on the corner of Central Park West overlooking the Museum of Natural History. Lorenz Hart, the lyricist who, with Richard Rodgers, created some of the best-loved musical comedies ever produced on Broadway, lived in the apartment next to ours. German governesses took care of my brother and me. Seeking more space and perhaps "the gentility" of Manhattan's East Side, we moved to a new apartment building on Park Avenue.

Summers during those pre–World War II years were spent at my grandparents' mansion in Rye, on Long Island Sound. My grandfather kept his luxury yacht tied to the estate's dock on one side, and my father his speedboat on the other.

My mother liked to say that I was a handful. I heard countless times about how I would chew on the curtains if my crib was placed close to the window, and more generally how I kept the nurse busy. Unlike my brother, who was the picture of health, I was less than robust. I had asthma, which meant I needed a lot of monitoring. Decades later my mother would tell my sister-in-law that she was the only one who loved me as a child.

My poor health may explain to some extent why I have so few memories of Rye. My only concrete recollection is a particular Fourth of July night when the fireworks scared me. After the war started, my grandparents sold the Rye mansion. Major gave his yacht to the Coast Guard, a story I remember because, like his chance to buy the Yankees franchise, it entered family legend.

The next stop was Crail Farm, a sprawling 250-acre property in the foothills of the Blue Ridge Mountains outside Hendersonville, North Carolina. Years later I was told that Major wanted the place as a fallback in the event Germany attacked New York City.

At the age of four in North Carolina, I went to kindergarten at a Catholic school run by an order of French nuns. Being sick with asthma during much of the damp winter, I had to repeat kindergarten. I was absent so often during the two years I went to that school that each time I went felt like the first day all over again, except a little worse. I was always the new kid who came to class and watched the other kids laugh and play. The nuns tried hard to be nice and get me involved, but I remained outside the circle.

Tenant families lived on the farm and worked it, growing crops and raising animals. They were white. I only knew where two of the farmers' houses were, but I never went inside them. I remember thinking vaguely that those homes were off-limits. Except for my brother, John, and Junior, a farm boy who was ordered to stay away after biting me, it was just grown-ups and ancient Appalachian foothills and the farmers, who rarely talked to me. When my brother and parents went horseback riding, the loneliness seemed endless. I felt like an alien wandering around in a strange land, terrified of every new sound and yet scared my reaction might set off one of those asthma attacks that made me feel as if every breath I managed to pull into my lungs was the last.

My father hired a young black man named Bill Rutherford while we were at Crail Farm, and he would continue with our family as a butler and all-around man until he died many years later. He was about the same age as my dad. Two women also worked for us—also black. They did the cooking and cleaning. In the evenings after dinner, all three disappeared to a gloomy-looking shack in a grove of towering pines behind the house.

From his very first day working for us, Bill made me feel happy. He was always smiling and ready to play with me, taking the time to lift me in the air or muss my hair no matter what else he was doing. That was part of his job, I suppose, but to me it felt like a lot of attention—more than I was used to.

It wasn't long before Bill was drafted into the navy during World War II, and got assigned to the Seabees. My father offered to match whatever part of his pay he sent back, and Bill followed through.

When my father himself was drafted, John and I went to live with Major and Bessie in Miami Beach, where they had an estate that looked out over the Atlantic from the spot where either the Fontainebleau or the Eden Roc now stands. In faded photographs of my brother and me in our monogrammed linen shirts, with our hair combed just right, we look like little princes.

I went to a public school in Miami Beach for a while, before being sent to another Catholic school, where the nuns were harsh and dogmatic. I'll never forget my first day, when the teacher told the other children not to mind me: "That little boy in the back doesn't say his prayers because he's Jewish," she said, as the children craned their heads to see the strange addition to their class. "You see, he doesn't believe in Jesus Christ."

There was murmuring, little hands and faces registering the information as I looked at my shoes pretending I wasn't the center of attention.

Shortly before my father returned from serving in the Army Air Corps somewhere in the Midwest, we moved back to New York City. I was seven, so my parents enrolled me at the neighborhood public school, PS 6, where both my father and my Grandma Bessie had gone. The class I landed in skipped forward because of wartime overcrowding. Because I had difficulty learning to read, my parents got me a tutor— the wealthy always knew how to make sure their children had every advantage.

Bill must have returned from the Seabees to work for my parents at about this time, but it is hard for me to remember as I can't even recall him or even my father being gone. Nor do I remember when Lorraina joined Bill. I knew she came from North Carolina, and I think her sister worked at the Crail Farm house. I was told they were married, but I never knew when and where. All I really knew was that I was happy to have both Bill and Lorraina around.

When John and I got into it, Bill was my protector—or at least that's how it seemed to me, though keeping the peace was in his interest, because if we wrecked the apartment it would only mean more work for him. A giant of a man in stature, no one was gentler. Bill was dignified, and so was his wife, Lorraina. They seemed to be part of each other— Lorraina tiny and beautiful, Bill big and kind. She cooked and cleaned while he served and did the heavy lifting. They were like a second set of parents. I used to love whiling away hour after hour in their matchbook-size room off the kitchen, just hanging out.

Lorraina had her own children from another marriage—a boy named Duby, and Sister Baby. My father had a stepfather, so I knew how that worked, but it was a different situation because his father had died, so there was never an issue about where he was going to live. But I had no idea about the man Lorraina had those kids with. I remember wondering who the father was when Lorraina mentioned Duby and Sister Baby. I imagined them living with their father or Lorraina's family in North Carolina. I do know that Lorraina missed her children because she said so. Even so, on a day-to-day basis she was more my mom than theirs. From time to time John and I talked about who took care of Duby and Sister Baby, but neither of us had the life experience to get very far in those conversations. There was something unreal about the way Lorraina and her kids lived compared with the way we did. I couldn't imagine being in their shoes. It seemed sad, but at the same time their life was abstract, and I didn't stay in those moods for a very long time. Over the years Lorraina brought Duby and Sister Baby to our apartment when they were very little. Those visits made the situation even harder for me to fathom.

When I asked my mother and father how Lorraina could live away from her children, I remember vague replies, as if I was asking something that was out of bounds or made them feel uncomfortable. I got the impression that I shouldn't think too much about things like that.

Seared into my brain, however, was the way my mother used to talk to both Bill and Lorraina as if they were children, using a high-pitched and condescending voice she used with no one else except servants. Her words escape me now, but not the feeling.

When I was ten years old, I came down with rheumatic fever. Being bedridden for a month brought my time at PS 6 to an end. I was enrolled at Riverdale Country School in the Bronx for the seventh and eighth grades to make sure I would be ready for Culver Military Academy in Indiana, where my brother had just started. To this day I am not sure why we were sent there.

Not exactly fitting in but always trying: That was my experience of childhood. I struggled and thought I had to prove myself. Being sick a lot of the time served only to amplify those feelings. The sole upside to being sick was that I got to spend more time with my mother, who was at her best when I was ill. She would play cards with me and help nurse me back to health. That summer my parents rented a lakefront house in Maine. We had lots of guests and, of course, Bill and Lorraina. By the end of our time there, I was in pretty good health.

Riverdale Country School was a hard slog of trying to make friends with kids who had known one another for a long time, and keeping up with the demands of the teachers. The school was a bus trip away at the outer reaches of the city, on a hill near the large homes of the wealthy. Still in recovery mode, I was behind the curve on the sports field. To make things just a little more difficult, I was nearsighted, and my parents had no idea. It took about a year before I complained and got glasses. In most other ways Riverdale was okay. There were no tough kids to avoid as there had been at PS 6. The message was that we were members of the elite, a select group who went to one of the city's finest private schools. I am almost certain there was not a nonwhite face on the campus—not among the students, faculty, administrators, or clerical workers. Maybe not even among the maintenance men and service people. Peering out of the bus windows on the way to Riverdale from Park Avenue, we saw black people as we traversed Harlem. It seemed as if they were contained in a separate world with garbage-strewn streets and sad-looking tenements all stuck together and falling apart. To us Harlem was a dangerous place that was best to pass through as quickly as possible. It was a foreign world, a hostile territory that existed between the well-maintained buildings that comprised my worlds at home and at school. As we rumbled toward Riverdale, however, we were safe and protected. With the 1948 presidential election approaching, we sang, "Dewey's in the White House, Truman's in the ash can!" Everyone seemed to be a Republican back then.

Grandma Bessie presided over Friday-night dinners for the Levy clan in a private dining room at the Park Royal Hotel on West Seventy-Third Street, where my great-grandparents, Moe and Esther, lived. Bessie's sisters and brothers and their families always showed up. Moe and Esther were kosher, but as far as I could see there was little religion among the Levy offspring. Family members gossiped that one of Bessie's brothers, Ralph, married a Catholic and the son of her sister Dee married a Protestant, which was another thing to talk about.

John and I received no religious training, and our family never went to temple, but that didn't seem to matter. My father's brother, Carl, had been captured during the war in the Battle of the Bulge and put in a concentration camp with other Jewish soldiers. He came home weighing eighty pounds. So even though we always had a Christmas tree and Easter-egg hunts, I knew we were Jewish and that there were people out there who really didn't like us. Without being taught, we learned that being Jewish was something that mattered.

Uncle Ralph's Catholic wife as well as my aunt Dee's daughter-in-law looked more or less as if they might be "one of us," and they were friendly enough, but still, when it came to the family they were outsiders, which meant they weren't part of the inner circle that got to sit at the dinner table where the family congregated on Friday nights after they were switched to the Hampshire House, the exclusive Central Park South hotel–co-op where my grandparents lived.

Bessie's sister Ruth Leeds and her husband, Al, who called me Blackie (which I hated), were sometimes there. On other evenings they would come after dinner, with their daughter, Helene, and her husband, Ross Newhouse.

"Why does Uncle Al call me Blackie?" I remember asking my father.

"He doesn't mean anything by it," my father told me. "You have dark hair."

Blackie was what someone might call a black man, and I didn't want to be black. Black people lived in Harlem. Whatever my feelings for Bill and Lorraina, and regardless of their feelings for me, I had already internalized America's racial hierarchy, and while I might never attain the same heights scaled by my fair-haired brother in that highly racialized scheme of things, I definitely didn't want to be a black person who served people, had to work all the time, and went home to scary neighborhoods. I also didn't like the thought of looking like black people because to me white was the only way to be. It was obvious: White skin was better than brown skin. Blond hair was better than dark hair. A narrow nose was better than a wide one. Uncle Al made it sound as if I were in the same league as a butler or a cook when he called me Blackie, and I wanted him to stop.

It was a complicated problem for a boy to navigate; Bill and Lorraina were central figures in my childhood. But there it was. They were black and I was white, and I liked being white. It didn't lessen my feelings for them, but I knew my color was better, and theirs marked them as lesser people. When Bill and Lorraina went off on Thursdays and Sundays after breakfast, I remember missing them terribly. As I grew older, my love for Bill and Lorraina took the form of thinking about them enough to wonder more about their situation, so I questioned my parents about the way they were treated. They invariably replied that "the help" had Thursdays and Sundays off, but it didn't seem that way. Bill and Lorraina worked parts of those days, which meant they worked every day of the week.

"That's the way it is," my parents said. "That's how everyone does it."

Because I wanted Bill and Lorraina around as much as possible, I was easily reassured. But something seemed not quite right to me. That said, I was a kid, and my focus was on myself. I was generally able to hold on to a perceived injustice, real or imagined, only if it related to me, and even then, not always and not for very long. My brother the golden boy. Uncle Al calling me Blackie. The tough kids from the other side of the tracks. Whatever. I remembered those things—what it felt like to be the underdog. But I certainly did not make the leap connecting my perceived grievances to the much-harder-to-comprehend status of being black.

The racial hierarchy had become ingrained. I knew it from the microcosm of our relationship with Bill and Lorraina. They were in our apartment to help, and they were paid salaries. My mother had a buzzer placed strategically in the dining room, and she used it when she wanted the help to do something. The relationship was hazy to me as a child, but I understood the broad strokes. The job description for domestic help in our household, had one existed, would not have included "Love and be loved by Lewis." They were there to work, and that was that. It was this divide between "the help" and me that provided my first introduction to the relationship between race and social hierarchy. Power was a birthright, which was manifested in the way my parents treated the servants. I suppose that—compared with some households—they did so gently and with everyone's humanity mostly intact.

I sensed that while Bill and Lorraina were completely available to my parents in their worker roles, their friendship and finer emotions were not. Those things had to be earned. I liked that thought, because they liked me. What I didn't see then was the big picture, where being pleasant and helping my parents raise me was part of the job description. Years later I began to understand that the complicated love that existed between me and Bill and Lorraina—all three of us wired not to engage in it entirely, or not in an open, uncomplicated way—had a lot to do with my lifelong attempts to change the pervasive racial dysfunction in our society. The fact that I never did ask Bill and Lorraina how they felt about me, or my not telling them how I felt about them, and that we had to rely on the hugs that adults and children give each other has stayed with me all my life.

When I was about twelve, my father gave me a book about the French resistance which I think was called *Paris Underground*. Its heroes defied the Nazis to get downed flyers out of France. They were underdogs, and I admired them. I imagined myself alongside them, a ragged crew fighting for something that mattered. I think my father intuited my rebel leanings and tried to be supportive. Soon after that book about the resistance, he had me reading Irving Stone's *Clarence Darrow for the Defense*.

My father's interest in the renowned "Attorney for the Damned" was that of a spectator. The stories were great. Darrow's cases were adapted into plays and movies, including *Inherit the Wind* and *Compulsion*. Darrow was a charismatic man who did important work—an American hero. I wanted to be a lawyer like him. I did eventually become a lawyer, though I wasn't often associated with the sort of high-profile cases that were Darrow's stock in trade. There was never a hanging tree outside the courthouse door when I served as counsel. With the exception of Hurricane Carter, none of my cases have been turned into movies. Like Hurricane's, however, I tended to take on hard-to-win or unwinnable cases—though I never thought that way—and other cases because they held the possibility of breaking down racial barriers in the United States. I eschewed the interference of special interests—corporate or otherwise—whose objectives were antagonistic to the cause. (This was not true of Darrow, since he occasionally worked for big-money entities, but my financial situation let me be more of a purist.) While my path diverged from Darrow's, his career blazed a trail for the kind of work that attracted me most. Like him, I came of age during the still-evolving uproar in America's cities, which were exploding with the anger of people too long kept down. The Harlem I experienced as a child on the bus ride to Riverdale Country School ceased being contained. The tone and tenor of that outrage reached a fever pitch.

With Darrow serving as my role model, I dared to believe in the impossible. He took on impossible cases and won. He made me want to become a lawyer. Thinking back to the time when my father gave me that Darrow book, I remember him being wistful, and how he told me of his regret that he had not become a lawyer.

"Why didn't you?" I asked.

He shrugged.

If he answered, I have no memory of what he said. I remember more his sense of resignation. Maybe that interchange planted a seed; I don't know. Maybe it made me think about how Bill and Lorraina led their lives; I don't remember. I do remember wondering a lot about it, and that I didn't feel comfortable with the thoughts I had—as if they were an invasion of my father's world. I never asked my father about it again. On some level I knew I didn't want to hear the answer, but that moment with my dad marked my fantasizing about doing something important with my life.

That was around the time that Uncle Al stopped calling me Blackie and started calling me Counselor.

3

Culver Military Academy
and Harvard

On May 17, 1954, with Culver Military Academy's commencement a few days away, something infinitely more important happened that would forever change the course of American life. There was no way I could know that it would be the cornerstone of my life's work. Back then, however, I missed it entirely.

As a cadet I was waiting for the marching band to blare the John Philip Sousa music that signaled the high spectacle of the garrison parade, with its precision marching, booming howitzers, and daring horsemanship. A little ambivalent, I was also thinking about the formal ball with the brilliant saber-arch salute honoring our regimental commander and his date. And I suppose I was also thinking about freedom from the strictures of military school as we headed off into the lazy days of summer, which would end with me entering my freshman year at Harvard.

It was no time for the news of the day, no matter how momentous. Not even if the United States Supreme Court ruled in a case that would put an end to state-mandated public school segregation. The Court based its decision in *Brown v. Board of Education* to no small degree on the theory that segregation taught black children that they were inferior to white children, doing permanent damage to their self-esteem. That, the court said, irreparably harmed them, affecting their ability to learn and function in society. *Brown* described the fallout from segregation in stark terms, stating forcefully that its effects were hard or impossible to undo.

Essentially Chief Justice Warren's opinion signaled what should have been obvious but what was not to most white Americans: that segregation was directly responsible not only for the entrenched social inequality between black and white Americans, but all manner of other social ills. Based on its findings, the Court ruled that the South's segregated schools violated the Constitution. Far more important than any of the speeches we cadets heard during our graduation was that ruling, joined by all nine justices, including one from the Deep South, which set the nation on a new course.

I have no memory of that decision. I am sure there was a story about the case in the *Indianapolis Star,* and I am equally sure I didn't read it. It probably led the nightly news too, though I had no way of listening at Culver. Faculty members must have talked about it, but not with us. Some, I am sure, would have applauded. But others might have reacted negatively. To put the ruling in perspective, Indiana was still home to school boards that openly segregated black from white children, and the Ku Klux Klan was still active in the state. Had I thought about it, I would have felt that the Supreme Court did the right thing. But I didn't think about it, although as one of a handful of Jews, I had a few experiences of another form of discrimination at Culver—anti-Semitism. Even then, however, I knew better than to compare my tame encounters with what it was like to be black.

Also at that point in my life, I considered segregation to be a Southern problem. I thought we were more enlightened in the North. Slaves hadn't built our roads or our grand public buildings. We hadn't based our culture and economy on Jim Crow rules. We celebrated Lincoln's birthday, and let blacks ride anywhere they wanted on the bus. We weren't still fighting the Civil War—but the South was, which was preposterous because we'd won it. I probably felt on some level that those backward Southerners needed to think more like us. In other words, I had no idea how widespread segregation was. Although slaves hadn't built our roads or public buildings, I never then thought about the all-white workforces and unions in the various trades that built and maintained everything important. I was surrounded by discrimination, but I didn't recognize it.

We were cloistered at Culver. The campus was located in a rural county. *Brown* was about public schools, and I hadn't attended public school since PS 6, so even if I had heard about the Supreme Court ruling the whole thing would still have been abstract.

Anyway, I was a teenager. That alone was enough to explain my lack of interest in the news. My days were occupied by being worried about the way I looked and being seriously agitated about not having a date for the ball. Going with my twenty-seven-year-old cousin, Helaine, was mortifying, even if she was beautiful. She came from New York City with my family to attend my graduation, and I was grateful to her, but everyone would know she wasn't a real date, and her presence only served to underscore the reality of my datelessness. That was way more important than some faraway Supreme Court ruling about what black children endured. Discrimination, to me, was personal. It was about being Jewish and dateless. Most of the other graduating cadets had dates, but in the wilds of Indiana, Christian girls almost never went out with Jewish guys. A friend of mine once offered to get me a blind date, but confided that he would have to tell the girl in advance that I was Jewish. It was humiliating. In addition to my excitement at going to Harvard, my outsider status as a Jew at Culver definitely contributed to my eagerness to move on. And I had heard it was easy to get dates in college.

Back in New York City, I had Bill and Lorraina to dote on me when I went to my grandparents' house. I assumed they would stay there forever. Domestic work was not a job where you could easily leave a family and work for another, because that required references and answers that could be hard to wrangle. Thinking of the past—with Bill and Lorraina living in the servant's room in our apartment off the pantry in a space just wide enough for a twin bed, a narrow passageway leading to a bathroom the size of two bath mats—was always pleasurable. That room had been a sanctuary before I was sent away to Culver. Curling up at the foot of their bed on the nights my parents were out on the town remains a fond memory. Whatever we talked about has been swallowed by the fog of time past, but the being-there part is imprinted on my memory like few other things from childhood—Bill with his hair slicked down and a stocking on his head, Lorraina in her robe and wearing a hairnet.

Still, I would see Bill and Lorraina at Major and Bessie's big Victorian house on a hilltop outside the city in a sleepy Westchester village, which they used for many years as a summer residence. I had spent a few summers there playing tennis at the country club where Major had been a founding member, and I remembered evenings at the house standing behind the men and looking at their hands while they played gin rummy. Major, I could see, was not one of the better players. He would hold high cards, and often got stuck with them when someone went gin or knocked. My dad was not like that. He was careful and held on to low cards. Bill would drive me to the club in Major's giant car every day and pick me up later. We would chat about one thing or another as we sat next to each other. Mainly he would ask me what I was up to. It was rare, if ever, that I asked him what was going on with him and Lorraina. The focus on me and not on him manifested a not-so-subtle sort of racism and classism of which I was unaware. Bill's life in my mind was fixed: He served my family. That was his role. And his life was as an appendage to my family's, so there was little he could tell me. But as his boy—his Skippy—the nickname he gave me when he came back from the war—I had wide-open opportunities in front of me, and I thought he would like hearing about that. Bill, however, must have known far better than I that our dynamic was changing. Bill was still the smiling, friendly presence that settled me down, but he was no longer my security blanket. He knew I was fast outgrowing him. He asked questions to be sociable, but he knew what was going to happen long before I did. He was going to become a friendly servant rather than a father figure.

On some level I was living in an imaginary world or, better, an imaginary state of mind. I loved Bill and Lorraina very much, and I assumed they loved me back, but our respective social positions made it hard to know how real that love was. They were domestic servants. They did not grow up in a privileged environment. But even if they had, how many kids got to fire submachine guns in the FBI headquarters or rub elbows with movie stars as John and I did when we visited the Warner Brothers studio and had our pictures taken with big stars like Doris Day, Virginia Mayo, and Ruth Roman.

I was thirteen years old when I was sent to Culver, following in the footsteps of my brother. My first roommate was Jewish. The administration probably thought we would be more comfortable with our own kind. Two of the smallest kids in the barracks, we knew why we were stuck together but didn't really talk about it. The idea was to fit in and act like everyone else, but even though I came from a completely nonobservant family, fitting in was difficult. I was Jewish in the eyes of the other boys, and that reality was never far from my mind.

Fortunately Culver's plebe system didn't care who was what. It was equally rough on everyone. Between the older cadets bossing plebes around, a demanding academic schedule, and mandatory athletics, there wasn't much time to think about being different. I learned to do what I was told and stay out of trouble. I even got promoted as the years went by, and eventually became a cadet officer. It didn't matter; I rarely felt at home at Culver. In part that was by design. Culver was engaged in character building, not mollycoddling. But even so I rarely felt a true sense of belonging. Although I had a few close friends, I never felt like one of the boys, as most of my classmates had never met a Jew. At times that made me feel special and maybe even a little bit smarter than the gentile majority. After all, I didn't believe in the virgin birth. Sure, maybe there was a Jesus, and maybe he was a great philosopher and charismatic leader, but if there was no virgin birth, it undercut the idea that he was the son of God. That they accepted those Jesus stories of miracles allowed me to harbor a false sense of superiority.

For the most part, however, being Jewish at Culver was not hard; it was simply the first time in my life that it was more than nothing. Race also wasn't a dominating issue for me, although at Culver it came up occasionally because of the North-South divide among the students. There was no talk of segregation, I think, because everyone had internalized that we as whites occupied a higher place in the world. That was just the way it was. While the uniform for cadets was a leveler, we all looked pretty much alike. Some of the Latino cadets from Central America, Mexico, and Cuba were darker, but they came from rich and powerful families. As to them, there was a crystal-clear Culver point of view even if their skin had a darker hue. They were honorary whites; so instructed, we rarely thought about whether they had any "colored blood." There was a different "normal" down there: "They're just like you," was the Culver message. "They're being trained to be leaders in their countries."

The unspoken message about the black waiters who served our meals was equally clear: "They're nothing like you." They were probably about the same age as we were, but their race raised an impenetrable wall that no one tried to breach. Three times a day we marched into the huge mess hall and sat at tables laid out with military precision by a bunch of black kids who were not being trained to be leaders and who were less than citizens in their own country. They were there to serve us, and after they brought our meals they were trained to disappear just like the help after supper when we lived at Crail Farm.

During my plebe year I hardly noticed the waiters, as I sat rigidly on the two outermost inches of my chair, ever ready to pass food to demanding upper classmen and answer their questions, no matter how frivolous.

As a "yearling," however, I could relax a little and observe the way things worked a little better, and the idea of those waiters started to bother me. At some point I learned that they had been recruited in the South and that they lived in a dormitory somewhere near the school, but I never knew where. During my four years at Culver, I never made any attempt to find out. Their dormitory was off-limits. And that was another Culver message: There was no reason for us to know how they lived. They didn't figure in our lives. It was the same for Bill and Lorraina and other people who worked for our family and friends; the less we knew about the black people who provided services to us, the better.

All we knew was that the black waiters stayed out of our territory, except to clean and serve. The South was a big place, and whatever its problems were, I was pretty sure they didn't concern me. I didn't know where the waiters came from and how they got to Culver. I didn't know what they did in their spare time, or what life was like for them when Culver was not in session. I remember it did seem odd that they never appeared anywhere other than that mess hall. We sometimes went into town on Saturday afternoons to the movies, and we never saw them there either. Probably there were rules, and they weren't allowed to be there.

The Southern contingent at Culver, which was very large, felt right at home with the system in the mess hall. They liked to sing "Dixie," and they liked their Confederate flags. They liked to argue that the South had beaten the hell out of the North in the Civil War, and they especially liked to be waited on by blacks. All the better if those blacks happened to be the same age. That bothered me, as did their bragging about knowing "how to talk to them."

I certainly didn't know how to talk to the black waiters, but I was equally certain that the Southerners didn't have a clue. The idea of those black boys living out there in the woods made me a little uneasy. I had no words for what I was feeling, no vocabulary for it. I could not cite any books to bolster my feelings with organized thought and argumentation. But another seed was planted in the fertile ground of my embryonic sense of where I stood on racial issues: They had every right to be angry at us, Northerners and Southerners alike. If I were in their shoes I certainly would be angry, I thought, watching a world of privilege and serving it, knowing that the opportunities that we white kids thoughtlessly enjoyed was something they would never know. Being Jewish might get me into a few fights and cause me to receive rejection letters from certain colleges, but I started to understand that was nothing compared to staying penned up in the woods and let out to serve white boys three times a day. Like most thoughts of unfairness, though, they were fleeting.

While I passed the summer before my senior year worried about where I was going to college, the waiters were going back to whatever they did in the South. Working on a farm, picking cotton, cleaning up after white people, always avoiding eye contact and saying, "Yes sir" and "Yes ma'am," tipping their hats, getting off the sidewalks so whites could walk by, and hoping nobody took offense because that might mean a late-night visit from a lynch mob. How was I supposed to know about any of that? The Southern boys said they treated them well and that "the coloreds" liked it that way. I was pretty sure they were wrong about that. What little I knew about the lynchings, chain gangs, and other horrors that polluted the South was enough to tell me that no black person liked things the way they were.

By my senior year I had a small circle of friends who had started to question the way things were. I talked about the waiters with them, wondering if they went to school, somehow knowing that they did not. Our little group was pretty much in agreement that it was unfair. We were critical of the attitudes of the Southern boys. We liked to say they had a "mental block" when it came to blacks. A few Southern friends felt the same way, but they were the exception to a fairly ironclad rule and would never say anything publicly. The republic of race was serious stuff.

I do remember one incident about race at Culver that made me think harder about the waiters and Southern attitudes. I wrestled there, and I was pretty good until I couldn't hold down my weight in my senior year. Then it was all over for me. I couldn't beat the bigger guys who, like me, were struggling to make weight for the class that I barely weighed enough to be in.

One afternoon, as our team was preparing for a match and I was struggling with my weight, a teammate announced some news that got everyone's attention.

"I hear there's a black kid on their team," he said.

"I wonder who's going to have to wrestle him?" another asked.

For the whole week that was the talk around the mats. Wrestling was the type of sport where you could get your face stuck in someone's armpit or crotch.

"What if he smells?" someone wondered.

The Southern boys didn't like the idea one bit. The rest of us kept our mouths shut.

"No remarks," the coach warned. "Just go out and fight him like you would anyone else."

We were cadets at a military school, and we did what we were told. The match came off without incident, but I didn't wrestle him because by then I was second string, and I am not sure who won. Also I don't recall if there was any consensus regarding the way the black kid smelled. We all smelled bad, but there was that expectation—certainly among the Southerners and maybe among us Northerners too—that there would be a very telling difference, and I knew those expectations a little from being Jewish. But with us it was not smell. I was never sure what it was.

The parallel to Bill and Lorraina couldn't have been more obvious, but it didn't occur to me then. It was perfectly fine for them to clean and work for us as long as they knew their place and did not interact with us as equals. Like the black wrestler, their presence among us was limited.

While Culver had some wonderful teachers who made history and literature come alive, and occasionally one who invited a few of us over to his home to discuss the "big questions," I don't remember any conversations about race, segregation, the waiters, or that wrestling match, and there was definitely never any discussion of the kinds of social theory that would try to justify or explain how Culver's form of apartheid fitted with the concepts of freedom and democracy we were being taught to defend.

At Harvard prejudice was subterranean, as was common in the North, where bias had adapted to changing social mores and gone into a sort of stealth mode. Admission quotas for Jews were gone. Of course there were still intimations of the old prejudices if you knew what to look for. When I was a freshman, my two assigned roommates were Jews. It was no more accidental than Sheridan Meyers and me in the same room at Culver. We belonged together was the message. Society tells you that, acts on it, and it becomes normal.

I can't say that I minded that my roommates were also Jewish. That provided familiarity while we learned the lay of the land. Having long since discovered that there could be some reaction to my being Jewish, there was something comforting about not having to get into issues about religion, or not having to wonder whether I would be viewed as somehow different.

Low-level anti-Semitism was a reality at Harvard, though it wasn't obvious. You heard it existed at certain social clubs. Then there was the famous Father Feeney, who was an endless fount of anti-Semitic bile. Feeney believed that Harvard's horned-beast men who killed Jesus were an "enemy far more dangerous than McCarthy."

Unlike at Culver, Jews at Harvard more often than not hung out with and dated other Jews. Maybe it was out of familiarity or comfort or culture. Maybe it had to do with religious beliefs, though not in my case. It was a bit of everything. At Culver my closest friends had been Protestants, but at Harvard I slowly migrated into a more Jewish world.

With regard to racial prejudice, the situation was quite different from Culver. In my junior year the senior class elected a black student, Clifford Alexander, who later went on to be the U.S. secretary of the army, as its first class marshal. Also there was a history of at least a few blacks attending Harvard, dating back to Richard Theodore Greener, who graduated four and a half years after the Thirteenth Amendment was ratified. That said, black students when I was there were few and far between.

"Only at Harvard," my friends and I said about Alexander becoming class marshal.

That history and Alexander's popularity notwithstanding, you would have been hard put to find many Harvard students, myself included, who had read a single book written by a black writer. Perhaps there was a mention of George Washington Carver or Booker T. Washington in something we were assigned, but I doubt if I learned a thing about Frederick Douglass, W. E. B. DuBois, Marcus Garvey, or Sojourner Truth, much less contemporary black leaders like Thurgood Marshall.

One of the famously great courses that American history majors like myself took was Arthur Schlesinger, Jr.'s, Intellectual History of the United States. Schlesinger probed the age of Andrew Jackson, the "Bull Moose" (or Progressive) Party, the closing of the frontier, and the New Deal. We studied President Wilson's international policies, but his racist attitudes and how he reversed the small progress blacks had made in the federal bureaucracies were somehow overlooked. I'm also pretty sure we weren't assigned Gunnar Myrdal's classic 1944 study of racism, *An American Dilemma*. Instead I remember focusing on the isms of the day— McCarthyism, communism, capitalism. Out of class, the issue of race was part of an unspoken "gentleman's code" forged in the Boston Brahmin furnace. Silence was golden. The blacks at Harvard defied everything that white society believed about them. They were exceptions to perceived stereotypes. In my experience the thing to do was to pretend that there was no chasm, no differences in our worlds.

Whatever lessons I had learned about being Jewish at Culver were put aside at Harvard. There I soon realized that I was one of many. At the daily student newspaper, the *Crimson*, where I spent much of my time, religion and race took a backseat to top-notch journalism. But while I had friends who were not Jewish, my contacts with black students never evolved into friendships. For example, I worked with Adele Logan, a Radcliffe student from a prominent black family, when I directed Gian Carlo Menotti's *The Consul* for the Harvard Opera Guild, which I founded with a couple of other students. Many of us who worked on the production became friends, but Adele, whose choreography on some very difficult scenes was wonderful, vanished the instant the final curtain came down. Never once had we talked about anything personal. We literally did not discuss anything that did not have to do with the opera. Considering that *The Consul* was about resistance to post–World War II totalitarianism, a discussion about race could well have come up. But it didn't, as neither of us tried to navigate the racial waters that separated us.

Only on the fringes of campus life was a transformation detectable. A handful of students were strumming guitars and talking about things I didn't study at Harvard. One conversation in particular that I recall was about the legendary singer Bessie Smith, who died after a horrible car accident; it was said she was turned away from a white hospital in the South.

"At a hospital?" I asked. "Did that really happen?"

"They let her die outside the door," I was assured. "The same thing could happen today."

I didn't know whether the story was accurate. But it made me think. Stories were coming out of the South about lynchings and how segregated everything was. I remember lying in bed replaying what I'd been told about Bessie Smith. The Hippocratic oath was ignored. Those doctors let her die, and for no other reason than the color of her skin. It boggled my mind. I wondered if the Southerners I had known at Culver would have let that happen. On and on these thoughts rippled out, troubling me. The doctors had to know it was wrong. But I don't remember connecting it to myself, or thinking about how my family treated Bill and Lorraina. Back then, their smiling faces and healthy looks covered up what I would later see as a connection.

The story of Bessie Smith, ironically, was where any similarities between being a Jew and being black in America ended for me. I was sure those same doctors would never leave me to die on the steps of a hospital, just as I was fairly certain that I could look at more or less anyone I pleased without being lynched. This was America, not Nazi Germany.

After college, anti-Semitism was rarely an issue for me, although I did have a passing incident where racism touched me. After graduating, I was stationed at Fort Sam Houston in Texas as an army officer for six months. Then, I worked in the theater before law school, and I lived in New York City. These were all places and, with regard to the military, a station in life, where anti-Semitism was not overt—or at least not to me. Race, however, was different. When I was stationed at Fort Sam, I attended an integrated dance somewhere off base at the edge of San Antonio and quickly learned a sharp lesson about the South. There was a local law, I was told later, that said you couldn't drink past midnight on the day of a local election, and there we were drinking past midnight. I was outside the dance hall when the cop cars came roaring into the parking lot. Standing by my car smoking a cigarette, I remarked to an approaching cop, "That's the biggest flashlight I've ever seen." He punched me in the face, and I spent the night in jail. The cops must have known that blacks and whites were dancing together, I thought. But being white and an officer as well, I was released the following morning.

Back in New York City, it seemed that many Jews thought another Holocaust could strike us at any time, even in America. But I rarely gave that a thought. Every now and then I would read in the newspapers about Jewish graves and temples being desecrated in Brooklyn. For me, however, such events seemed to occur in a different world.

Slowly, however, thoughts about race prejudice were penetrating my thinking. Southern school-integration struggles and lynchings would be on the news, and I would tell friends the story of being slugged in Texas. But day to day I lived in an all-white world and didn't seem to notice the absence of black people wherever I went. Of course there were still Bill and Lorraina, but they seemed like an appendage to our extended family, rather than two hardworking individuals surviving in an uncaring environment, always there, always welcoming. At the outer edges of my thinking, perhaps things were beginning to pile up, however: the waiters at Culver, Bessie Smith, the segregation when I visited my grandparents in Miami Beach, that incident in Texas, and awakening thoughts about Bill and Lorraina. But my focus was on getting a job in the theater. Seeds had been planted, but they were still far from being ready to sprout.

4

Bill Rutherford

It was more than the usual kindness of the family butler. I used to think it had to do with my brother so clearly being the favored child. John was good at sports and a solid student. He didn't need any special treatment. I missed a lot of school because of various illnesses, and I was continually falling behind in school. We were a study in contrasts.

As a child I didn't try to parse the relationship. I loved that Bill Rutherford called me Skippy. He paid attention to me. Whether I was Skippy the kid who got skipped or it was just the name that came into Bill's head, I was thrilled to have a nickname.

I don't know why Bill and Lorraina stopped working for my parents. I was at Culver when they went to work for Grandma Bessie and Major. Maybe they really had been there to be like a second set of parents, and after I was sent to Culver they were no longer needed. Maybe my mother and father wanted to simplify. Bill and Lorraina had always been there to make our lives—school and sports and shows and concerts, social events, and all the rest—a little easier. They were there to keep the apartment spotless and to cook whatever my mother ordered by phone from Gristede's. There was a laundress who appeared once a week, too. I took it all for granted and really didn't think about how other families did things.

My mother definitely liked that buzzer in our dining room that called Bill to bring this or that. There was small talk—how we were doing in school, what was going on with the sports we played or followed. Dinner was the time we were supposed to be together.

Occasionally my father and mother talked about matters pertaining to the household economy or the economy of the allied households that fell under Grandma Bessie's protectorship. And while that sort of thing happens in all kinds of homes, the focus was on Bessie, from whom all good things apparently came. Although I had little understanding of the mechanics of our family's life, Bessie was the center of my parents' attention. As I later understood, we stood to benefit from a society that stayed more or less the same, preserving our position on top. To say that money and privilege were the reasons my parents were not social activists would be too simple. However, few people question the order of things when it is to their benefit that nothing changes. There was no upside for my parents to agonize over the treatment of black people in the South, or of the help, or anything else.

Oceans of social and emotional change and growth long since covered, I'm not sure, however, that the whys and wherefores matter much. The specific social dynamic in our home was what mattered to me. We had domestic help. That help was black. At some point they got sent somewhere else within the family to do more of the same, and a relationship that mattered a lot to me changed in ways I didn't understand.

Talking about maintaining the status quo, that probably applied to Bill and Lorraina too. They had escaped the South. As far as I knew they didn't participate in the civil rights movement. They had jobs that kept them busy from morning till night as butler, chauffeur, bootblack, heavy lifter, cook, and lady's maid. They served three meals a day except Thursdays and Sundays, when they served only one or two. It was their job to put the kitchen back together after those meals. It didn't matter if the air conditioner was on; there would be sweat on their brows when they were working. But they seemed content. Or maybe that's how I needed to see them. Smiles are easy to forge. It never occurred to me until much later in life to wonder about things like that. To me they were just Bill and Lorraina, always there, always smiling, ready to give me a hug.

I write about them not only because they meant a lot to me, but also because they mean something in the big picture. Racism flourishes in the blind spots that even the most conscientious people have. Although history was my favorite subject in school, I lost sight of what little I knew about the South when it came to Bill and Lorraina, two people who, despite their employment status and placement in the American caste system, were dear to me. As I grew older and was able to understand better, I blocked thoughts about what their lives had been like before they came to my family, let alone about their lives up North. It was not intentional. It was hard to accommodate both the reality and my feelings about that reality, even though I had enough of the facts. They were raised in the South when Jim Crow was still the law of the land and black men were regularly lynched for crimes ranging from garden-variety forms of disrespect to a lingering gaze in the direction of a white woman. Doing quick math on my fingers, I think they were within the age range to have family members who had been slaves. I wondered about that. Bill was light-skinned, and I would have to guess that there were white people in his genealogy—a grandmother who happened to be at the wrong place at the wrong time or some other equally troubling explanation. The possibilities were nothing I wanted to ask about. No matter how close I thought we were, a question so pointedly focused on the main insult to our intimacy—the black-white divide—was unthinkable.

Up North the whip and the lynch mob were considered the barbaric manifestations of unenlightened bigots nostalgic for a time that thankfully had gone the way of slavery and the seven-day workweek. But still Bill and Lorraina were tied to their more-or-less seven-day-a-week jobs. In the Hampshire House the entire staff (except for certain household servants) was white, as far as I knew, which included the doormen, the front-desk personnel, the restaurant waiters, even the back-elevator servicemen. It was a closed shop to people of color. And while Bill and Lorraina might have been able to find jobs working for some other wealthy white people, it would not have been easy. They weren't slaves, but they weren't exactly free to leave either. A black servant needed references from his or her present and/or previous employer, which was tricky. In Bill and Lorraina's case there would have to be a job for a married couple—as well as an explanation as to why they no longer worked for the Warner family, why they left my parents, and a lot of thinking and wondering on the part of their prospective employers—which meant that for Bill and Lorraina, changing jobs was not something they thought too much about. They were free to leave, but if they wanted to live together and earn a salary, they were nowhere near free in the way that people think of freedom. They occupied a place in society that predictably assured their past would also be their future.

As the civil rights movement picked up steam, I assumed Bill and Lorraina were not involved in it. They benefited in the ways any person of color did at the time, but it seemed as if they did so quietly. Maybe they sent a few dollars to the NAACP every now and then, but if they did, I didn't know about it.

In conversations with Bill, the sort of things liberal students discussed just never came up, whether it was Bull Connor unleashing dogs that attacked civil rights protesters, the 16th Street Baptist Church bombing in Birmingham that killed those four girls, burning buses, or mass arrests. Bill seemed far removed from that struggle.

Of course most white people I knew, especially those of my parents' generation, were far removed from the struggle for equality too. Many thought back then that Jim Crow segregation of black and white in the South could be undone without affecting the upper echelons of society. As a teenager I reflected my parents' attitudes and understanding of the situation. As I learned much later, I was wrong. Without Jim Crow laws, there was up North almost as much segregation and just enough tolerance to keep racial intolerance, prejudice, and bigotry from boiling over—that is, until a black family tried to move into a white neighborhood almost anywhere in the North, and whites burned crosses or attacked their homes and threatened their lives. Then, in the 1960s, when racial unrest and the black power movement shattered their complacency, whites were shocked and angered when blacks reacted violently to the deprivations they suffered. As I grew older, however, I began to see that Bill and Lorraina were expected to have no needs or wants themselves, and in some ways treated like the servers were treated at Culver. As I became more aware, I asked careful questions that were gently half answered or ignored. Still, it was not hard to go about my life as a passive agent of the status quo.

When Bill and Lorraina left to work for my grandparents, it didn't hit the heights of drama or even register much in the way of change. As far as I was concerned they were elsewhere working for the family.

I didn't mind too much, because I knew I would see them. The big smile and hug were the way we greeted one another after the longer and longer absences from the comforts so stitched into the experience of growing up with them, but the little betrayals of our racial and social caste differences proliferated. They were still "there," even though I was growing and changing, because that was their job. I saw them at the weekend house in Westchester County during the summer and down in Miami Beach over the Christmas holidays. I still found my way to their room and flopped down on the bed and talked to them, as I had in my childhood days, but I was no longer the same person and our relationship had changed. I no longer needed them. I was becoming, without my knowing it, another white man they worked for. I came and went as I pleased, taking for granted their always being there.

Bill, never too probing, would ask me about my life.

"Doing well?" he'd say.

"Everything's going great," I would typically reply.

"That's wonderful."

We each recited our parts. Bill still sometimes called me Skippy, and that felt good.

In Miami Beach I knew that blacks were getting tired of sitting in the back of the buses. They didn't want to get up to let white people sit down. Because we stayed in a wealthy, whites-only colony, I rarely saw the segregation although it was in front of my eyes. But when I did, like on the buses, I felt embarrassed—perhaps even guilty—about being a white person. In New York it was easier to maintain illusions. In the South, even in Yankee-packed Miami Beach, the reality of the coming racial wars was hard to miss.

As I grew older, family dinner discussion did occasionally turn to racial issues, but the conversations never went anywhere: "Things are fine the way they are," Major would say. "Those damned fools are only stirring up trouble."

Sometimes Major turned to Bill for confirmation: "They like it the way it is, isn't that right, Bill?"

"Anything you say, sir," Bill invariably replied.

And that was the end of it. We knew it was a bad idea to rile Major. But his total disregard for Bill's personhood was a denial of his humanity, and I could not help being aware of it. Bill did his thing regardless of Major's insensitivity. He served the meals in stately fashion, making a production of moving dishes and trays in and out of the dining room. Grandma Bessie's finger on the tinkling bell announced our readiness for each new course. With an ever-so-slight bow, Bill brought in the tray.

"I think I'll take the end piece. It looks so good."

"As you wish, sir." The words were delivered with a deferential nod, the tray lowered from the left to just the right level.

Every now and then one of the women said, "William serves so beautifully."

"Thank you, ma'am," Bill would reply. "You are so kind."

As much as I wanted to take my place at the dinner table, being waited on like the adult family members was hard, and I began to shrink from the table's rituals. There was nothing I could say to Bill when he served me that didn't bring with it the risk of a courteous response, which to me would be hurtful.

I looked into his eyes when he passed the tray.

"Thank you," I said.

I wished he could somehow understand that I wasn't one of them. I wanted to be a grown-up, but not to become a master. At the end of each meal, I sneaked off to the kitchen to prove that I was different from the other adults at the table.

The older I got, the harder our relationship became to navigate. After dinner at my grandmother's, I started staying with the adults, and my trips to the kitchen became more perfunctory. Bill was still Bill, and I had become Lewis. But Bill was more reserved. I know now that this was not because he had changed, but because I had. Wordsworth wrote that the child is the father of the man, and in that respect Skippy was still around, and Bill was still a keystone in my developing sensitivity to race. But my childhood was fading into adulthood, and while certain things survived, my relationship with Bill and Lorraina was changing. Each time I saw Bill, it was slipping further and further away.

Sometimes I felt the pang of loss, but often I managed to desensitize myself to the pain of our drifting apart, or simply to ignore it because

I was focused on what seemed like a new world. Bill was slowly becoming a mythical figure from my past. I carried his warmth and caring inside me as a seed that turned into a life in the civil rights movement, but the days of needing him had passed. Around this time, Bill changed the rules. Between my subtle detachment and Bill's, it was no longer possible for me to indulge in the fiction that I was still his boy. He soon stopped calling me Lewis. I became "Mr. Lewis." And for a while I pretended not to hear him. It was like some of the other new ministrations that I rejected, like the ritual around my coat.

"May I take your coat?" Bill would ask, as though I were a visitor who required special treatment.

"I got it," I would reply, smiling.

But "Mr. Lewis" was too much. It wrecked my sense of belonging. I thought about talking to Bill about it, but I couldn't. Every time I ran through the conversation mentally, it seemed impossible. I imagined asking him if there was a way for us to turn back the clock. But in the end, saying anything to Bill about what he was calling me seemed like a violation of some unspoken rules of our social contract. And it was. Talking about it was too threatening. It felt wrong. That was racism's domain, and I was part of the problem.

If I asked Bill why he was calling me "Mr. Lewis," I had no idea what he would say. Maybe, I worried, he would have told me the truth: "Because that is what you have become."

But I doubt that would have happened. There were other forms of subterfuge open to him. He could have claimed that Bessie and Major wanted it that way. If I pleaded with him to stop, I figured he might. But even then, wouldn't my pleading be interpreted as a command? And wouldn't I hear the echo of that command in whatever he called me after that?

Filled with anxiety, I talked to Lorraina about it a few times. She nodded when I told her I felt that Bill was shutting me out, and that it hurt because I loved him very much.

"I don't want to be anything but Lewis or Skippy to him," I said.

"I know," she said.

We looked at each other, both of us sad.

"Can you say something to him?" I asked her. "I'm afraid anything I say to him will make it worse."

Lorraina was touched, but her choices were limited. Fear probably made it harder for her too. She shook her head and told me that Bill still loved me.

"That's his way," she explained.

I protested.

"It is too hard for him any other way," she said smiling. "You've got to accept it. The Lord makes people the way they are. And you will be a good man," she said, holding me by the shoulders, "just like Bill is a good man."

5

Kitty Muldoon

Becoming a civil rights lawyer wasn't exactly a fallback position, though I did work in the theater for a while before I went to law school and subsequently joined the movement. It would be more accurate to say it was part of my evolution. Race issues started to intrude at Culver Military Academy. Perhaps a dormant seed had already been planted with Bill and Lorraina, but there were other influences, like the blacks who served meals at Culver. They were our age. We cadets treated them like nonentities, and they lived somewhere out of sight, invisible. Then in Florida, the segregated buses, and the folksingers' stories at Harvard, and in Texas, the night in jail for going to an integrated dance, and the goings-on in the South as the effort to end Jim Crow heated up—it all added up and started to occupy a larger and larger place in my mind.

The increasingly visible battle against racial injustice probably lurked beneath the surface of my fantasies of becoming a stage director too. I saw the theater as a place where the important issues of the day could come to life. I loved Henrik Ibsen, George Bernard Shaw, Arthur Miller, Tennessee Williams, Lorraine Hansberry, and others for how they were able to change the way people looked at the world. American musical theater used lyrics to get to people's hearts and minds. So many songs come to mind: *Show Boat*'s "Ol' Man River" and "You've Got to Be Carefully Taught" from *South Pacific*, and of course all those numbers in *West Side Story*. Then there was Menotti's *The Consul*, which I had directed at Harvard. All these spoke to injustice. I was drawn to characters who cried out for liberation. Then there was that mournful song I first heard at Harvard, "Strange Fruit." Billie Holiday is probably better known for it, but when I listened to Josh White's version, I felt as if I'd witnessed with my own eyes the horrible truth of lynching in the South. In many ways theater was my first revolt from the more conventional path taken by my brother of going to a top law school and then joining a well-regarded law firm. I had a few good but low-paying theatrical jobs—including an onstage appearance feeding laugh lines to Academy Award winner Melvyn Douglas in the Broadway production of Gore Vidal's *The Best Man*, before deciding that this was not the place for me.

Melvyn Douglas aside, the most important gig of my short-lived show-business career was a revival of *Babes in Arms*, the musical by Richard Rodgers and Lorenz Hart, our old neighbor before we moved to Park Avenue. It was on the set of that production that I met Kitty Muldoon, who became my wife of more than half a century. She was playing the ingenue; I was the assistant stage manager. We fell in love.

To my eyes Kitty was one of a kind. To describe her I would have to use every positive adjective in the dictionary. She was beautiful, caring, unspoiled, filled with fun, had only good words for everyone, a great listener, and—despite being only a high school graduate—someone who read a little of everything, knew more than a little about history and art, and was the most emotionally intelligent person I'd ever met. She also had a great soprano voice and knew hundreds of songs, though she couldn't read a note of music. I'd never met anyone like her in the theater, at college, or among the various girls who populated my world at home. Kitty had heartbreak in her story too, which deepened the rivers of her soul and I think made her a more kindred spirit. When she was a teenager, her baby brother, Johnny, died. She was in charge, babysitting, when a neighborhood friend got into a car across the street from their house and released the emergency brake. It rolled and struck her little brother. The family's tragedy was never more than a few moments out of her thoughts, and in many ways probably shaped her life. In addition to her other qualities, Kitty did not appear to have a prejudiced bone in her body. Kitty's best friend was a comedian named Mitzi McCall. Like many Jews during that era, she changed her name (from Steiner) to get more work. Also, Kitty's mother, Irene, had eloped with a Jewish boy when she was a teenager, but the families forced them to get the marriage annulled. The Jewish family supposedly sat shiva for Irene's short-lived husband, who, they proclaimed, was dead to them for marrying outside the faith. It was a hard lesson in intolerance, and one that made Irene adamant about teaching her children to put prejudice aside. Kitty was a regular churchgoer back when we met, and I knew all about going to church from Culver, where we were marched to the school's nondenominational Protestant church for vespers twice a week, as well as for the Sunday service. "Onward Christian Soldiers" and "Stout-Hearted Men" were among the choir's standard offerings. Religious services were not among my post-Culver activities, but I was so smitten with Kitty that I joined her every Sunday because I wanted her to know that I could accept her religious beliefs. Catholicism was new to me. I had no experience with kneeling, crossing myself, or breathing in the incense. I didn't know about the prayer candles, and I wasn't sure what I thought about it all. But I liked the Latin a lot. It was mysterious.

The rift between Protestants and Catholics was a bigger deal to Kitty. It didn't mean very much to me. When I mentioned "Onward Christian Soldiers," she informed me: "We don't sing that. It's Protestant."

I will never forget the night we went to the Gate of Horn in Chicago's Rice Hotel after the *Babes in Arms* show that night in Highland Park's tent theater. We sat in that club listening to Josh White. He sang "Strange Fruit," which was a test of sorts. Had Kitty hated it, I don't know what I would have done—but I might not have felt the same way about her. I needed to be sure Kitty got it.

After *Babes in Arms* closed, I didn't see Kitty for about seven months. She lived with her parents, who had long ago moved from Pittsburgh to Altadena so she could attend the Pasadena Playhouse. Quickly Kitty was cast in *Les Girls*, which played in Las Vegas's Desert Inn. I was working too—first on a Tennessee Williams play in New York and then in London as the producer's assistant in Rodgers and Hammerstein's *Flower Drum Song*. The following spring Kitty came back to New York as a Miss Rheingold finalist. Six months later we were engaged.

I was twenty-three. According to her passport and driver's license she was two years older than I. Ten years later, while we were on vacation,

Kitty brought up our age difference: "Darling, what if I were to tell you I'm a little bit older than you think I am?"

"How the hell old are you?" I shot back, echoing the prejudice of the day about marrying an "older woman." Had I been nicer, she might not have chopped a year off the real number. It wasn't until my seventieth birthday that her age came up again: "Darling," she started in exactly the same way. "What would you say if I told you I'm a little older than you think I am?

"How old are you?" I asked. She added the missing year. "That's sad," I said. "I'll have one year less to love you." Sometimes you learn with age. The age difference was never a big deal, but other things were. While Kitty's family didn't care that I was Jewish, my mother cared a lot that Kitty didn't come from a wealthy family. Somehow she decided that it was best to ascribe her disapproval to the religious difference. The insanity when I told her that Kitty and I were getting married in a Catholic church was memorable. She didn't want to know about the church wedding.

"Your grandmother won't come," she fumed.

I thought it was all a show. Bessie wouldn't miss my wedding, but the damage was done. Kitty was hurt, and I felt that was the real goal.

My mother had been unrelentingly miserable to Kitty from the moment she laid eyes on her—no kind words, no taking her out to lunch, not even the tiniest present as a gesture of goodwill after we announced our engagement. Nothing. She wanted Kitty to know that she wasn't welcome—that she was and would remain an outsider. Trying to dictate the terms of our wedding merely offered another way for her to send that message. I stayed silent when all this happened—an unwilling but complicit agent of my mother's agenda. It was not my finest moment. To Kitty, not getting married in a Catholic church was not getting married at all, so we ended up having a secret church wedding without my parents, and then another one for my family at my grandparents' place in Miami Beach. In the pictures that were taken at that wedding, there is one of Kitty and me with Bill and Lorraina. Sadly, or more to the point, that photo did not make it into the wedding album.

The irony of expecting prejudice from Kitty's family when there was none (or very little), while my mother's snobbery masquerading as prejudice forced us to have two separate weddings, was exquisite. I should have been furious, but I went into survival mode. I wanted to get through the whole thing without being disowned.

Making our real wedding easy, a close friend, John Eyre, set up the church ceremony. He had connections in the New York Diocese and somehow arranged for us to get married on Holy Thursday, the day before Good Friday. Standing in for her father, John accompanied Kitty down the aisle. Kindly as Irene was, she wasn't going to share the occasion with Jack Muldoon, with whom she was on the outs. My brother, John, served as my best man. A few friends were there, and of course we had Kitty's two disabled aunts from Erie, Pennsylvania, who wouldn't have missed our wedding for the world.

Being a Jew married to a gorgeous Irish Catholic girl made me feel like a stranger from another world. I was afraid the more doctrinaire members of the Catholic Church might take a dim view of one of their own marrying a Jew, as the boys from the South had when wrestling a black kid at Culver. Of course there was a difference. When I left the church after our marriage, I didn't fear for my life because I had flouted a cultural convention. There would be no thugs waiting for me, much less a lynch mob. It seems unlikely that the black wrestler's feelings were the same as mine. While he was not in danger at Culver, I feel certain he was on heightened alert.

Twenty-three going on fifteen is what I felt like when I got married, and there I was in church, all the crosses covered with dark fabric, and all I could think was that "they" had done that because Kitty was marrying a Jew. I believed they thought they had to protect the crosses from the affront. It was unsettling. The reality was that the crosses were covered because it was Holy Week. But there was no way I could know that when I walked down the aisle. I loved Kitty, I was committed to her, and even though I wondered what I was getting myself into, I wasn't about to say a word. The red-cheeked priest, Father O'Pray, had a twinkle in his eyes as he did his thing. It was short and simple. Walking out of the church, married, I breathed a sigh of relief and put the covered crosses out of my mind. That afternoon John Eyre and his wife, Susan, threw us a party. Afterward we went straight to Miami Beach for what my family thought was our marriage the next day. I've long since forgotten the lies we must have told about why none of Kitty's family showed up. But then again, my parents didn't care. I was marrying into an Irish cop's family, not into the family of a Catholic millionaire or aristocrat. The Irish Catholic part was meaningless. My parents would have been delighted if I had married into the Kennedy family. The problem was class. The irony of Kitty Muldoon, a cop's daughter, born without sufficient pedigree, was that she would become the most educated member of the Steel family, with two master's degrees, a Ph.D., and a career as a psychoanalyst.

Over the years my parents never once visited Kitty's family, even when they vacationed near them in California. When they went to Palm Springs, they visited Lottie and Harold Mirisch, who produced *Some Like It Hot*, *West Side Story*, *The Pink Panther*, and other blockbusters. But Ruth and Arthur had no time to see the Muldoons.

When I joined Kitty's family in that slow dance where strangers are supposed to love each other or at least be nice, I sensed a few mild intimations of anti-Semitism. It wasn't much—some loose words said in jest or the automatic kind said without any intended malice, like that old chestnut, "Jews can't go to heaven." What I saw as anti-Semitic, however, could have been something else. I can't be sure. Perhaps I was oversensitive and too quick to apply an incorrect label. It could have been me, I can't be sure. Sometimes I think it may be impossible to grow up Jewish in the United States, even in New York City, without getting a taste of the very real—sublimated, modulated, insinuated—prejudice against Jews out there. So maybe I jumped too quickly while staying with the Muldoons. There were what I took to be concrete things; Grandpa Duffy, sister Mary's grandfather in-law, dousing me with a glass of whiskey being the most memorable. But maybe even that was not anti-Semitism; it could have been his playful way of welcoming me into the family.

The glaring difference between my family and Kitty's was that the Steels were rich and the Muldoons were not. My father was happily married; he never laid a hand on John or me. He traveled the world and went to an Ivy League college. His kids were also college graduates, one a lawyer and the other on his way. Of Jack's four children, Kitty was the best educated; she had two college credits and two years of drama school.

That Jack Muldoon wasn't the best husband goes well beyond universal relativism. As for his fathering, three out of his four children found him hard to take. But none of that mattered to Kitty. She loved him as only a favorite child can.

Jack was raised in an orphanage by an order of monks in Pittsburgh, and the story was that he was abused by the brothers there. It seemed to me that he became a cop so no one could hurt him again. The blackjack he carried around in the back pocket of his uniform was an insurance policy. He also recited poetry, read history, sang old Irish songs in a beautiful tenor voice, and could tell stories with a wry sense of humor.

Almost the first thing out of Jack's mouth when we met was, "I hear they have a lot of pinkos at Harvard." God knows how I replied to that.

Only Kitty knew how to handle Jack's moods, always staying on his good side. It didn't hurt that she was the apple of his eye. She could glide over the pitfalls of daily life with Jack when everyone else had to walk on eggshells. Having heard the family stories for more than five decades, I believe the takeaway is that Kitty symbolized everything Jack wanted to be. It was almost as if she were a reflection of his better self.

Jack and I got along all right. He adored Kitty and wanted the best for her. I benefited from that. She loved him. I adored her. But that didn't stop Jack from reciting his version of the Cohen and McCarthy story in two distinct dialects, Irish brogue, and Yiddish that to this day Kitty can do perfectly: McCarthy had a brickyard, and Cohen had nothing. So Cohen baited McCarthy—calling him names and taunting—till McCarthy threw his bricks at him. Cohen kept up the harangue till McCarthy had no more bricks. Then Cohen took all those bricks and built a grand hotel. He called it "Ireland."

However, I was never sure whether that was a "crafty Jew" story. If Jack held any real prejudices against Jews, he hid them from me. There was no way he'd let something like my religious background get in the way of his special child marrying into the Warner family.

When we visited California we always stayed with Kitty's sister Mary. She had married Jim Duffy, a died-in-the-wool American Irishman who drank beer and loved the "ould sod." In the beginning I was always on my guard in their home.

As far as I was concerned, the Muldoon-Duffy clan belonged to a different tribe. I downed a Scotch or two from time to time and I liked to have a few beers now and then, but drinking was not my thing. Because I saw myself as being so different, I thought they would consider me an intruder who had married their prize girl. And that made me feel like the odd man out. And the sense of being a Jew was always there, someone who did not believe in their Jesus Christ or the Virgin Mary, or for that matter the God of both the Jews and the Catholics.

Over the years, however, I drew close to Mary, Jim, and their children, Jimmy and Erin. Jim and I became good friends. He retired as the general manager of his local pipefitter's union, after integrating it with blacks, Latinos, and women, all the time retaining the respect of his white members. Jim marched with Cesar Chavez during the farmworker strikes and became a progressive voice in Southern California. His son became a public defender handling death-penalty cases, and Erin is one of my daughter's closest friends.

Ten years after we were married Kitty overheard me telling the story of how the church covered all the crosses for our wedding.

"That had nothing to do with you being Jewish!" she exclaimed. "It was the Thursday before Good Friday. The crosses are always covered."

Afterward she marveled that I had kept that to myself for all those years.

"What was I to think?" I replied.

When we moved into our first apartment, Kitty put up a cross in the hallway to our bedroom. I looked at it a lot. Sometimes I ignored it. But sometimes it made me feel anxious. Looking at it sideways, out of the corners of my eyes, I started to fear that it was going to come between us. It was Kitty's cross, I told myself, and her religion, and she should be able to be herself in her own home. If I wanted to put up a mezuzah by our door, Kitty would have had no objection.

That Kitty had a right to hang her cross in her own home, however, was not a feeling shared by my mother. When my parents visited, I saw my mother eye the cross, but she said nothing. She waited till she had a way to use that sighting to her advantage. The opportunity arose the next time we were on the phone.

"Grandma Bessie will never come to your apartment if you keep that cross up," she said in her archest tone.

I disputed that, but she was insistent.

"You must tell her in advance, so that she can tell you without having to see it," she scolded me. "Or I will do it."

When I told Kitty about the call, she felt trapped. She was alone in New York City without the support of her own family, which had always been a big part of her life. It wasn't easy trying to integrate herself into a different culture, with a mother-in-law who saw her as a shanty Irish showgirl who had seduced her gullible son. It was hard for Kitty to understand and accept that she would never be able to win over my mother the way she had everyone else. Ruth was all pretense and show. Her status within our family, and the way she was perceived by the tiny society of well-heeled Jews she cared about, was her overriding concern. Kitty was pretty, and people liked her. She had an easy way about her and no guile—and that was anathema to my mother.

I tried to assure Kitty that I would stand by her if she wanted to keep the cross up. I told her that my mother was blowing things out of proportion, that my grandmother wouldn't be upset in the least.

Kitty had a good relationship with Bessie. It seemed absurd even to think about whether she would accept Kitty's cross as the natural symbol of her religious belief. It was a given. But my mother managed to cast that into doubt, which was infuriating because being Jewish meant nothing to her. She even gave a fleeting thought to becoming Unitarian, but apparently that lasted through only one Sunday service. Years later she read a few books on Zen Buddhism. It was just a passing thing, although after my father died and she was in her late eighties, Ruth claimed she was a Buddhist. I joked and said she was a "Jew-Boo." She tried that out on a few friends and soon began calling herself that.

While my mother didn't have a religious bone in her body, religion was important to Bessie. So Kitty's religion was a plus. Bessie had heard that Pope Plus XII saved many Jews during the war, even hiding some of them in the Vatican. He was a good pope, she always said, and after

Kitty became part of her family, Bessie always served fish at her Friday dinners.

But Kitty was deeply insecure about her status in the family, I was a weakling, and that business about the crucifix gnawed at her. Bessie was supporting us at the time, and Ruth had her ear.

"You're wrong." That's what I should have said to Ruth about the cross. "It's not coming down no matter what."

Instead I told Kitty, "If you tell me you want the cross to stay up, it will stay up." Looking for guidance and the comfort of home, Kitty cried to her mother, Irene, the peacemaker. She soothed Kitty and told her to accept the situation for what it was, and the crucifix came down.

Kitty was deeply hurt. She let me to know I had not been a pillar of fortitude. I told her to put it back up if she wanted, but that wasn't the same thing as putting a nail in the wall and hanging it back up myself.

It wasn't long after that we purchased a painting of Jesus by an artist named Joachim Probst, who painted luminous pictures of saints and other religious figures. It hangs outside our bedroom today, not as a religious symbol but in homage to a man who sought a better way of life for the poor, and a more peaceful world.

While we were on vacation in Rome a few years later, my father arranged for us to attend a papal audience in the Vatican. Among the guests milling around the chapel, we waited for the Lord's vicar to appear. Pope Paul VI glided in, all in white. To me he looked like how I imagined a medieval artist would paint Satan. I stared at those bushy black eyebrows perched above his deep-set dark eyes and looked for a sign of warmth in his long, severe face. Not a trace of a smile or a twinkle in his eyes softened his features.

"He looks like the devil," I whispered.

Kitty shushed me.

The pope was doing his duty, allowing himself to be seen. He blessed all the trinkets and saints' medals people brought and disappeared whence he came. Kitty was delighted. She had seen the pope and had treasures for all of her family. I don't think my little comment about the satanic-looking pope—which I have happily repeated many times since then—diminished the experience, though I suspect Kitty would say that I was just being my ornery self.

Over the years Kitty drifted away from Sunday churchgoing, saving her attendance for Christmas, Easter, and sometimes Ash Wednesday. She also goes with her sisters, Mary and Dolores, when they are together. The falling-off began with an incident at confession that was sparked by her mother. She had told the priest she was going to use birth control, and that her mother had told her it was all right—that it was her own personal sin. The priest said her mother would burn in hell. Kitty left the confessional with tears running down her face. She considered her mother a saintly woman. Despite her mother's advice that she just go to another priest, Kitty's questioning of the dogmas of her faith grew. Certain mainstays fell away, but her sense of belonging remained.

Many years later, when we were in our seventies, we went to San Juan Capistrano, the California town famous for its migratory swallows, to spend the day and see its old Catholic mission.

"I'm going to buy a cross there," Kitty said on the drive down from Mary's house, "to replace the one Ruth made me take down."

In the gift shop, with me looking over her shoulder, Kitty purchased a small crucifix.

"She can't tell me to take it down anymore," Kitty said. Later, on the drive back, she told me something I had never known before.

"The cross Ruth made me take down," she said, "was in my little brother's coffin before we buried him."

Prior to hearing that, I had always done a little mental dance about the cross. Kitty, of course, could put the cross wherever she wanted. But now I saw the cross in a wholly different light—as a remembrance of Johnny and the darkest part of her life. I was glad she purchased that cross and that it now hangs in our home, closing that chapter in our life.

6

Starting at the NAACP

Contrary to Ruth's admonishments, Grandma Bessie never retaliated because of Kitty's religious background or any other reason. She kept us afloat after I graduated while I was in law school and Kitty had her swan song in show business—with Jimmy Durante at the Copacabana—shortly before we married. There were also the occasional television commercials, but Kitty had decided to get an education, keep up her acting and singing on the side, and start a family. A regular at family dinners, she developed a caring relationship with Grandma Bessie and got along well with Major, who sometimes would roll up to Kitty in his Cadillac, chauffeured by Bill, to whisk her away from NYU to the Aqueduct racetrack, where they would spend the day playing the ponies.

"Here's a twenty, blondie," Major would say, handing her the crisp bill on his way to place his bets.

"How'd you do?" Major would ask her at the end of the day.

"Not too good, I'm afraid," she would usually say. "I lost the twenty." That was Major's cue to hand her another twenty.

"But don't ever come back," he'd joke.

Meanwhile, after law school, I applied to a few law firms and to the U.S. Attorney's Office. My lack of enthusiasm and ambivalence were obvious, however, and my failure to get a single job offer came as no surprise. I just did not see myself at a desk, pushing papers, at a time when the country was in an uproar over civil rights activists trying to desegregate the South. Even though Kitty was about to have our first child, I was not ready to settle down. There had to be a better way to lead my life, and I could not get those media images of youthful blacks, joined by young whites from up North, being brutally attacked by Southern mobs, aided and abetted by the local police, out of my mind. That was a different America from the one I imagined. John F. Kennedy, a Harvard man like me, had urged all of us who had rallied to him: "Ask what you can do for your country." I wanted to be able to say, "I hear you," but I could not do that by remaining on the sidelines.

The woman who answered the phone told me I could talk to one of the general counsel's assistants if I wanted to learn more about volunteering at the NAACP.

I met Maria Marcus in the cramped quarters allocated to the NAACP's legal staff at Freedom House, which was at 20 West Fortieth Street across from the New York Public Library. The busy office of my imagination, bustling with lawyers, gave way to a nearly deserted office suite. Maria was there with Princene Hutcherson, secretary to the NAACP's general counsel, Robert L. Carter. He and Barbara Morris, the only other attorney, were out, working on a case.

Maria was white and perhaps five years older than I. She was friendly and conveyed a sense of urgency. It was among her jobs to coordinate the work, and she needed help. I told her I had graduated first in my class and had been the editor in chief of the *Law Review*. She told me there was plenty to do, and I could start right away. Maria sent me—nervous but excited—to the New York City Bar Association's library a few blocks away to look up the court procedures of a Southern state where the NAACP had been sued. I did that and rushed back with the information, ready for my next assignment. By the end of that first week, Maria started to treat me like a staff member.

The NAACP worked through a branch structure, with its national office there to develop policy and programs, push Congress and the president to pass civil rights laws, coordinate with like-minded organizations, and protect its members on the front lines of the civil rights movement when they came under attack. For example, in the South some NAACP branches were boycotting businesses that refused to serve or hire blacks. Some of the targeted establishments retaliated by suing the local NAACP branches, and occasionally the national office was named in those lawsuits. The cases were heard by hostile judges and all-white juries, calling into question the survival of the entire organization. A First Amendment expert, Carter and his attorneys invoked freedom of speech and the right of assembly, but those issues were often complicated by what proprietors claimed was the threatening behavior of the demonstrators. Only rarely did the national office have any control over those demonstrations. It set policies, but the branches did their own thing—then turning to the legal staff to defend them.

"The other organizations will come and go," Maria told me, referring to the more militant groups like the Student Nonviolent Coordinating Committee, "but it will be up to the NAACP to pick up the pieces and go on."

To keep the branches functioning and to protect the national office, someone had to crank out the legal papers to oppose all the Southern lawsuits that were coming our way.

I learned quickly and started looking for ways to counterattack. Soon I was invited to staff meetings to discuss cases, where I began to focus on the work's broader implications. Carter's office was often empty because he was meeting with NAACP activists and organizers around the country. But it was his vision that guided our work.

Maria helped me get my bearings. She was married to a corporate lawyer and had two young children. Maria was in love with the law, and she spoke in quasi-mystical terms about her father, who had served as a judge in pre-Hitler Austria. Carter, she thought, was cut from the same cloth: Both were great men committed to justice.

Everyone called Carter Bob, even though he was a larger-than-life character. When I arrived he had recently saved the NAACP from what might have been a crippling blow by winning a series of Supreme Court cases. At issue were the NAACP membership lists, which were kept secret so that individuals could join without fear of reprisal or retaliation. The first case was called *NAACP v. Alabama*. Bob won another Supreme Court decision, *NAACP v. Button*, repulsing Southern attacks on NAACP attorneys for allegedly concocting lawsuits on behalf of branch members instead of individuals who fitted the organization's stated mission. *Button* overturned a state supreme court ruling that subjected local branch attorneys associated with the NAACP to severe sanctions on the grounds that group representation was illegal.

Maria also gave me a thumbnail sketch of the tangled history that resulted in Bob's becoming NAACP general counsel rather than head of the NAACP Legal Defense and Education Fund (LDF), which had a large staff of civil rights attorneys. The story went like this: Thurgood Marshall had headed the LDF. Bob had been his longtime chief assistant before Marshall became a U.S. circuit court judge, then the U.S. solicitor general, and finally the first black Supreme Court justice. As Marshall's assistant, Carter had played a key role in developing the legal strategy that prevailed in the Supreme Court's *Brown v. Board of Education* decision, and had won a series of Supreme Court cases that were stepping-stones leading up to *Brown*. Bob was also behind the social-science testimony cited in *Brown* that segregation caused irreparable harm to a black child's self-esteem.

Seven years Bob's junior, Jack Greenberg, who was white, had played a much lesser role in the NAACP's legal battles and was not nearly as creative. Despite that, Marshall handpicked Greenberg as his successor at the LDF and steered Carter over to the NAACP as its general counsel.

Maria explained the various theories as to why that happened. One involved a personal conflict between the two men. Another had to do with fund-raising. LDF was a tax-exempt organization, and some thought a white person could raise more money from wealthy whites.

"Others thought that Bob would challenge Marshall's status as 'Mr. Civil Rights,'" Maria told me. Also, some people theorized that it would help Marshall climb the white judicial ladder if he placed a white rather than a black at the helm of the LDF.

Bob, however, had refused to be sidetracked into an administrative job that would be responsible for internal NAACP matters and leave civil rights litigation to the LDF. Instead he developed an aggressive legal agenda for the NAACP, which involved attacking segregation in the North, where it was not based on Jim Crow legal codes but instead on more subtle, less overt forms of racism. In essence Bob believed that in the long run, the South would slowly adopt the Northern forms of racism, and blacks would still find their children trapped in segregated schools and housing, and limited in their job opportunities. By contrast the LDF effort was almost entirely focused on the South, bringing lawsuits against school boards and other public authorities that openly refused to obey Supreme Court rulings prohibiting segregation.

Under Bob's careful direction, the NAACP legal office was working on a number of challenges to segregation in Northern public schools, where officials claimed that if any racial segregation existed it was the unintentional result of real estate ownership and housing patterns. Bob was convinced that Northern school administrators intentionally used school-district boundaries to segregate black children, but he thought it was a fool's errand to argue about geography. To do so, he believed, would push the NAACP into the trap of trying to prove intentional segregation in thousands of heavily segregated school districts. To make that challenge even more difficult, most schools had at least some black children attending with whites.

Bob believed that if he pushed the *Brown* decision to its logical conclusion, the courts should rule that public school boards could not maintain predominantly black schools and predominantly white schools in the same district because black children would suffer the same type of psychological harm they suffered in Jim Crow schools, which was just as unconstitutional as total segregation. It was the effect of the actual segregation that resulted, no matter the cause, rather than the intent of public officials, that was the focus of his cases. Those targeted in this Northern campaign, as I will call it, countered that the NAACP was engaged in social engineering, and that its attempts to balance the races would require racial quotas, something that never crossed the minds of the Supreme Court justices when they decided *Brown*.

By the time I arrived at Freedom House in 1963, the opening round of this struggle to desegregate the Northern schools had been fought and lost in Gary, Indiana. The decision of George Beamer, the federal judge who heard *Bell v. School City of Gary, Indiana*, was that there was nothing illegal about the school segregation that existed. The kinds of segregation caused by housing patterns and the neighborhood-school plan, which placed children in schools near their homes, wasn't a violation of the Constitution, he ruled. It constituted de facto, or unintentional, segregation, not de jure, or officially created, segregation.

Therefore *Brown* didn't apply, Judge Beamer concluded. On behalf of the black children and their parents, Bob, appealed, and on October 31, 1963, the U.S. Court of Appeals for the Seventh Circuit upheld Beamer's ruling.

Bob didn't seem to be particularly fazed by the defeat. He had hoped the Northern judges would accept his legal concept, but was confident that the Supreme Court, which had unanimously decided *Brown*, would understand his argument and look beyond those Latin phrases, *de facto* and *de jure,* to the word that followed them both: "segregation." To test his theory Bob requested that the Supreme Court review the *Gary* decision. At the same time Bob, Barbara, and Maria were engaged in a series of cases aimed at closed-shop unions. Their claim was that the National Labor Relations Board (NLRB) had the authority to force segregated local unions supplying labor to the same employer, with the white unions controlling all the higher-paying jobs, to integrate. In 1963 the NLRB agreed, but its ruling was under attack in the federal courts, which had the final say. But segregated local unions were only a small part of the problem. In the building trades, for example, the unions that controlled the jobs through collective-bargaining agreements were all-white. The same was true in many other industries where there were no black unions to integrate and whites-only unions controlled all the work.

To hasten the process of opening up these jobs, Bob decided to take on the liberal establishment that had made a habit of talking out of both sides of its mouth, courting the unions for votes while engaging in lip service about supporting black equality. Disregarding the combined political power of both the construction unions and the politicians who had voted for and supported massive public construction contracts, Bob had decided to take the David and Goliath route. The NAACP legal staff, on behalf of Lloyd Gaynor, sued the governor of New York, Nelson Rockefeller (the same man who, eight years later, ordered the Attica attack), as well as the city of New York and its mayor, Robert F. Wagner, for authorizing multi-million-dollar projects. In one fell swoop Bob had figured out a way to open up virtually all the trades, since the state and city contracts involved everything from heavy-equipment operators to welders and iron and sheet-metal workers to electricians, carpenters, plumbers, and pipe fitters. It was a daring move. If the onus fell on public officials to ensure equal rights in the workplace, at least on public projects, all the local unions and contractors that otherwise would have had to be dragged one by one before administrative agencies or courts would be brought to heel at the same time. The case was called *Gaynor v. Rockefeller*, and Bob had commenced it just as I had started to volunteer at the NAACP.

Even without *Gaynor*, which by itself was a huge undertaking, the NAACP's legal staff was already overwhelmed. The Northern school cases were moving forward, the NLRB test cases were still unresolved in the federal courts, and the various boycott and demonstration cases arising in the South came in over the transom nonstop.

I remember the worried look on Maria's face as she surveyed the papers on her desk. Barbara Morris was more vocal.

"This has to be a joke," she groused as new mountains of cases materialized on her desk. She directed the comment at Bob's office, but it was empty. "If he's got a plan, I'd sure like to hear about it. Maybe it's a secret, but there's a whole lot of late-night work sitting here waiting to get done and not a whole lot of hands to do it."

Barbara had a point: The pressure was mounting.

Pressure, however, was second nature to me. It was the theater all over again: The show had to go on. But there was so much more at stake. There was a thrill associated with being needed, appreciated, and useful. The more time I spent at Freedom House, the more the fog of those feelings I had regarding the unfairness of American race relations lifted. I felt the pieces of my life coming together. I only wanted to be down there helping out. Part of it, I sensed was payback for Bill and Lorraina, who had given me so much time, caring, and love and had gotten so little in return. But another part was something more. I was creating an identity outside the mold of my family. I was already straddling two tribes, one wealthy Jewish and the other working-class Irish, in my marriage. Now I was touching the outer borders of a third. I could still be a Warner grandchild and yet be free from some of its inherent restraints. Yet there was fear, too. I was in over my head, and if I made a mistake my well-meaning efforts could cause more harm than good in an arena where the stakes were so high. I can handle it, I kept telling myself. This is what happens when you become a grown-up. It's what life's all about.

Every day there was a project waiting for me. Soon I was working on *Gaynor* as well as the Southern demonstration cases. A few other volunteers showed up from time to time to pick up legal papers and drop off drafts. Like me, they were almost always white and Jewish. Some, like Sandy Katz and Anne Franklin, were very good. But I was the only one who was beginning to think of the NAACP office as a second home.

One day Maria asked me why I was volunteering so much of my time. I made up the answer. I told her that I came from a wealthy family and had been taught that I should give back to society.

"Noblesse oblige," she said, with an odd smile.

In my parents' eyes, my volunteer work at the NAACP raised questions. I was the second son, who had tried his hand in New York theater, had not gone to a top law school, married an actress, had a child, and was not a great example of responsibility in action. So when a job at a law firm finally came along, engineered through my father's contacts, I felt I had to take it. But I was determined to continue volunteering for the NAACP. Fortunately my employer, Abe Pomerantz, was left-leaning, and he liked the idea of me spending time as a volunteer at the NAACP. So he agreed I could work at Freedom House one day a week.

I liked Pomerantz. He espoused socialist views while simultaneously charging big fees to those who could afford them. He had made his name and his money suing directors of large corporations for lining their pockets at the expense of their shareholders, as well as representing some rich clients who wanted a bigger piece of the action. It was interesting stuff, but I suffered through one deadly research assignment after another. Pomerantz had also defended Valentin Gubitchev, the Soviet diplomat accused of bribing a Department of Justice employee named Judith Coplon to obtain state secrets. It was one of the major communist witch-hunt cases of the McCarthy era, but that case was long over by the time I was hired.

I had been trying to think of an apt excuse to escape the confines of Abe's law firm, Pomerantz Levy Haudek & Block, so I could get back to the law library and work on my NAACP cases, when I heard the news that President Kennedy had been assassinated. I was horrified. For all of Kennedy's equivocations, he had called upon all of us, and especially those of us who were young, privileged, and educated like him, to work for the betterment of the nation. Kennedy's death moved me deeply. I felt as if something in me was going to die if I ignored his request to find a way to express my love of country through good work. And that way was right in front of me. Soon I found myself slipping off more and more to the library or to Freedom House.

The more time I spent at the NAACP, the more I wondered how Bob and Barbara viewed the white people who worked there. Besides Maria and me, there were the white volunteer lawyers who made occasional appearances at Freedom House. Sometimes I worried that Bob and Barbara merely tolerated us as helpful hands, even though there was plenty of evidence to the contrary. In my experience whites had always lorded it over blacks. Also there was Jack Greenberg, who had usurped Bob at the LDF. Put the two things together, and that seemed like reason enough for them to be on their guard.

Outwardly we all got along. Bob was the boss and leader I mostly saw at meetings. He called me "What Name," but it wasn't a race thing. He called a lot of people that.

I was mostly silent at the NAACP staff meetings that I was invited to attend, but when I had something useful to add, or when Maria put in a good word, Bob always acknowledged me. I felt that Barbara could go either way in terms of how she actually felt about us white interlopers, but despite my misgivings she always treated me well. At some point it became clear that whatever my racial insecurities were, they were infinitely more manageable than the ever-expanding apathy that I felt for the dire solemnities of a day job where my main objective was to facilitate the pursuit of wealth by our already-rich clients as well as large fees for the partners.

In contrast to the deadly seriousness of the Pomerantz firm, I liked going to the NAACP office. The staffers were appreciative and told me so. I could flit in and out, have ideas, make suggestions, do legal research, draft legal papers, and be generally clever—all of which appealed to me. Also, there was always humor in the air—maybe gallows humor—but still, it was not all work and no play. But there was a weightlessness to it all because I wasn't truly responsible for anything.

I was still a volunteer when the *Gaynor* appeal was decided. Although a couple of the judges had given Bob a tough time at the oral argument, I thought we were going to win. After all, Harold Stevens was one of the five judges at the appellate court; he was black, and our case seemed strong.

When I read the opinion I remember thinking the conclusion must be a mistake. The beginning sounded as if Judge Stevens agreed with our argument. "The racial policies of exclusion by some of the defendant unions," he wrote, "are of so long duration and so widely known that the courts might, if they so elected, take judicial notice of the fact." That seemed to mean the NAACP would be spared the burden of proving what was beyond any question true.

Stevens also recognized that "unions exercise a virtual monopoly of skilled crafts in the construction industry and their policies effectively bar [all blacks] from employment. . . ." Again, that is what we said.

Stevens added that the court had to presume that both Rockefeller and Wagner "know that [the antidiscrimination] laws are not self-executing and depend for their effectiveness upon the sincerity and depth of conviction of public enforcement officials." Another great finding. Then the bottom fell out.

Judge Stevens had two reasons to explain his adverse ruling: "Courts will not presume that such officials will fail or refuse to perform the duties of their office," he declared, as if that negated all he had written before.

Second, Stevens ruled that we should have joined the contractors who were doing the work on the state and city projects. Even if the contractors were necessary, however, the judge ignored the fact that the standard rule of law for not joining a party (like those ancillary contractors) in a multiparty case is to give the plaintiffs the chance to add them. After we had all read Stevens's decision, I joined Maria and Barbara in Bob's office, where we talked about the next move. Quickly everyone agreed we should appeal to New York's highest court, the court of appeals. The decision made no sense, and to start all over again and name the contractors would create endless delay. I was hoping Bob would explain why Stevens ruled against the NAACP, but I held back, afraid of asking him to bad-mouth another black man, as in my world I had heard Jews saying bad things about other Jews in private, but not before "mixed" company. In my family, for example, we were more careful about what we said when we were with non-Jews. Also, we rarely talked about why my parents changed our name from Siegel to Steel. Of course there was a family prec-edent, since Warner had somehow emerged from either Wonsal or Won-skolaser, and many other Jews had also anglicized their names.

We became the Steels when I was five, during World War II, after we moved to Crail Farm, which Major had purchased because he feared New York City might get attacked by the Germans. Although my dad never explained why our names changed, my mother came up with the explanation that they did not want people to think we were Germans. True or not, I never believed that was the reason.

So, without Bob's input, I figured maybe Stevens was afraid that if he voted to keep our suit alive, he and other blacks struggling to have a voice would be marginalized even more than they already were, just as many Jewish leaders had been reluctant to press Franklin Roosevelt to take whatever action our armed forces could have carried out to stop or at least impede the Holocaust.

After our meeting I tried asking Barbara about Judge Stevens. She waved off my question and said he'd been a judge for so long he'd forgot-ten what the real world was like. "Don't be worried about it," she added. But I did worry. It would take me many years to internalize how difficult it was for one individual to stand up to group thinking, and why it was so important that there be a critical mass of minority representation in any situation where the group thinking of the majority could effectively bring about self-censorship, whether it was one black kid in an all-white class or one black jurist on an all-white court.

7

Getting My Feet Wet

The letter informing me that I had passed the New York bar examination came in the fall of 1963. The admissions ceremony took place in the same courtroom where Harold Stevens and his fellow appellate judges had ruled against the NAACP in *Gaynor*.

The courthouse was on Twenty-Fifth Street overlooking Madison Square Park, which was gray and pruned back for winter. Once again five judges sat on the raised platform behind the beautifully hand-carved bench. The inductees were virtually all white and male. We sat in plush chairs under the domed ceiling, with the faces of famous judges set in stained glass peering down, literally, from on high. With the robes and shafts of morning light, it felt almost like a religious ceremony. There was a similar feeling of quiet and reflection. I had earned the right to be there. I was delighted, and I felt a mixture of pride and humility.

The stories I had heard while volunteering at Freedom House about the many ways racism had become hard-wired into our jurisprudence system, however, flickered through my mind. I now had some understanding about how hard it was to show judges where the law failed when it came to black citizens. I could see from my volunteer work at the NAACP how the smallest gains required Herculean strength, but somehow the stony reality of that knowledge dissolved in this setting. The feel in that ornate courtroom was informed by pride—both personal and patriotic. I had earned the right to be a part of this world. Quickly, however, the reality that I was beginning to see at the NAACP took over. As

I glanced up at the judges on the ceiling, there in the glass dome was Roger Taney, a former chief justice of the United States Supreme Court. It had to be him, I thought, the *Dred Scott* judge; there couldn't be two Roger Taneys.

Shortly before the Civil War, Taney had authored the *Dred Scott* decision, which made the consignment of slaves to endless bondage a matter of settled law. This courthouse had been built thirty years after the abolition of slavery. But now, looking up, I didn't care that Taney might have earned his place in the pantheon that floated above us on the basis of other decisions that had nothing to do with slavery. I felt my anger boiling up. This was no role model for me or anyone else to admire. Better a hole where the cold rain of November might get in than him! I wanted so badly to belong to the priesthood that practiced in this courtroom, but Taney's presence had tainted the ceremony.

That evening, after my negative feelings had dissipated, a bunch of us went to the Playboy Club to celebrate—not my idea. The club was new and occupied an entire building on Fifty-Ninth Street east of Fifth Avenue. Catering solely to a well-heeled crowd—looking exclusively white— the club issued symbolic keys to its members. The decor featured a lot of marble, overwrought brass, and crystal that screamed a spurious sort of elegance. It was the Culver mess hall for grown-up cadets, except that here there were girls, or—as I learned to say many years later—young women, in bunny outfits instead of black teenagers who lived somewhere in the woods. We ate upstairs in a softly lit dining room with pleasant music piped in—the whole thing an ornate put-on designed to foster the illusion of our importance. Like the courthouse I had left only a few hours earlier, this was a club that wanted its members to feel special. As for Kitty, who was eight months pregnant, and our other female companions, they acted as if it was a special place for them too, instead of what it was: a tease calculated to entice males to feel entitlement to fantasy pleasures.

The waitresses bent low as they served us, and we tried to peek without getting caught. Our wives tried to dismiss our sideways glances as one of those things that boys do. And I did not then see the connection between the Culver waiters and the young women in bunny costumes. As for Chief Justice Taney, my outrage had long faded. New Year's passed, and I continued living my legal double life working for Abe Pomerantz and volunteering at the NAACP's legal department.

Then, in February, Maria told me about an opportunity at the Eleanor Roosevelt Foundation, which had just started a program that funded paid one-year fellowships for people who wanted to do civil rights or other social-service-oriented work. Bob would support me if I applied for a grant, Maria said. If my application was successful, I would work full-time at the NAACP as an assistant counsel, and carry my own caseload. After that year was up, if all went well, Maria thought Bob could convert my job into a permanent position.

I took the opportunity home with a little trepidation. Kitty had given up a budding career in musical comedy to marry me, and she had become a college student and had our first child. That was what she wanted. But she had paid a price in terms of her professional aspirations.

Separated from her family and friends back in Los Angeles, Kitty found herself in a far different environment. Back home she had been the star of her Irish Catholic working-class family. In New York she was struggling to become accepted in a basically college-educated Jewish culture that had no connection to her past life. I hadn't been a great help getting her acclimated, either. Often moody about the effort it took to keep up the pretense of interest working for Pomerantz, unsure about my role as husband and father, and afraid of what the future might hold for me, family money–wise, if I strayed too far from the conventional mold, I was feeling prey to a sort of ill-defined pressure to "do the right thing" even though I had no idea what that was. The prospect of working for the NAACP excited me, but it was a job that would force me to work long hours and travel to the South, where I was pretty sure Jewish civil rights attorneys were not exactly welcome.

But Kitty didn't hesitate. She knew where my heart was and had seen enough of our family's dynamics to understand that fighting injustice could make me into the person she wanted me to be.

Everyone heard the news.

"Lewis has joined the legal staff. He's working for us full-time," the NAACP staff at Freedom House was told.

And just like that, in May 1964, I became a civil rights lawyer, someone who was supposed to know the law and be ready to engage in battle with opponents in the South, who were ready to go to extremes to defend their "way of life," and in the North—who lived a lot like me. Despite my veneer of self-possession, every time I contemplated standing up for people who were struggling to free themselves from the weight of history and a racist system that I had begun to understand and was inextricably a part of, I felt unsure of myself.

Adding to my fears, there was a group of black people in leadership positions whom I had barely met. Gloster Current, the director of all the NAACP branches and one of the people who helped steer the NAACP through many of its most turbulent years, was the friendliest. He would come by the office with a legal issue or problem, looking for advice, and was always appreciative of any help we could give him. The director of publicity, Henry Moon, and John Morsell, who was the deputy executive director, also dropped in from time to time. But both were older and seemed distant. The NAACP's executive director, Roy Wilkins, was a slight-looking, light-skinned presence at Freedom House. Distinguished and urbane, he hardly ever came out of his office unless he was going on the road. The most tangible difference between my role as a volunteer and full-time employment was that Maria no longer played go-between and protector for me. Now I knew I would have to work hard to develop meaningful relationships with Bob as my boss and Barbara, who was a far more experienced lawyer. At the Pomerantz firm I had the experience of working with superiors. But they had been white, as had all my teachers, professors, army officers, camp counselors, summer-job bosses. Bill Rutherford had laid down the law for me now and then when I was a boy. But this was different. I would have to look beyond race, as race had always put me above those with black skin. What helped was that I had already developed a deep respect for both Bob and Barbara. Still, I remember feeling a fairly constant low-level anxiety about inadvertently exposing some hidden—or worse—subconscious racial prejudice lurking in my thinking. I worried all the time about saying the wrong thing. Equally troubling was a gnawing doubt regarding my commitment to equality: I feared that I might find out things about myself while working as a full-time civil rights lawyer that I didn't want to know.

Then there was the outside world of the civil rights movement, about which I knew little. The NAACP was only one of many civil rights organizations fighting for the allegiance of different black constituencies while simultaneously waging a multifaceted, several-front war against the widespread backlash seeking to weaken or ignore what the civil rights movement had accomplished in the decade since *Brown v. Board of Education*, culminating with the passage of the 1964 Civil Rights Act.

By the time I joined the legal staff, I was becoming aware through the media coverage that there were influential leaders in the Movement who thought the NAACP was too mainstream, too willing to acquiesce to whites retaining their hold on power. For example, the board president, Kivie Kaplan, was white, which was a defining characteristic from the organization's inception, and therefore it could not be trusted.

The organizations I had to learn about included Martin Luther King, Jr.'s, Southern Christian Leadership Conference (SCLC), which emerged during the 1955–56 Montgomery Bus Boycott and made King the country's most visible civil rights leader. From what I heard, the NAACP and SCLC were competitors, and Wilkins resented King's rise to prominence. It was all pretty disorienting, and I didn't feel comfortable asking anyone in our office for direction.

A year earlier I hadn't left Kitty and our baby, Janine, in New York to attend the March on Washington. And now I knew I had not only missed out on Martin Luther King's "I Have a Dream" speech, but on all the gossip on the NAACP bus that had taken the staff to the march and back.

When I started working full-time at the NAACP, a new civil rights law was about to take effect, pushed through Congress by President Lyndon Johnson. On paper the new law appeared to be strong. It would make discrimination illegal under a wide variety of circumstances. In theory it would open up jobs and public accommodations, including hotels and restaurants, to all, regardless of their race. But even before it was signed into law, civil rights lawyers were making noise about it, complaining that it would be hard to enforce and that there would be little voluntary compliance.

Tired of waiting, and because the act had no voting rights provisions, the more aggressive activist groups were getting ready to launch what they called the Mississippi Summer Project. Under the plan Northern students, black and white, would travel all over Mississippi trying to register blacks to vote, defying the segregationists who had killed or beaten anyone suspected of being a civil rights activist and burned down their homes and churches. All over the South activists were looking to Mississippi to give them inspiration and courage and calling us for legal advice and other kinds of support. Wedged into our already crowded offices at Freedom House, I dived into an endless stream of questions and requests for help that came in through the association's more than eighteen hundred branches. One was trying to start a boycott somewhere, another was planning a march. If a judge ordered the NAACP not to demonstrate or conduct a boycott, we were asked for advice about how to respond. Often the branch would decide what to do without talking to us. At other times we would be asked to get demonstrators out of jail or oppose lawsuits seeking damages. In the South, LDF generally handled school segregation cases, so we rarely had that burden. In the North, however, branches would call to find out how much support we could provide if a school board refused to desegregate.

The national office at Freedom House had a small staff that could not respond to all the inquiries that poured down on them on a daily basis. The higher-ups at the association were swamped by the unending crises that threatened it, so it was all hands on deck, whether that meant Gloster Current or the NAACP's education director, June Shagaloff, or the labor director, Herb Hill, or even a new assistant counsel like me. Whoever was around and willing to spare a few minutes did what they could in the daily life at Freedom House.

Often I tried to get Barbara to take the phone calls that came my way because I had a hard time understanding the accents of callers from the Deep South.

"You handle it, hon," she would push back, singing out to me.

I'd take the calls and do the best I could. When I did understand the accent on the other end of the line, I scribbled furiously to take down what was said and promised to get back with an answer, sighing with relief when I managed to escape the caller. Sometimes I had no idea what I'd been told. That's just the way it was.

When Barbara was inclined to educate me, she explained that most of the time the people who were calling were asking about the legality of actions they had no intention of undertaking.

"It's mostly just talk," she told me. "And anyway, if we tried to give real advice to everyone who called us, we'd never have time to get anything done. Most of the time those people aren't looking for any particular answer; they just want to know they're connected to a place where they could get help if they needed it. And you're the lucky one to give them that assurance."

I got what she was saying, but the person on the other end of the line had my name. It was fine for Barbara to be so cool about it. She was attuned to her own people. I wasn't.

What am I doing here? I'd ask myself at odd moments, when my anxiety had me in its grip. It was hard for most people to understand that the NAACP's national office—the headquarters of that august organization—had virtually no control over the chaos that was the civil rights movement during the 1960s. We were caught up in the same maelstrom as everyone else. At least on the surface the world I came from appeared more orderly. Right or wrong, leaders had answers to questions about how to proceed. At the NAACP, however, even those staffers who could pick up the nuances of what was being said "out there" were often powerless to do anything about it. Just too many people involved, all in their own worlds, too far away. The local branches of the NAACP had to make things happen as best they could. Or they could back off and wait, and things would stay the same. Barbara's cavalier attitude was a coping mechanism. It was her way of dealing with a stressful reality. As for me, the very fact that I didn't know what to do or how best to help was a magnification of what propelled me toward the NAACP in the first place.

A few weeks after joining the legal staff, I attended a retreat sponsored by the Eleanor Roosevelt Foundation as part of the fellowship that paid for my position at the legal department. There were about forty of us at the retreat. We found ourselves thirty-five miles north of New York City in a converted mansion. The idea was to immerse us in a process of racial exploration and understanding to open us up to the problems we would confront. The retreat location was self-contained. Many of us never left the grounds the entire time, and no one except invited lecturers and support staff intruded on our isolation. Long sessions, led by skilled group leaders, were devoted to the examination of our feelings and beliefs when it came not only to race but to a whole kaleidoscope of social issues ranging from gender to religion, family, and politics. Hungry for change, we quickly made real progress in revealing little pieces of ourselves, and finding we could survive the inevitable questions and challenges that followed.

I had to overcome my fear that the black attendees would either ridicule me or feel alienated by a white guy who wanted to talk about the confusion occasioned by his relationship with a butler and a maid. In response some of the black attendees talked about the pain of having their mothers or fathers work endless hours for white families at their expense. They told me what it was like to have parents they rarely saw, who came home exhausted and filled with resentment. Although they fought to conceal their emotions, I could feel their pent-up anger, and heard an affirmation of what I had always suspected about Duby and Sister Baby— that my gain was their loss. Without a thought, I had taken their place in important ways. I felt as if I was on slippery ground. My love of Bill and Lorraina was built on the degradation of their primary relationships with two children, an affront that was generative, creating the potential for dire social consequences. While I learned from my new black confidants what it was like to be on the losing side of my relationship with Bill and Lorraina, they got to hear something about white guilt. Bill and Lorraina had given me the nurturing that helped me to sense the pain inflicted by a racial caste system. It was hard to imagine my being at the retreat without that relationship.

My internal conflicts at least began to find a way to be expressed. I could better understand black anger even in so-called integrated areas of the country. And I began to see why it was so hard to create a solid bridge between black and white people in the United States. We, the whites, had all the advantages of a caste system, and they were trying to create a life for themselves in an oppressive environment. In the meantime it seemed to be the consensus among the attendees at Tarrytown that we could begin the process of reaching out and being open to the difficulties ahead. When white people heard the basis of black anger expressed in a reflective mode, there was an opening for understanding. For their part the black attendees seemed willing to believe that at least the whites in attendance were ready to work with them to foster a more egalitarian society. And that made the isolation of all of us at the retreat easier to handle, creating some space for us to come together in that protective setting.

Lectures and seminars also created an intellectual framework for our experience. Historians, social psychologists, activists, writers, and musicians visited us. We learned about the cruelty of slavery and the evolution of dispossession, how blacks were terrorized in the South after the Civil War and penned into urban ghettos in the North. We studied black resistance to prejudice in the United States and elsewhere, in countries like Algeria. We learned about black survival and the high price black people paid to exist in a hostile country that created new forms of bondage in the South and treated them as invisible in the North. Every second of our waking day was devoted to learning more about the issues that would drive us in our work as civil rights activists. The thoughtfulness with which the program was created and run, the caring of the participants toward one another, the high quality of the presentations, as well as my own desperate need to find the inner logic between the way I grew up and the work I was starting to do at the NAACP, were liberating. I began to feel I belonged to the struggle and that I could contribute.

I left the retreat house filled with respect for black Americans who were ready to make our country live up to its promises. Though I remained inexorably part of the problem, cleaving to the advantages that flowed from my wealthy family, I felt much more ready to take the emotional risk of interacting with both black and white people to help create a more just society. I was one person starting to move in two distinct cultural worlds at the same time.

8

Dealing with Fear

"Well, you have to go sooner or later," Barbara Morris said in her laconic way. "It might as well be sooner."

I'd been working at the NAACP for a few months.

Barbara had spent a lot of time in the South, handling a variety of cases. There were a few racially charged criminal trials and lots of work with our Southern branches. In her early thirties, Barbara was an attractive, self-assured black woman with straight black hair. She seemed to have a read on everyone. Her looks, dress, and manner were consistent with somebody who had gone to the right schools and hung out in the right places. She thrived in a way I thought would be impossible for a black woman in the South. Even in the North, however, segregation was the quiet rule, and powerful women, black or white, were the exception.

Barbara had clocked the requisite hours driving the back roads of the South in search of witnesses, and she'd done hard time in courtrooms where the locals bridled at the presence of a strong-willed black woman. That she had a bully pulpit—or at least the wherewithal to speak forcefully to white men in the Deep South—was almost unthinkable. Often she was in mortal danger. In a word, Barbara had serious grit. She also had a sense of style. I was drawn in by the easy way she told terrifying stories about her travels through Jim Crow territory, among them being followed on deserted highways as she drove between towns looking for witnesses.

"I tell you . . . ," she would say with a chuckle.

Barbara knew I was anxious about working in the South. But I had to go. That was the way it was. Civil rights lawyers had to go where the cases were, and they were generally not in places with a lot of racial harmony. I remember wondering if maybe Barbara felt that white Movement lawyers had a little more to prove than their black counterparts. The reality, however, was more complicated. Sure, I needed to pay my dues. But I had something to prove that was much deeper than anything that was going on between Barbara and me. In the summer of 1964 a civil rights attorney would have to be fundamentally unbalanced not to be nervous about heading South—especially for the first time. It was a dangerous place to challenge a centuries-old racial caste system. Less than a year had passed since Medgar Evers—an NAACP field secretary at the time—was assassinated in Jackson, Mississippi. He had pulled into his driveway after picking up new T-shirts emblazoned with the legend Jim Crow Must Go, when a bullet from an Enfield M1917 rifle hit him in the back. He didn't die right away. Byron De La Beckwith, a fertilizer salesman and member of the White Citizens' Council and the Ku Klux Klan, was arrested eventually, but he got some "good ol' boy" treatment and walked away from criminal charges until—nearly three decades later—the times bad changed sufficiently that he was prosecuted and put away for good.

Compounding the feeling that I was heading toward a place where I could get killed, three young civil rights volunteers disappeared in Mississippi right before I was sent to Baton Rouge. The disappearance of Andrew Goodman, Michael Schwerner, and James Chaney gripped the nation and was the lead story on all the nightly news programs. The three activists went missing in Neshoba County not long after Deputy Sheriff Cecil Price stopped their blue station wagon on bogus speeding charges. Sam Bowers, the Imperial Wizard of the Ku Klux Klan splinter group White Knights of the Ku Klux Klan, had issued an order to kill Michael Schwerner in particular. That conspiracy was the reason Price had the car's plate numbers in advance. He arrested all three. And then the plan to kill them was put into play. Chaney, Goodman, and Schwerner were released on their own recognizance in the middle of the night in a county considered among the more dangerous ones for civil rights workers. Forty-four days later their bodies were found in an earthen dam near Philadelphia, Mississippi.

Six years before going to Baton Rouge, I had visited New Orleans on my way to Fort Sam Houston in San Antonio for officer training. I had signed up for the Reserve Officers' Training Corps (ROTC) program when I was a sophomore at Harvard. If there was another war like Korea, which had just ended, and there was still a draft, I didn't want to be a private.

That said, the ROTC program was no cakewalk. I had developed an attitude problem. Trouble started after the appearance of a snarky article that I wrote for the *Harvard Crimson*. Col. Trevor N. Dupuy, professor of military science and tactics, took issue with my view that the ROTC was more tolerated than admired at Harvard. As Dupuy soured on me, so I soured on the program. But I stuck with it and at graduation was commissioned a second lieutenant in the Army Reserves, assigned to the Medical Service Corps.

To begin my active-duty assignment, my dad suggested a road trip—a sort of ritual of the soon-to-be empty nest. Grandma Bessie had given me a shiny new blue Plymouth convertible for graduation, so the drive seemed like a good way to check it out. We would travel down the East Coast to Jacksonville, Florida, where my dad owned a movie theater called the St. John's that was managed by my mother's brother. I didn't give it a thought at the time, but Jacksonville being in the Deep South, the theater must have been segregated.

My dad loved to drive, and we had a good time following the coastal roads, chatting about nothing much. He wasn't big on fatherly advice or philosophical ruminations, and there was very little if any drama in his emotional makeup. Life didn't seem to trouble him much. He appeared to be content. I was not. I remember there was no talk about the future—his or mine—which seemed a little odd to me. I was going off to the army for a six-month stint, and that was it. When it was over he and my mother might be home or they might be on one of their many trips to see the world. We didn't have much in the way of missing one another. I think he saw me as a difficult son and never quite knew how to open up to me. Maybe he wanted to strengthen whatever father-son bond we had before it slipped away. Whatever. We enjoyed each other's company on the ride down. It felt good being with my father, all by ourselves for a few days, talking about nothing much, eating at the Howard Johnson's along the highways, looking at the scenery out the car windows.

I was nervous about reporting for active duty, but I kept that to myself. The Medical Service Corps was a little scary. I knew nothing about military medicine. We were not taught about the wounds of war at Culver or at Harvard, and I had taken no science courses there. I saw no blood or broken bones when I directed *The Consul* for the Harvard Opera Guild. Commanding had never been my thing, discussion and persuasion being more my approach to getting things done. Even as a cadet officer at Culver, I had avoided bossing the plebes around. Perhaps that had something to do with feeling like an outsider myself. For sure, I'd never barked orders to carry a stretcher or drive an ambulance or anything else. Others in the ROTC program seemed to like the idea of command, while I had come to look at authority with a skeptical eye. But I was not about to talk about my concerns with my dad.

The overnight stay in Jacksonville was uneventful. We had dinner with my uncle Shel and aunt Harriet at their lovely home on the St. John's River. A black maid served us. She smiled and treated me as if I were a young master. I smiled the way a regular person would—not a master— and tried to act as if she were a real person—not a servant. But I was a master, and she treated me the way I supposed she might any other white man—that big smile meant to hide true feelings. I had traded that kind of smile at the homes of friends and relatives more times than I could count, but I felt the conflict. Later I would learn that Florida led the country in lynchings and had a long history of whites torching black areas. I knew much less then, but I was still self-conscious when it came to my relationship with black people who served in white homes. I wanted warmth and attention, which I got from Bill and Lorraina, and hoped to keep that by signaling that I was their friend and, despite my preppy clothes, not on the way to becoming a white master.

The next morning I drove west toward the Gulf Coast and New Orleans. Alone, I started to feel apprehensive. I was in the Deep South, a young Jewish kid, driving a shiny new car with New York plates. Northern Jews weren't exactly welcome down South, especially outside a few big cities. I could sense the hostility on those lonely roads, especially toward the likes of me with my curly black hair and my horn-rimmed glasses. I was hyperaware that I didn't look like "them." Whites down there were pretty sure the North was once again trying to impose its views on the South, but the first attempts at integration associated with the civil rights movement had not rippled out to the small towns I was driving through—gas stations still had their Whites Only signs on restrooms. Restaurants didn't need any signs to let folks passing by know who was welcome and who was not. In fact it didn't seem that signs were necessary anywhere. Looking in car windows in the towns I passed through, I saw only whites.

I remember wondering where the blacks were—where they lived, where they worked, and—more important to me—I wondered how Bill felt when he was down here. He had to be completely on edge if I felt the way I did. It was better when my father was in the car with me. "They" would be far less likely to hassle him. He seemed more like one of them. Alone, I kept the top up and drove carefully.

I stopped off in New Orleans, where a friend from Culver met me. I let him take the wheel of my snappy new car. Speeding through the center of town, we were stopped by the police. But my friend, who was related to former governor Huey Long, hardly blinked an eye. Like magic, the cops tipped their hats and let us go. It was quite different from the experience I would have a few months later at that integrated dance outside Fort Sam Houston, where I stupidly remarked on the size of a cop's flashlight and he punched me in the face before dumping me in a paddy wagon and depositing me in the local lockup with an assortment of drunks and whoever else they picked up that night. With the traffic stop behind us, my Culver pal whisked me off to check out a nightclub featuring drag queens doing some crazy dance numbers. We listened to jazz on Bourbon Street, and we ate crabs on a pier on Lake Pontchartrain. That was New Orleans, my friend said. There was another New Orleans—the Ninth Ward and many other impoverished areas—but it was invisible to me.

Prior to Barbara telling me that I had to go down South sooner or later, these were my only experiences of that part of the world.

In 1964 Baton Rouge was under the thumb of a racial reactionary and a tough-talking backroom boss named Leander Perez. The local NAACP's first target in its campaign to crack the policy of total segregation was the state capitol's cafeteria. But the branch's efforts had stalled under the watchful eyes and nightsticks of a thuggish ring of state troopers.

It was a time when public officials at all levels, from governor right down to local sheriffs, were in open defiance of the law of the land. The Supreme Court had ruled that the Constitution prohibited segregation in any public facility. The law was routinely being flouted. I was not going to Baton Rouge to push a new or complex legal theory. The legal precedent had already been set. Instead I was going there to show the Louisiana NAACP leadership that my boss, Robert Carter, had a growing legal staff that could help them.

Two black men dressed in business suits met me at the airport. They were officers from the local chapter of the NAACP. We shook hands and headed for the parking lot.

"Your door lights are broken," I told them as we drove off the parking lot into the darkness.

The man driving looked puzzled for a moment, as if he were processing my ignorance about Movement work in the South.

"They've been disconnected," he told me.

We stopped outside a small blacks-only motel. The lightless street was deserted and silent.

"It's getting late," the other man said. "We'll have plenty of time to talk in the morning."

Alone in that bare-bones room, I was scared. I wondered if we had been followed. Why had they abandoned me there? It felt as if I had been left to fend for myself, and all I could think about was the disappearance of Chaney, Schwerner, and Goodman. I pushed the dresser against the door of my tin-roofed cell. I looked around at the motel room the way an intruder would see it, and decided to put a pillow where my head would be if I were sleeping in the bed. Then I wrapped myself in a sheet and lay down on the floor between the beds. Every bug landing on that tin roof set my teeth on edge. I was terrified. I lay there watching the shadows for the slightest change, and the raking light from passing cars move across the ceiling and down the wall. I barely managed to control my fear. Somewhere "out there" nameless, faceless people wanted to kill me, and there was no one to protect me. The colleagues I came to help had left me, a Jew from New York City, in a black motel to get snatched by the Ku Klux Klan and killed in some godforsaken swamp. I was the one who needed help. I felt like a sacrificial lamb and a lost soldier sleepwalking in someone else's war. Every time I willed my eyes closed, some sound or another—simple creaks, the tin roof moving in the wind, or a car going by—made my eyes pop open again. Then it was morning.

The local NAACP guys who had dropped me off at the motel brought me to the capitol and showed me the "Closed" sign on the cafeteria door. We walked over to the federal courthouse, and I filed a civil rights complaint with the clerk. The idea was to get an immediate hearing. We were in luck. The judge was available, and so was an assistant Louisiana attorney general.

I don't remember the judge's name, but he was famously unfriendly to interference from Yankees like me, especially when it came to race issues.

We greeted each other cordially.

"What's this case about?" he drawled.

As I started to explain that Negroes had a constitutional right to eat in the statehouse cafeteria, the judge looked at my colleagues from the local NAACP and then back at me.

"Down here we call them *Nigras*," he said. Then he swiveled back to me with a smile and added, "No offense intended."

He looked pleased with himself.

I glanced over at my associates. Their faces were frozen. I turned back to look at the judge. A part of me thought he wouldn't have said that to a non-Jew, and all the hurt of being called a "kike" washed over me. The anti-Semitism I experienced at Culver was long gone, but the way it flashed through my mind when he said "Nigra" was as if it were happening all over again. That said, this was no cadet I could wrestle to the floor. I couldn't demand he take it back. This was a federal judge appointed to the bench for life by the president of the United States. None of my preparation was any good. It didn't matter that I'd been warned he was a race baiter—one of several openly racist federal judges whom President Kennedy appointed to appease the South. He was testing me.

With Bob's indomitable approach to racists playing in the back of my mind, I let instinct guide me: "My clients are called Negroes," I said.

"The court is adjourned."

That was the reply. Without another word the judge disappeared through a courtroom door. I stood speechless.

"What happens now?" I asked the clerk.

He flashed a smile at me.

"Court's over," the clerk said. "You can go now."

Alone at my table in the courtroom, I wondered if I had done the right thing. We had made no progress, and the judge was gone. I walked back to my clients, worried about their reaction. To my relief, they were pleased.

"You did fine," they told me, laughing about the way the judge had fled his bench.

I called Bob in New York to tell him what happened and to ask for instructions.

"You've done enough," Carter replied. "Come on home."

Catching an afternoon plane back to New Orleans, I made a late flight to New York. A few days later the bodies of Andrew Goodman, Michael Schwerner, and James Chaney were found buried in the Bogue Chitto Swamp. I was horror-stuck as I watched the television coverage. Goodman and Schwerner were young Jewish men like me. Chaney was black. The fear I had experienced in that motel room bubbled to the surface as I saw the evening news. If these men could be brutally murdered and buried in a muddy grave, so could I. Oddly, however, there was something about my one day in the South and these killings that made me want to go on more than ever. I sensed that this was what things looked like when a dying part of society ran scared. Just as the federal judge in Baton Rouge thought he could put a halt to the changing status of African Americans by abandoning his own courtroom, those racists in Mississippi thought they could kill two Jews and a black man without fear of punishment. In fact the killers considered themselves public-spirited citizens fighting the "good fight" to protect their communities from an alien invasion. The South was a place where the murder of a black man was on a lesser level than the destruction of property. Lynching was carried out in public, sometimes with the full participation of law enforcement, and those "public-spirited" communitarians made no bones about what would happen if anyone snitched to the Feds about the parties responsible. For civil rights workers, the killings served as a warning that the South's rural back roads were dangerous, and for me that meant trying to stay out of harm's way as far as possible. But even so, I felt a determination growing inside me to go wherever I was sent and do my work no matter the consequences.

The deaths of Chaney, Goodman, and Schwerner marked a change in me. That was the moment in time when I became a more dedicated part of the Movement, rather than an isolated individual left to sink or swim on my own. That was when I felt like a part of something huge and important. That sleepless night in the motel had been a test. It was the last time I would doubt my peers or the situations I found myself in with them. Letting me fend for myself for a few hours in that motel in the Negro part of town offered me a fleeting sense of what my black counterparts in the Movement did every instant of their lives. It was an object lesson about why putting me up in one of their homes carried unacceptable risk for them and for their families—as well as for me. That night in the motel taught me the most important lesson a person can get: that I had a lot to learn.

As much as I wanted to face that judge again, there was no return to Baton Rouge. The motel where I stayed was burned to the ground later that summer. The lawsuit I filed to integrate the capitol cafeteria languished. A local NAACP attorney worked on it until the following year, when the cafeteria was quietly reopened to white and black people, and the lawsuit was dropped.

9

Robert L. Carter's Northern Campaign

Cuyahoga means "crooked river." It comes from an Iroquois dialect that was spoken along the slow-flowing switchbacks that now divide the city of Cleveland before emptying into Lake Erie. Between 1868 and 1969 the waterway caught fire no fewer than thirteen times, and in the 1960s, it became a sort of cause célèbre for being one of the most polluted rivers in America, with the stretch between Cleveland and Akron completely devoid of fish.

In addition to its fame as dead water, the Cuyahoga is probably best known for serving as the dividing line between the white and the black areas of town in what is still one of the nation's most segregated cities.

In 1960 almost none of Cleveland's black population lived in the suburbs. Around 98 percent of the city's black population was concentrated in ghettos east of the Cuyahoga River.

The schools were terrible. Unqualified teachers were employed to work in them, and they were so overcrowded on the black side of town that there was a waiting list for kindergarten. Those lucky enough to get a spot for their children found the schools in the black neighborhoods so overenrolled that they were on half-day sessions. So kids were going to school in shifts, which put a strain on families where often both parents had to punch a work clock.

Across the river, white flight was already a reality, with white families having left in large numbers for the rapidly forming suburbs around the city. As a result schools on the west side of town were underenrolled.

To reduce the overcrowding, some black kids were bused to the white side of town, where they were completely segregated within the white schools. They ate separately, were taught separately, and were allowed to go to the bathroom only once a day. The busing angered both whites and blacks. Whites didn't like black kids being shipped into their neighborhood schools, and blacks didn't like their kids being completely segregated in those schools. As tensions flared in the city, the board of education decided to build new schools on the east side of the Cuyahoga and return the black students to those buildings when they were completed. The end result would obviously harden the patterns of segregation and freeze them in place. The school board justified what it was doing based on a rule of thumb known as the neighborhood school plan, used almost universally in U.S. cities, which placed kids in schools near their homes, but it ignored the rule whenever it suited its purposes.

The Congress of Racial Equality (CORE), a newly emerging civil rights organization, had played a big role in shaping a response to Cleveland's schools. Working with a local group called the United Freedom Movement (UFM), which the local NAACP helped form in 1963, CORE played a leading role in opposing the board's plan. When the board of education announced its intention to quickly build new schools on the east side, CORE and UFM organized demonstrations at the proposed sites. Then, on April 7, 1964, the Reverend Bruce W. Klunder, a white Presbyterian minister who headed the local CORE chapter, was killed by a bulldozer.

I had been aware of the deaths of civil rights workers in the South and the vicious attacks inflicted on the Freedom Riders, but this one was different. It was in the North, and much closer to home. Klunder and I were the same age, but unlike me he was on the front lines of civil rights activism, while until then I had been working the seams of the Movement from the safety of Freedom House in New York City. Around the time of Klunder's death, the NAACP began a lawsuit in federal court to stop the board of education from further segregating the Cleveland schools. The case was called *Craggett v. Board of Education of Cleveland City*. The lead plaintiff was a student named Charles Craggett. Bob and local NAACP lawyers sought a preliminary injunction to stop the school construction until the court could hold a full trial to determine the legality of the board's plan, which the NAACP argued violated the Constitution. After a hearing Judge Girard Kalbfleisch ruled that the board's building program would not cause prohibited public school segregation under the Supreme Court's *Brown* ruling, and denied an injunction. Carter and the local NAACP attorneys immediately decided to appeal. And that meant another major project for our office.

That's where I came into the picture. Maria and Barbara, who normally drafted the important briefs, had more work than they could handle, and Bob was constantly on the road. There was everything from boycotts, the constant drumroll of demonstration arrests, school cases, and labor-related cases. A fairly pure form of chaos existed in the NAACP legal office, as there were only so many hours in the day or night to get the work done. That's the reason it wasn't entirely a shock when Bob told me that, despite my inexperience, I would be putting together the appeal of the *Craggett* case. Still, this would be my first assignment on a key school case involving Bob's Northern campaign strategy.

As with most of the work I did as assistant counsel, it just kind of happened. Bob told me what he needed, talked me through the case, handed me an accordion file bursting with court papers, transcripts, and exhibits, and, on his way to the next thing, said something about me having ten days to get the brief done.

I must have looked stunned.

"Don't worry," he said. "Barbara and Maria will help if you run into any problems."

I doubt that changed the look on my face.

Barbara was working with Bob at the time preparing for trial in a school segregation case against the Springfield, Massachusetts, public school board, so she was completely up to date on the case law I would need to know for the appeal. She told me to read Bob's latest Supreme Court win in the *Prince Edward County, Virginia,* school case along with two other cases: a Long Island, New York, district court win and *Bell v. School City of Gary*, the Indiana case that was lost at trial and on appeal before the U.S. Court of Appeals for the Seventh Circuit on October 31, 1963. After reading those decisions, I reread the 1954 *Brown v. Board of Education* decision as well as the very weak Supreme Court follow-up decision in 1955, which was called *Brown II*. That second decision provided instructions to the federal trial courts about how *Brown* should be applied, signaling that the NAACP's work would not be easy, as the justices only required school boards to desegregate with "all deliberate speed" and instructed judges to be respectful of the problems that Southern school boards faced. Translated into lay language, the Court said, No rush. Barbara was a big help. I was filled with doubt. Although I didn't fully understand the scope of Bob's goal with the Northern campaign, I understood that he wanted to expand *Brown* to the North.

Bob told me to press the concept that segregation no matter what its cause resulted in damage to a child's self-esteem that was unlikely ever to be undone. This formulation came directly from Chief Justice Warren's original *Brown* opinion, and Bob, who had seen the need for the underpinning psychological evidence in that case, wanted the courts to adopt that concept in the North. Under his approach, it didn't matter whether a school board intended to segregate its children by race, and it didn't matter if there were a few white children enrolled at a black school or a few black children in white schools. What should matter, he argued, was the harm done to black children by segregation. In short, Bob wanted to move away from having to prove that school boards intended to segregate children. Given the number of school systems in the country, having to prove intent would require endless litigation that could go either way depending on whom the judges believed. The goal was to create a broader standard for integration that could be applied quickly and effectively anywhere in the country.

When I read the *Prince Edward County* decision, however, I found nothing to support Bob's theory. Prince Edward County was wedded to the Jim Crow laws that required school segregation. Its school board had tried to avoid integration by shutting down the county's public schools and offering to pay parents to send their kids to so-called private schools, which would segregate black and white children by creating racially separate schools. Intent, or de jure segregation, was obvious by the very nature of the plan, and the Supreme Court decision made clear that that was the key ingredient. By contrast, in *Bell v. School City of Gary*, the Indiana federal appeals court unequivocally found that unintentional, or de facto, segregation caused by a neighborhood-school plan did not violate the Constitution. While the Cleveland case was in the sixth circuit of the federal court system, the *Bell* decision was in the seventh, so it would not bind the sixth-circuit judges. But that court could look to the *Bell* decision for guidance, and there were judges from Kentucky as well as Ohio and Michigan who sat on the sixth circuit. So depending on which judges heard our case, and their mind-sets, it could follow the lead of the seventh circuit and uphold Judge Kalbfleisch's decision. As I worked to outline our Cleveland brief, it seemed to me that intent would be crucial, but Bob wanted me to argue only the impact of segregation and the psychological result. I turned to Barbara and Maria, and they agreed we should include an intent argument. So I wrote a draft for Bob's review that contained both his theory—with its goal of expanding *Brown* to include impact as a determining factor—as well as an argument based on the intent to keep children as segregated as possible.

The next thing I knew Bob stuck his head out of his office.

"Now, Lewis," he semiscolded, "that's not what I wanted. You should be arguing only our theory that it is the effect of segregation that counts, not the intent of school officials. If we argue intent, we'll be fighting Northern school segregation one school-district boundary line after another. It'll be another hundred years before we get those schools integrated. Effect is the only way to make *Brown* work."

"Barbara and Maria agreed that we needed to take both approaches in order to have a chance at winning," I countered.

The three of us marched into Bob's office to thrash out the issue. Finally Bob agreed that I could include an intentional-segregation argument in the brief as long as it was secondary to his effect theory.

"Thank God," Barbara sighed as we left Bob's office. "Springfield's school board changed the school lines so white children can transfer out of heavily Negro schools, and I was worried Bob wouldn't want to put that into evidence. But without that evidence I think we could lose the case. Bob's theory is the only way we are ever to achieve integration on a nationwide basis, but our clients want us to win, and so do I."

I did, too.

I was a newcomer to the civil rights activism that was happening everywhere, and here I was working with one of the country's most renowned civil rights lawyers. I understood what Bob was trying to do, but my perspective was much narrower.

As I look back now, I see the conflict between trying to win individual cases versus Bob's focus on finding more reliable ways to win cases by breaking through at a more basic and easier-to-prove level, using impact, or the effect of a practice, rather than its intent. Bob's point of view was informed by years of working on civil rights cases. He had gone through struggles before considering the benefits of taking an expansive approach versus a narrower one.

Before the 1954 *Brown* decision, Bob's approach to ending Southern school segregation was to engage in a frontal attack. There were critics in the civil rights community, however, who thought he was being too aggressive. They wanted to avoid an all-out attack, advocating instead for the enforcement of the Supreme Court's "separate but equal" doctrine in *Plessy v. Ferguson*, which in theory required Southern school boards to provide the same quality of education to blacks and whites. Bob's critics argued that it would cost hundreds of millions of dollars to provide separate schools that were really equal for black kids, and that would create a huge financial incentive to end segregation. Critics also worried that a frontal assault would lose based on the *Plessy* case. But Bob won over the NAACP's chief lawyer and decision maker, Thurgood Marshall, and prevailed. Now he was trying to attempt a different kind of big-picture attack up North.

Bob's whole approach to the law was strategy first. He constantly looked for remedies that would cut through the morass of racism and bring about real change or at least make change possible somewhere down the line, with the addition of supporting case law. That was also the impetus for *Gaynor v. Rockefeller*, the employment case I was working on at this time, and it was the idea behind his NLRB cases in the South, which fought against mirror black and white unions for the same trades in the same company, in which blacks got only the most menial jobs. To state it in its starkest terms, Bob was unwilling to sacrifice another generation of black kids if he could help it. To avoid that he was always trying to get precedent-setting cases before the Supreme Court. That was the goal. Push through, expand, and win at the highest level.

A few years into my work at the NAACP, I asked Bob about his strategy. I remember the frown that torqued his face.

"If we win, we make some progress," he told me in no uncertain terms. "And if we lose, we've lost nothing. Our children are in terrible schools, so if we lose we are where we started out. We'll come back and try again."

Being white, I'd been given something to ponder.

But in the Cleveland case I was very focused on the appeal issues, and nervous. Our case seemed strong. The public schools fell neatly to one side or the other of Cuyahoga's crooked color line, which divided the city.

Public school segregation in Cleveland was nearly total, and the few aberrations from the rule were just that: out of the ordinary. When CORE and UFM first started pushing back against the horrible school conditions on the east side of Cleveland, the school board agreed to bus children from the overcrowded black schools into underutilized white schools. Once there, however, those bused kids were kept so totally separated that invisible walls might have been keeping blacks and whites apart. CORE and UFM had done a good job pushing until the NAACP could get a legal foothold. Ongoing pressure resulted in some concessions from the school board, which announced that the children from both sides of town would be having nonclassroom-related activities together. On the white side of town that was a powder keg that exploded immediately. Within a week the board assured the white community that it would stop transporting students into their schools as soon as possible. All this was part of the hearing record from which I drew the facts for our appeal.

To carry out its promise, the school board, as I saw it, helped our case by speeding up the school construction program on sites that were unfit for schools, which occasioned more opposition from CORE and UFM. Because the city was doing everything in reaction to the warring factions on either side of the Cuyahoga, building sites were picked hastily—in fact, so quickly and with so little thought that the city planning commission recommended against construction at many of the specified locations because they either couldn't accommodate the proposed buildings and playgrounds, or the traffic patterns in the area were too dangerous for foot traffic. The board, however, ignored the planning commission and began the process of awarding construction contracts, which is when CORE and UFM members started to protest at the sites, and Rev. Klunder was crushed under the treads of a bulldozer.

When coupled with the city's neighborhood-school-district policy, the sites chosen ensured that the new schools would keep black kids on the east side of the river, and Cleveland's schools segregated. Beyond the slightest doubt the board's intent became obvious when the local NAACP unearthed a plan to zone one of the newly built schools, which was in a white residential area, so that its students would all come from outside the "neighborhood," a coded way of saying that the new school would be for black kids and the local neighborhood school would remain white. We can't lose, I thought.

Judge Kalbfleisch didn't understand, or had chosen not to understand, what all of the clamor was about. From his perspective the board was trying to build new schools, which would benefit the Negro community, and the NAACP lawyers for some reason that was more or less indecipherable to him had decided that it was a good idea to stop progress. In the judge's mind a new school was clear evidence of equal treatment. Viewing Bob and his colleagues as obstructionists, Kalbfleisch wrote: "The members of a school board are elected to office. It is inherent in the democratic process that a body politic is subjected to pressures. To infer an unconstitutional design when that body exercises its discretion in accord with law requires substantial evidence. The most this Court will infer from the facts is that the board desired to end transportation classes as soon as possible for the reason its general policy was to maintain neighborhood schools—a concept which has been declared constitutional."

In our appeal brief my job was to pull all the facts together and argue that the court should stop construction until after the NAACP received a full trial. Worried, I asked Bob how a trial would help if the judge had already made up his mind.

"Kalbfleisch might say something in the ruling that could help us later on," he replied. "He's old, too. He could be retired before the trial. Don't worry about him. Anything can happen."

After that group meeting in Bob's office about my first draft, I worked around the clock with Barbara's and Maria's help revising the fifty-page brief and then whisked it down to our printer, making final changes on the hot-metal galleys at the shop. Magically the booklet appeared, smelling of new ink. My name was right under Bob's on the cover.

About a month later we flew to Cincinnati, where the appeals court held its sessions. At the courthouse our attorneys from Cleveland surrounded Bob and congratulated him on our brief. I sat at the counsel table under the eyes of the three judges when Bob rose to argue. Even though I didn't have a speaking part, my heart was pounding.

Not more than a minute went by before one of the judges chastised Bob, and it was my fault. The Supreme Court had overturned one of the cases that I cited for legal authority about the standard for reversing a preliminary injunction decision. The point it spoke to was procedural and relatively minor, but it had been my job to make sure that everything in our brief was still good law, and it was plain as day that I had failed in this fundamental task. There was my boss being forced to apologize for my mistake. He gave me just the slightest downward glance and continued his argument. I turned crimson.

The rest of the argument went no better. Watching helplessly, I sensed that the judges enjoyed giving Bob a hard time. They seemed to resent his assertiveness, and the idea that a black man could lecture them about equality did not appear to sit well with them. When the argument was over, the judges reserved their decision. Outside the courtroom our Cleveland attorneys were worried. Bob appeared unperturbed; it was just another day in court. When we were alone, however, he turned to me: "Don't ever do that to me again, boy."

A few weeks after the argument the court denied our appeal in a short, perfunctory decision. I had prepared myself for the loss, but the lack of any meaningful attempt by the judges to analyze the case caught me by surprise. Courts normally write explanatory opinions that detail the facts and discuss the competing legal concepts if the matter before them turns on a serious issue. The object is not only to resolve disputes but also to offer guidance to the legal profession with regard to how similar controversies should be viewed in the future. These judges, however, treated the idea of the rights of minority children in a major city's entire school system as though they were unimportant. It was as if we hadn't presented them with anything of substance requiring hard thought and careful analysis. We might as well have been fighting a parking ticket, it seemed.

I was tortured by the horrible, even grandiose thought that my mistake had cost us the case. But I also wondered whether Bob's assertiveness had offended the judges. Perhaps if he had not adopted that knowing, professorial tone, we could have done better. It was an ugly line of thought, but I kept rolling it around in my head. I had seen white lawyers argue assertively in court, and none of them had Bob's track record. But white people heard black people differently. It wasn't just words with meanings. There was a meaning attached to an empowered black man, and it seemed to me that these appellate judges saw his stance as far too righteous. While I finally decided that a white lawyer would have had the same result, because the object was still an assault on a racial fortress that was being protected by a white school board, I could not stop thinking about that sort of implacable prejudice. I was confused and shaken, but Bob had already moved on to the next opportunity to expand the law. My background at Culver, Harvard, and in the military trained me on one objective: winning. In race cases, however, it was so easy to lose. The lesson I had to learn from Bob was to look back only to see how you could sharpen your arguments for the next time: Move on. The work awaited.

10

The Cincinnati School Case

Japanese knotweed is an invasive plant species that came to North America toward the end of the nineteenth century. It goes by many names. In some English-speaking countries it's called "fleeceflower." Other names include "pea shooters," "Hancock's curse," "elephant ears," "monkeyweed" "donkey rhubarb," as well as American, Japanese, and Mexican bamboo (though it's not bamboo).

The plant has a complex root system that makes it hard to kill. Only after years of cutting the visible parts can the subterranean roots be weakened enough to kill the plant. You have to destroy the root system to eradicate knotweed, and even then there's a good chance it will rear up again. (In England the roots and soil that result from knotweed removal are controlled by strictly enforced laws.)

The civil rights cases we fought to mitigate the effects of racism in America were—and still remain—like Hancock's Curse. It often seems to me that the roots run deeper than we can ever reach. John Hancock's famous flourish on the Declaration of Independence presents an apt, if accidental, symbol here, since much of the civil rights movement stems from the Founding Fathers' failure in the Constitution to extend the "unalienable rights" of the Declaration of Independence to nonwhite people, and instead accepts slavery with its infamous three-fifths-of-a-man formulation. That systemic, pervasive failure of moral imagination and its Civil War aftermath were the reasons Bob fought on as many fronts as possible with multiple cases that stood at least a shot of winding up in front of Chief Justice Warren's Supreme Court, which for a brief period appeared open to extending the Constitution's guarantees to people of color. Always with an eye on finding new ways to cut through the knotweed of racism in its countless manifestations, Bob knew that the roots of the problem remained untouched deep beneath the surface of the soil. Bob understood that racism in the North, with its unspoken codes, was a less visible but equally invidious and destructive version of the strain in the South, with its church bombings and lynching mobs. The key to breaking the back of public school segregation, he believed, was in the North.

Bob was hardly alone in this realization. In his book *All Eyes Are Upon Us: Race and Politics from Boston to Brooklyn*, Jason Sokol points out, "Through the 1960s, scholars as well as civil rights leaders questioned the racial meaning of the Mason-Dixon line. In 1961, historian Leon Litwack opened *North of Slavery* with a trenchant observation: the Mason-Dixon line 'is a convenient but often misleading geographical division.'"

Jim Crow laws are a thing of the past, although the Supreme Court's 2013 decision striking down key sections of the Voting Rights Act could, with the passage of voter identification laws in areas where there is a long history of racial suppression of the black vote, lead to their partial reestablishment. The hard truth today is that in all the years since *Brown*, and notwithstanding all the other state and federal laws written to promote equal rights that have been passed since the Civil War, racism remains a grave problem in the United States. A recent report by UCLA's Civil Rights Project, called Brown *at 60: Great Progress, a Long Retreat and an Uncertain Future*, found that while schools in the South are significantly less segregated than they were before the landmark decision, things are actually worse in the rest of the country: "In the Northeast, schools are more intensely segregated for black students—meaning that in some cases they comprise 90 to 100 percent of a school's population—than they were before 1968."

Bob's focus on the North was prescient. He was a giant in the Movement long before I met him. He started working at the NAACP Legal Defense and Educational Fund in 1944, as an assistant counsel to Thurgood Marshall, straight out of the U.S. Army Air Corps, where he had almost been court-martialed for his resistance to racial segregation. Besides *Brown*, there was a long list of other big cases, but the 1958 case, *NAACP v. Alabama*, stood out because the Supreme Court decided in favor of the NAACP, thus protecting its membership lists from public scrutiny and removing a tool of intimidation used in the South after *Brown* was decided. The opposition never ceased looking for ways to maintain segregation. Bob's objective was to make advances while protecting the ground already taken. Always looking to reinforce existing case law that would advance civil rights and take new issues to the nation's highest court, Bob argued or coargued and won an unimaginable twenty-one of twenty-two cases that he brought or helped bring before the U.S. Supreme Court.

On the road day after day and month after month, traveling in Jim Crow railcars or driving on Jim Crow roads, where danger was never more than an instant away for any black man, Bob always built toward an all-out attack on *Plessy v. Ferguson* and on school segregation. Some of his earliest cases challenged the so-called separate-but-equal doctrine of *Plessy*. By the time I was getting ready to leave Culver in 1954, Bob had argued school segregation cases in Southern or border-state courtrooms, which were joined together in *Brown* before the United States Supreme Court.

As Bob began to focus his attention northward, I slowly began to look around me. Maybe I already knew in vague terms that the white construction of race was one-sided. I sensed that from Bill and Lorraina. I saw just the tiniest tip of the iceberg at Culver and Harvard. I watched the television coverage of the Freedom Rides and the sit-ins, and I remember the fury of the mobs that tried to block the integration of a school in Little Rock. My eyes were opened by news accounts about those coward bombers—churches attacked, children killed, random people lynched—but until I started to work for the NAACP, I didn't understand the harsh realities of racism in the North.

In the summer of 1964, right after I became an NAACP lawyer, Bob traveled to Mississippi to investigate the disappearance of three civil rights workers, James Chaney, Andrew Goodman, and Michael Schwerner. While he was there the county attorney, Rayford Jones, kept calling Bob by his first name—he said "Robert"—rather than "Mr. Carter." Bob knew there had been a conspiracy to kill Chaney and his companions, and still he stood up to Jones. Bob called Jones "Rayford," an unheard-of violation of Mississippi's racial rules.

That was around the time I met my first Southern judge in Baton Rouge, but otherwise my days were spent at Freedom House preparing for trial in another of the Northern campaign cases against the Cincinnati school board, while Bob was in Neshoba County. Bob was hopeful that this new round of cases in Cincinnati and Springfield would offset the disappointments in the Gary, Indiana, case, as well as in Cleveland.

Soon I was off to Cincinnati to supervise our trial preparation. My plane landed at an airport in Kentucky across the Ohio River from the "Queen City." Since slavery had been abolished, Cincinnati was a terminal city for the so-called great migration. Blacks traveled north to escape Jim Crow laws and to find work in industrial jobs that whites also wanted. What they found in Cincinnati's flat downtown, surrounded by seven hills, was another kind of segregation, one that wasn't as evident as Jim Crow but whose effect was to lock the city's black children into mostly segregated schools while keeping the great majority of them out of white schools.

In the 1960s the black population was crammed into downtown Cincinnati, living in small worn-out houses or packed into old working-class apartments that were often literally falling apart, in the shadows of defunct factories. Jobs were moving out to the suburbs along with the city's white population. The inner-city blacks were trapped. As urban renewal projects tore down their neighborhoods, they were forced into ghettos at the base of the hills, as well as a few of the more rundown arteries that led to the suburbs.

Bob told me to work with Norris Muldrow, a volunteer attorney at the local NAACP branch to prepare the case, which was called *Tina Deal v. Cincinnati Board of Education*. A small but powerful-looking black man in his thirties, Norris had worked his way through law school, attending at night, and was a single practitioner. He was one of the few lawyers in the city who served the black community. We met at the downtown Hilton, where I was staying, his briefcase bulging with legal papers, maps, and other documents that he thought might help us put together the case. Norris suggested a drive around the city, so I could get a feel for the various neighborhoods and schools. While we drove around, he told me about the case, stopping the tour repeatedly to drop in on or call this or that client, with me fuming as I waited in his car, not entirely sympathetic to his day filled with too many people with too many problems.

The Cincinnati Board of Education had operated a small number of totally segregated elementary schools, which it called "voluntary Negro schools," until 1955. Norris said that recently there had been NAACP demonstrations that led to halfhearted promises to look into the segregation issue, and the appointment of one lone black member to the school board, but absolutely no action was taken to integrate the schools, and the demonstrations had petered out.

"They just wait you out," Norris said. "And people have to get back to work. They're relying on us to do the job."

When it closed these "voluntary" schools, the board's administrators put most of the students into nearly all-black schools. Since then segregation among the elementary schools was maintained by the careful placement of new buildings within gerrymandered district lines, and crazy, crisscrossing busing patterns that could exist only for the purpose of keeping white and black children separate. There was a little more integration at the junior high and high school levels, but board officials had worked hard to limit black attendance in the more elite white schools. The few schools with large numbers of both black and white students were disadvantaged in every way and were in poor neighborhoods.

After we had talked and driven around, I told Norris what I knew he didn't want to hear: "Carter doesn't want us to argue that the school board intentionally segregated these schools."

His face registered disbelief.

"Someone has to call them on what they've done," Norris finally responded. "How can we pretend like all this segregation is an accident? The community won't put up with it, and I won't either. I don't care how much time it takes me. I want everyone to see these people for what they are. And I really don't care whether or not Robert L. Carter has some theory about how to win a Northern school case. This is my town, and my NAACP branch, and I will prove, single-handedly if I have to, that Cincinnati segregates its schools on purpose and cheats black schoolchildren out of a decent education the same way Southern cities do."

Having seen the severity of the segregation problem in Cincinnati, I was with him.

"I'll talk to Carter and get back to you," I told him.

Back in New York, Bob was irritated. He lectured me for not persuading Norris to drop his intent proof, but agreed we couldn't stop him.

"Argue both," he instructed.

I called Norris to tell him the news, and suggested that we try to harmonize our approaches. He would develop the case for intentional segregation, and I would work with him to get the evidence and obtain the experts I would need to prove Bob's psychological-impact approach, comparing the performance of children at mainly black and mainly white schools, as well as comparing the facilities, the courses offered, and the teacher qualifications.

A few weeks later, Norris's insistence paid its first dividend.

We were in Judge John W. Peck's federal court chamber, and he was listening to the school board's well-regarded lawyer, C. R. Beirne, explain how our case was no different from the *Gary* case. Beirne was telling the judge that he should apply the *Bell* and Cleveland rulings, require us to prove intentional and not de facto segregation, and dismiss our case if we couldn't.

Judge Peck nodded his agreement.

"How can you win?" he asked Norris and me.

"We have evidence of intentional segregation," Norris replied. "And we can prove in addition that the black schools were inferior and that, as such, they harmed the children who were forced to attend them, but we need access to the board's files to develop our proof."

Shaking his head dubiously, Peck said he would grant our request to inspect the board's records before deciding whether we could have a trial.

"Just put him in a room with the files," Peck instructed Beirne, looking over at Muldrow, "and have your people tell him where to find the different types of documents."

When I reported back, Bob didn't like the sound of things.

"We're only going to win these cases in the Supreme Court," he reminded me. "Giving free rein to a local attorney just slows us down. But fine, it's already in play. Get a professor of education to analyze the data Muldrow gets for you, so long as you do it with no money because we can't pay anyone."

By the early fall, Norris had dug out reams of helpful documents from the board's files, including some evidence of intentional segregation based on reports in the board's possession showing how its administrators drew school-district boundary lines and designed crazy-quilt bus patterns, and reports documenting how high-majority black schools had less-qualified teachers, fewer substitutes, and inferior facilities. Meanwhile I had found a professor of education at Antioch College named Philip Rothman, who was willing to help us with the impact part of the case and document the black schools' inferiority.

On September 25, 1964, however, we got some bad news. A federal appeals court rejected Bob's de facto segregation argument in *Downs v. Board of Education of Kansas City*, another case that he hoped might make it to the Supreme Court. Again the case provided an example of school administrators openly segregating students, but Carter had tried to expand the scope of *Brown* and had lost. Because the Kansas City schools had been openly segregated until after *Brown*, Bob thought the Supreme Court might review the court of appeals decision, and was disappointed when it denied a review in 1965.

The Springfield case took place as Norris and I were getting ready for trial. The outcome there, after a five-day trial, provided a glimmer of hope. Judge George Sweeney ruled that the city's neighborhood-school policy was not a subterfuge for intentional segregation. However, drawing on the testimony of the NAACP's social psychologist, Thomas F. Pettigrew, Sweeney agreed that racial isolation in the public schools damaged the self-image of black children and limited their educational progress, denying them equal protection of the law under the Fourteenth Amendment: "It is neither just nor sensible to proscribe segregation having its basis in affirmative state action while at the same time failing to provide a remedy for segregation which grows out of discrimination in housing, or other economic or social factors," Judge Sweeney reasoned.

In Springfield, where the public schoolchildren were more than 80 percent white, any school that was "appreciably more than fifty percent non-white" was segregated, the judge determined. He ordered the board to submit a plan to eliminate, if possible, "within the framework of effective educational procedures," the racial concentrations. One week later, however, Sweeney allowed the school board to appeal before developing that desegregation plan.

At our next court conference in Cincinnati, I gave Judge Peck the Springfield opinion, but he was not impressed. Instead he framed the legal issue as containing only one question: Did a school board have "an affirmative duty to balance races?" When Norris and I tried to explain that our charges were much broader, Judge Peck frowned.

"You're clouding and obscuring the issues," he replied, but added reluctantly, "I'm not going to dismiss your case."

We got our trial a few months later, in June. By then we had put together an exhibit book containing a short history of the Negro "voluntary" schools, including a chronology of when the black children were transferred into other schools and their racial compositions, two of which were still all-black. Our exhibits featured maps of the variously odd-shaped school-district boundary lines as well as the system's most suspicious bus routes, as well as comparisons between black and white schools.

Following up on what Barbara had told me was a weakness in Judge Sweeney's Springfield decision—that there was no proof of government involvement in the city's housing segregation, we also focused on that issue. That led us to develop evidence that the Cincinnati officials responsible for public housing had segregated their projects, which was then reflected in the racial composition of the public schools.

"Everyone knows how cities get segregated," Bob had grumbled when I told him about our new evidence. "You won't be proving anything everyone doesn't already know."

"If everyone knows how cities get segregated," I replied, "white people sure spend a lot of time denying it."

"You do like getting in the last word, don't you?" Bob said, before giving us the go-ahead.

Like the Springfield trial, *Deal* lasted five days. Norris and I hammered away at school board members, trying to get them to admit that segregation was part of the system's history and that its legacy had carried over into the present era, but they denied having anything more than rudimentary knowledge about how their system operated. That was left to the administrators, they said. Even Calvin Conliffe, the board's recently appointed sole black member, hid behind that wall of feigned ignorance.

When I called Assistant Superintendent John Shreve, the administrator who was responsible for the actual districting of schools, I asked Judge Peck for permission to cross-examine him as an adverse witness. Unless my request was granted, I faced the prospect of having Peck block me from challenging anything Shreve might say under an arcane doctrine that a lawyer must accept whatever his own witness testifies to as the truth. But the judge stopped me cold.

"I take no offense at being called idealistic, if you care to do that," he lectured me. "But I have enough idealism to be absolutely convinced, until the contrary is shown, that public servants are just exactly what is connoted by that term. They are serving the public, not an individual master."

I questioned Shreve anyway, determined to show Peck how wrong he was.

"Be careful," Bob warned me.

Using board documents Shreve could hardly dispute, I examined him about the factors he considered when deciding where to locate new schools and how to district them, and got him to admit he considered "community homogeneity" a "plus factor" when locating new schools.

"Isn't race a part of community homogeneity?" I pressed Shreve.

"Racial similarities are not, in and of themselves," he hedged.

Frustrated, I retreated. Bob gave me an encouraging look when I sat down.

"You did fine," he whispered. "But you have to learn to quit when you are ahead."

Switching to safer ground, I had Philip Rothman explain his charts, which showed that the children in the 80 percent or more black schools actually lost some of their learning ability as measured by standardized IQ tests as they progressed through the grades. By comparison the children in the 80 percent or more white schools gained IQ points.

"Children have equivalent basic ability to learn regardless of their race," Rothman testified. He explained that black children were damaged by segregation in two ways: It caused them to develop negative self-images and it led administrators and teachers to stereotype them as being unable to succeed.

Rothman also presented charts showing how the predominantly black schools were short-changed in terms of teachers, programs, and facilities. He discussed what a "neighborhood school" was in a racially divided city like Cincinnati, where the term could be used to mean anything the administrators wanted. Some school districts extended for miles and had odd shapes, while others were small and compact, he pointed out. Some schools were located in the middle of their districts, while others were perched on a border. In Cincinnati, Rothman concluded, neighborhood-school planning subverted the ideal of the public school as a melting pot for American democracy that brought together children from all strata of society, from all ethnic groups, to induct them into the American way of life. Early-childhood experiences and socioeconomic class as well as race played important roles in pupil performance, Rothman readily agreed when Beirne cross-examined him. But racial isolation, he reiterated, contributed significantly.

Lee Rainwater was up next. He was a nationally recognized expert in human development from Washington University in St. Louis who presented still more testimony on the effect of segregation on learning.

Our next witness was Joseph Murray. Our object was to show how government contributed to the creation of ghettos. Murray worked for Cincinnati's Department of Urban Development and was in charge of the relocation services provided to families displaced by government action. Subpoenaed, he was uncomfortable as he sat in the witness chair and admitted that his department used race to decide where people went.

"There are certain areas," he said, "in which Negroes are not accepted."

Robert Coates, the deputy executive director of the Ohio Civil Rights Commission, followed Murray. His agency documented housing discrimination in Cincinnati, as well as other cities, and had issued a report that detailed the private and municipal measures used to create segregated neighborhoods. When I tried to put that report into evidence, Judge Peck immediately sustained Beirne's objection, cutting me off. Earlier Peck had also rejected a memorandum Muldrow had unearthed in the board of education files that proved school officials had reviewed reports from a private research organization that pinpointed where blacks lived and what type of housing they occupied. In my view that memo went hand in glove with Shreve's admission that the school administrators had favored "community homogeneity" when determining the boundaries of particular "neighborhood" school districts. Peck, however, was letting us know that the city's complicity in Cincinnati's housing segregation wasn't going to figure in this case, no matter what evidence we put before him.

Hitting a dead end, Norris called some of the black schoolchildren's parents, among them Jacqueline Stonom, who told Peck about her child's experience at a predominantly white school where the black children were kept completely separate, as had taken place in Cleveland. She also told the judge about confronting the school superintendent, Wendell Pierce, who admitted that her child had been segregated and brushed her aside.

Impatient, Judge Peck interrupted Stonom's testimony, obviously discounting her, which made her all the more vehement.

Seeing that exchange, I was seething. I had watched white people, sometimes the very white people who had raised me, and later myself, close our eyes to the needs of black people. I had sensed how painful it was for Lorraina Rutherford to be separated from her children while she lived with us.

If I were black, I would have believed Stonom, I thought, shocking myself by how quickly my own doubts about her honesty vanished, and how sure I had suddenly become that the color of our skin had such a profound effect on what we saw and heard as well as what we believed.

After Jacqueline Stonom left the stand, her head held high and her eyes flashing defiance, we finished our presentation. Immediately Beirne asked Judge Peck to dismiss our case, arguing that we had not proved that the board was guilty of intentional segregation.

Peck said he would decide Beirne's motion after the board presented its factual witnesses, but before it had to present its experts. The signal was plain: In Peck's mind, motive was the key.

To satisfy Judge Peck, Beirne called a few board members and administrators, who all hewed to the line that each school's racial composition was a reflection of the city's housing patterns, over which they had no control. Superintendent Pierce joined the chorus as the board's last witness.

When it was time to prove that Cincinnati-style segregation was harmful to black children, Bob took over the cross-examination.

Pierce agreed with Bob that segregation in the South was damaging to black children because it conveyed a societal judgment that blacks were inferior. But things were different in Cincinnati, he maintained.

"Have you read the reports available that say the effect is similar to the South?" Bob asked.

"No," Pierce responded. "My assistants may have, but I don't believe the experts have reached a generally accepted view."

"So how do you explain a totally black school where all the kids live in a totally black housing project? Does that resemble the South?" Bob asked.

"Not a great situation," Pierce replied, "but the children had many contacts with white administrators and teachers." Then he added, beginning to sound defensive, "Now, I am not saying in my statement, Mr. Carter, that there are not things that should be improved in terms of the treatment of the Negro, you understand that," he said. "I feel very strongly in terms of employment, housing, all these other aspects. I am saying, though, that I think there is a marked difference between a Southern approach to this, societally speaking, and Cincinnati."

Norris and I could see that Pierce was getting a little weary. Keep asking questions so that he will have to come back tomorrow, we urged Bob. Half an hour later, the judge adjourned court.

The next morning Pierce was asserting that the Cincinnati schools were not harming black children. "All kinds of people are Negroes," he explained, "just as you have all kinds of whites.

"In other words," Pierce continued, "the idea that every school that has a predominance of Negroes, that they are depressed, that they feel they are not getting an education, you know, that this is a horrible place—this is not true. Mr. Carter. At least from my experience going to the schools."

It was a good answer, but Bob wasn't through with him.

"Don't standardized tests demonstrate underachievement in those schools?" he asked.

"But Mr. Carter, the reason for that, as I have stated many times, is related to the heredity, the out-of-school environment, and we are attempting to compensate for that," Pierce answered.

"I see," Bob replied, barely concealing the undertone of menace in his voice. "What do you think heredity has to do with it?"

"Well," Pierce replied, "you are born with certain potentials."

Bob closed in on the racial insult, asking if heredity was the reason black children underperformed on the standardized tests.

"I am not saying that," Pierce said, but he had gone too far and could not pull back entirely. "I say it is just one factor in it."

"Well, that would be a factor?" Bob asked, staring at the superintendent.

"Yes, one factor," Pierce replied.

The contest was over. Released from the witness stand, Pierce retreated to the back of the courtroom, having just demonstrated as far as I was concerned that the attitudes of school officials in Cincinnati mirrored those in the South.

The trial, at least for now, was over. Judge Peck had to decide if he was going to dismiss the case, or ask the Cincinnati Board of Education to defend its position with expert testimony.

Flying back to New York, I was euphoric. It seemed a sure thing.

"Peck had to comprehend the significance of Pierce's heredity remark," I enthused to Bob. "Put that together with John Shreve's admission that homogeneity was a positive factor in school districting, and it couldn't be more clear."

"Don't be ridiculous," Bob replied. "That judge didn't understand a thing."

11

NAACP Battles

Our second child, Brian, was born in 1965. His birth was a bright spot in what, workwise, was a very hard year. It started with a big NAACP loss. New York's highest court—the court of appeals—decided against us in *Gaynor v. Rockefeller.*

Bob's objective in *Gaynor* was to make the highest public officials responsible for the institutional exclusion of black workers by the all-white "father and son" unions and their hiring halls that was the norm on construction projects built under their auspices. After Judge Stevens had ruled against us in the appellate division, everyone had pitched in to write what we all felt was a compelling brief to the New York court of appeals.

That court announced its decision in early 1965. Stanley Fuld wrote the opinion for all seven judges. It was a slap in the face. All our arguments were rejected in cold, hard prose. The plaintiffs couldn't sue jointly as a class, Fuld wrote, and Rockefeller, Wagner, and their contracting public officials had not acquiesced to union membership practices. The decision contained not an ounce of understanding of the problem the NAACP was attempting to confront. Instead it referred our clients—and anyone who had a similar complaint—to the New York State Commission for Human Rights, a severely underfunded, weak-kneed agency that took years to decide even the smallest case. In other words, there was no remedy. Salt in the wound was the fact that Rockefeller appointed the human rights commissioners the court had ruled should decide such matters.

I was furious about the outcome. As I saw it, the court had rendered a purely political decision. We had sued two of the most powerful politicians, Rockefeller, a Republican, and Wagner, a Democrat. Both claimed to be liberals when it came to race. Without any allies, not one of the seven judges wrote a dissent. Complain to someone else, Judge Fuld told us. In lockstep, the other judges had agreed.

"Oh well, what did you expect?" Barbara had said, dismissively.

"How could they do it?" I fumed.

"Well, they did it," Barbara replied, "and they meant it." She chuckled at my naïveté, as if white folks couldn't possibly understand. At least that's the way I heard her.

When I joined the NAACP it was at least in part because of Bill and Lorraina. They had given me love and warm affection, and I desperately wanted to do something for them—repay them for their kindness to me, for all the nights Lorraina spent away from Duby and Sister Baby, and for what Bill had to do to make his life bearable. I wanted to make up for the slights Bill experienced serving my grandfather, with his asking Bill to agree that Negroes were satisfied with the way things were.

I needed victories to make that right, not defeats. I wanted to be there for Bill the way he'd been there for me.

But losses, rather than victories, were my lot, at least in my first few years at the NAACP. And there had been a lot of them. We lost the Cleveland school case in 1964. Then that same year we lost the Springfield school case in the First Circuit Court of Appeals. Also, as Bob predicted on the return flight from Cincinnati, Judge Peck dismissed my first school desegregation case as trial counsel.

The *Gaynor* loss was also huge. Not only was Stanley Fuld no longer a giant of the law in my eyes, Judge Stevens didn't seem so fainthearted. The lone black judge in that appellate division, he probably knew better than anyone that our case was preordained to fail. The state courts were not going to hold this governor and this mayor responsible for union practices, even if they knowingly ignored the state's human rights law, and the equal protection clauses of the federal and state constitutions. Stevens also was the only judge who discussed both the discrimination practices of the unions and the open acceptance of those practices by the public officials involved, while warning us that certain defeat awaited us. In his own way Stevens was implicitly saying that justice could be blind in the most negative of ways. And that was something I was just beginning to learn, but something that Bob and Barbara knew only too well.

Coming from one of the country's most highly respected courts, the unanimous *Gaynor* decision seriously undermined the idea that the NAACP was going to open up the public construction industry to black workers. Right or wrong, however, I remember still believing that I could reach the Stanley Fulds of the world and make them listen to me. I vowed to keep on fighting to prove myself not only to Bob, but to Bill Rutherford as well.

At the same time the loss parted the curtains on something I needed to understand. The entire struggle in which we were engaged meant something different to Bob. The heavy demarcation lines between white and black were reality he faced all his life. He knew he would have to face racism one way or another in the courts, in the streets where taxis passed him by, or almost anywhere that whites ignored or threatened him and treated him as a lesser person. Such losses were part of what it meant to be a black person in America, and a burning reason to keep on fighting. To him losses were part of the struggle. I didn't expect losses. I wanted something to take back to Bill, something to free me from feeling that I had taken part in a great wrong. I wanted to win.

The civil rights movement was not the ideal place for a young lawyer who measured success by wins, especially as the mood of white and black America alike turned bitterly angry following the passage of the Civil Rights Act of 1964. After its passage President Lyndon B. Johnson promised a War on Poverty, but to the blacks trapped in their ghettos, that was just more empty words. An ascendant militancy decried the lack of change, as moderates like Roy Wilkins kept hoping for incremental progress.

The schools, North and South, were still segregated. Most blacks living in cities, and especially the poor, were squeezed into white-owned, high-rent buildings, many of which were falling apart and never maintained. To escape the summer heat, people camped out on stoops and even in the streets. Across the nation police watched blacks suspiciously when they ventured out of the ghettos. Virtually all the cops were white, and they were quick to arrest blacks for whatever crimes came to mind. Black-on-white crimes led to coerced confessions and beatings. The sentences were more severe, including many more death-penalty convictions. Black incarceration rates were on the rise. Black unemployment was double the rate among whites, and when blacks did find work, it was in generally poorly paid menial jobs. There were so few black lawyers in the United States that Bob half seriously said he knew almost all of them. Black doctors were few and far between. The plumbers, pipe fitters, carpenters, electricians, and all the other craft-union men were white, and it was just a fact of life that their apprenticeship programs were closed to blacks.

For their part, most whites thought they'd done enough. They were angered by the unrest. In the North many whites thought the fight had been about segregation in the South. They had done no harm, and were just hardworking people trying to keep their neighborhoods intact, and if that meant keeping blacks out, it was okay because they had their own neighborhoods.

Demonstrations spread in the North over schools, housing, and jobs. As blacks became more demanding, whites dug in. In this atmosphere almost anything could spark an explosion.

When violence broke out in black neighborhoods, the media tended to call it a "riot," but those incidents were more like miniuprisings or rebellions. Blacks destroyed blocks of businesses and stores in their own neighborhoods—many white-owned, some not—leading to finger-pointing among whites, who saw such behavior as proof that segregation, or to give it another name, exclusion, was a good thing. The major racial explosions lasted days on end—from Newark to Detroit to the Watts section of Los Angeles—where thirty-four people died over a five-day stretch, and more than a thousand were injured. Hundreds of buildings and cars were set on fire and destroyed.

For the NAACP legal department, it was a hard few years. There were more demonstrations, and more cases filed when private businesses sued the NAACP for engaging in boycotts and picketing, and local police in more and more municipalities started arresting leaders to crush public demonstrations. In April 1966 we lost a case called *Overstreet v. NAACP* that threatened the organization's very survival, when the Supreme Court decided five to four against reviewing a Georgia supreme court decision that had upheld a large damages award against our national office for its purported involvement in a boycott conducted against a local market. For years Southern courts had tried to come up with ways to threaten the NAACP, and Bob had beaten them back. But now we had lost, and the fear was that there would be dozens of copycat cases aimed at putting the NAACP out of business. But the NAACP received an influx of donations to help it weather the storm, and thankfully we were not inundated with new lawsuits.

The North had its fair share of demonstration cases too, and I was assigned to handle some of them. In Springfield, Massachusetts, a thousand activists had marched a mile and a half past a thousand National Guardsmen armed with bayonets, 250 state troopers, and all 360 members of the Springfield police department. I was the lead attorney in a court action to stop police interference with lawful demonstrations there, and to enjoin the criminal prosecutions of the leaders. We tried that case and lost despite the wild stories police told—or maybe it all hung on that one grinning police officer's testimony that he couldn't understand what the marchers were saying because they were speaking "African." The testimony of our witnesses was clear, consistent, and credible. The city did not even call the mayor or the police chief; it did not matter. A year later I lost a similar demonstration-and-mass-arrest case in Hartford, Connecticut. In both cases we had presented witness after witness who testified that the marchers had been peaceful. In both cases the judges accepted whatever the cops said. In both the authorities eventually dismissed the criminal prosecutions. But in both the demonstrations had been broken.

In the South I was equally frustrated. I represented three student leaders at Bluefield State College, which is in the coal country of West Virginia. The college had been historically black but was being converted to a white college due to overcrowding at the state's white institutions. The black president had been replaced with a white man. There were mass demonstrations and some property damage. Although there was no proof that our clients, who led the black protests, had caused the damage or advocated it, a federal judge upheld their expulsion. True, we won a demonstration case involving all-black South Carolina State College that same year. A year later, however, state police shot wildly into a crowd of demonstrators, killing three South Carolina State students and wounding twenty-eight others, in what became known as the Orangeburg Massacre.

On the school segregation front the Supreme Court declined to review the adverse decision of the court of appeals in the Cincinnati school case, which triggered another district-court-level review of a few outstanding questions relating to school boundary lines and bus routes. We were preparing to file more Northern campaign cases, but the picture there was certainly becoming bleaker.

Two years after *Gaynor v. Rockefeller*, in 1967, the Columbus branch of the NAACP propelled us into an almost identical case involving construction jobs at Ohio State University.

Bowing to NAACP pressure, Governor James A. Rhodes had signed a state executive order in 1966 that required contractors to include in their public construction bids an assurance that their workforces would not be closed to blacks. The next year Ohio officials called for bids on a new Ohio State University medical science building. It was a $12,800,000 construction project. The contractors refused to sign the assurances, so the state director of public works, Alfred Gienow, obtained a waiver. It was the same old story, an order with no enforcement.

I fielded the calls from the branch office in Columbus, and promised to talk about the situation with Bob, but the *Gaynor* decision had made us gun-shy. Also, I had enough on my plate without a reprise of that case. Kitty was pregnant with Patrick, and we had an exhausting caseload. Picking up on my ambivalence, the local NAACP branch filed a federal suit on its own, modeling it on *Gaynor*. The complaint named Governor Rhodes, Alfred Gienow, and John Gardner, who was President Johnson's secretary of Health, Education, and Welfare. When the judge ordered a hearing for the following week, the local attorneys in Columbus asked us to send someone out to make the presentation in court.

David G. McConnell, a white science professor at the university and the chairman of the local NAACP branch's labor and industry committee, had spent a long time developing contacts and creating a list of black candidates for admission to the unions of the all-white building trades. He found William Ethridge and Jerome Welch, who had been denied union membership application forms, and after they agreed to be plaintiffs in the suit, McConnell also brought two local attorneys on board.

William J. Davis and Irwin Barkin prepared the legal papers. Davis was a well-known local black lawyer with a reputation for speaking his mind, but he was a single practitioner and his time was limited. Barkin was much more accessible. He had a small law firm that worked on labor cases, and was already representing Ethridge in a snail-like Ohio Civil Rights Commission proceeding against a major electrical contractor and the local electrical workers' union. But Barkin also represented unions in his practice, which made it impossible for him to be the lead attorney.

Worried about another loss, I talked to Bob about negotiating a settlement.

"If we look weak, we'll never get anywhere," Bob said. "The goal is to change the law, not open up a few jobs."

"If I handle the negotiation right the judge might view us as the reasonable ones here."

Carter was skeptical, but said it was my call.

"But remember," he said as I left his office, "we're not giving away the case."

I flew to Columbus the weekend before the hearing. McConnell whisked me away to his university office so we could figure out what to do when we went before Judge Joseph P. Kinneary.

Although there were some troubling similarities to *Gaynor*—specifically that the plaintiffs never actually sought work at a job site—to my mind there was a bigger problem: Secretary Gardner was named because his agency had promised the university half the construction budget. Like many Johnson appointees, he had a pro-civil-rights reputation. But to sue a Democratic appointee distracted attention from the conduct of a Republican governor and his administrators, and was a bad move in front of a judge who owed his appointment to President Johnson.

McConnell was adamant about suing Secretary Gardner. As an NAACP attorney, I couldn't drop him from the suit over McConnell's objection, especially when black militants around the country were assailing Johnson for his escalation of the Vietnam War while crippling black poverty persisted at home. So I decided that until we got into court it was McConnell's show on that particular issue.

Judge Kinneary called all the attorneys into his chambers at the federal courthouse in Columbus's main post office building at nine thirty on a chilly Monday morning in March. After William Davis introduced me, I suggested that Ohio voluntarily agree not to sign the construction contracts for two weeks to allow us time to negotiate a resolution. Receptive to that idea, Kinneary directed the state's attorneys to consult with their clients and come back at one thirty. Breathing a sigh of relief, I now at least had time to talk to the people we had subpoenaed as witnesses, and get some idea about what I could expect them to say on the witness stand.

At one thirty, Ohio Assistant Attorney General William Hoiles reported that Mr. Gienow did not want anything to delay the project and did not feel that this was a matter for the federal courts. With that, Judge Kinneary ordered us to put on our case.

Halfway into my opening statement, the judge interrupted me: "Will you be seeking relief against Secretary Gardner?"

"If the state officials were ordered not to sign the construction contracts, there would be no reason for the federal officials to make money available for the project," I replied, trying to thread a needle that kept the peace with both McConnell and Robert Draper, the U.S. attorney representing Gardner. Draper didn't buy it, arguing that the court had no jurisdiction over the secretary and should dismiss the case against him.

Kinneary wanted to hear our evidence before he made up his mind, so he asked me to call our first witness.

I called William Ethridge. In his thirties, he had worked as an electrician for more than fourteen years at North American Aviation installing equipment, reading blueprints, and on all phases of the electrical work there. In addition he moonlighted for a local contractor doing commercial and residential wiring. He testified that he had tried to join the electrical union local in 1966 and 1967, but had not even been able to get an application. He had also been rejected for jobs that required union membership before, and he wanted to work on the medical building, which required union membership. The whole thing took ten minutes.

The brief cross-examinations mounted by Draper and Hoiles were aimed at establishing that Ethridge never tried to get hired. Given the loss in the *Gaynor* case, I was worried, so I recalled Ethridge.

"I have a family to support," he said, "and I cannot continue to run all over the city and let my feelings be hurt by these same people every time."

Next up was Jerome Welch, who operated heavy equipment. After a few preliminaries, Judge Kinneary exercised his prerogative to question the witnesses, asking him if he was able to operate the same equipment that the union workers would use.

"Similar," Welch replied.

I held my breath waiting for the follow-up questions about how long it would take to learn how to operate the exact same equipment, but they didn't come from the judge or Draper and Hoiles.

Two contractors, John Myers, a plumbing and pipe-fitting contractor, and J. Parker Garwick, the project's general contractor, were next. When I asked Myers why he had refused to sign the assurance about hiring black workers he said the union hiring hall was all-white, so there was no way to make it happen. Similarly, Garwick testified that, other than laborers—by far the lowest-paid workers on the job—his workers had to come from a union hiring hall. Even so, he had provided the state his assurance that he would hire blacks.

"How can you comply with the assurance?" I asked Garwick.

"By asking the unions for Negroes," he answered.

"And what would happen if none were sent?"

Garwick shrugged. "Well, I wouldn't hire nonunion workers, because if I did, we wouldn't have any other men on the job."

Having gotten this far in less than an hour, I called Ellis Ross, the executive director of the Ohio Civil Rights Commission, to testify that Ohio officials knew blacks were excluded from most of the building trades. Ross was black, but he owed his job to Governor Rhodes.

"Watch out for him," McConnell had warned me. "He's dangerous."

I had talked to Ross during the morning break. Despite the friendly facade, he managed to slip away from every hard question. I needed Ross, but didn't want him to hurt me.

The Ohio Civil Rights Commission had surveyed the racial composition of the craft unions that supplied workers to Ohio State University.

"And what were the findings?" I asked.

"The result," Ross replied, "was that in general there seemed to be an absence of Negroes."

"And does 'absence' mean total lack of blacks?"

He agreed that it meant a total lack of blacks.

"If you conducted the same survey on the Ohio State campus today," I pressed, "would the situation be the same?"

"It would."

I didn't want to push him any further.

McConnell thought my next witness might illustrate the uglier side of the union race problem. We had already established that the electric workers' local was all-white, but Daniel Bricker, its business manager, was especially hated in the black community, and there was a good chance he'd shoot off his legendary mouth in front of the judge.

A puffy middle-aged man, Bricker was only too happy to say that he had given the state assurances he would provide them with black workers on the Ohio State project.

"How many Negroes do you have as members?" I asked.

"What do you classify as a Negro?" Bricker said, staring at me blankly.

Responding to the wise-guy act, Judge Kinneary pointed to some of our supporters in court: "The four gentlemen seated in that row are Negroes. That's what the counsel means by a Negro. I think it is common knowledge what a Negro is," he snapped.

"We don't have any," Bricker cheerfully admitted, before rejoining his snickering supporters.

I followed with Park Pixley of the Associated General Contractors of America, which negotiated collective-bargaining agreements between contractors and craft unions. He said contractors were allowed to hire nonunion workers if the union locals couldn't supply them. That meant Ohio officials could enforce the requirement that contractors employ black workers, whether or not they were union members.

The day's final witness was the director of public works, Alfred Gienow, who had obtained the compliance waiver. I asked him if the state knew there was discrimination among the unions.

"We made a head count at Ohio State and found something along that line, yes."

Judge Kinneary took over. He asked Gienow what he would do about the absence of black workers on the project.

"Well, sir," Gienow replied, "I am an engineer, not a lawyer."

"But what would you do?" Kinneary asked.

"The state would void the contract."

"Would you do that?" Kinneary demanded.

"Oh, certainly. That's spelled out in the executive order," Gienow replied.

My heart thumped with excitement. I knew for a fact that the state had never cancelled a contract for that reason and was ready to pounce, but Judge Kinneary waved me off.

"I am not going to permit any more questions of this witness," Kinneary announced, and called us into chambers.

There he said he would hold another hearing in May where we would have to prove that our clients lacked adequate remedies against racial discrimination in the construction trades, under both Ohio law and the Civil Rights Act of 1964, and that there had been irreparable harm—the standard for issuing an injunction.

I listened, and worried that we were heading down the same dead-end road as in *Gaynor v. Rockefeller.* Then a hopeful sign came in the form of a promise, extracted by the judge, that no contracts would be awarded before the court's decision in May. The more I thought about that, the more I focused on the good things we achieved that day, and I started to believe that we actually had a shot at winning.

My face was distorted in the little jet window, beyond it the complete darkness of night.

In one afternoon I had somehow navigated the stories and evasions of eleven witnesses. As I thought about the case, it became clear how big a part good fortune and chance could play in the law's development. Without William Ethridge and Jerome Welch coming forward, without the hard work of David McConnell and Bob's tireless efforts and innovative theories about how to expand civil rights law, and without my contributions we would have no case. That word "we" resonated in my mind. It had taken all of us to get this far. It was my job to get us over the top, and this was my chance. I had wanted deliverance from the feeling that I was somehow separate and apart from real civil rights lawyers who changed the laws, and this was my opportunity. We could convince the judge. There had to be a way.

I said nothing of the day's accomplishment to the man strapped in next to me. Having tried talking about my work on other flights, slowly working around to what I did after listening to my neighbor's stories about his job, family, and traveling, I knew better. Most of the guys I met on those planes cared a lot more about safe neighborhoods, good schools, and secure jobs than they did about racial equality—if they cared about social issues at all. "Good luck with what you're doing" was a common good-bye at the end of a flight, a hint of distaste in it.

Back in the office my mind settled on a particular phrase from the hearing: "the absence of Negroes." It haunted me. Whites were used to the absence of Negroes. To us, blacks were almost always absent. They were absent from our neighborhoods and absent when we went to restaurants. They weren't on planes. You hardly ever saw them in the theater. Most of the time they were absent from the movies and TV shows we watched, or they had bit parts that were absurdly stereotyped. There was an absence of Negroes in almost all the books we read, and the only appearances they made in the newspapers belonged to sports figures, entertainers, and criminals. Sure, they were in our homes as help, knew the details of our lives, but we avoided knowing about their cares and troubles, and once out of sight they were out of mind. Absence was the preferred status.

So it was a major moment when Judge Kinneary asked me to explain why the "absence of Negroes" mattered in this lawsuit. I got to work. It would be easy to prove that Ethridge and Welch had no remedy. The Ohio Civil Rights Commission had never placed a single black with a construction union, which meant that Ohio's antidiscrimination laws provided no realistic remedy. The new federal civil rights laws had been in effect for two years, but there hadn't been a single lawsuit against a construction trade union in Ohio that made it to trial. If Judge Kinneary stopped construction, the state officials could find a way to get blacks on the job.

The other issue raised by Kinneary was irreparable harm. While Ethridge and Welch would probably make more money on the Ohio State project, the difference in pay didn't rise to the high standard required to prove irreparable harm, a legal concept used for centuries by judges to thwart litigants who wanted a court to force someone to do or refrain from doing this or that thing. And in this case, the object, at least initially, was to stop construction on a building that could lead to discoveries that would help thousands of people, black as well as white.

Then it occurred to me that thirteen years earlier, Thurgood Marshall and Bob Carter had used psychological testimony to convince the Supreme Court that school segregation taught black children they were inferior to whites, and that the damage inflicted in the process was unlikely ever to be undone—in other words: irreparable harm.

I tried it out on Bob.

"If a black child grows up walking by construction sites where every single worker is white, doesn't that send the message they aren't good enough to be construction workers—that they will never get a shot at a job like that, and doesn't that amount to the same sort of psychological damage as in the *Brown* case?"

"Everyone knows that," Bob said dismissively.

"Most white people don't," I replied. "Anyway, you could say the same thing about school segregation—everyone knew it hurt kids' self-esteem—and yet that's how you convinced the Supreme Court it had to do something about it."

"I'm not so sure what most white people knew then," Bob replied. "But it's worth a try. Be careful not to overreach or take chances that will lose us credibility with the judge."

I was ecstatic.

"And don't expect me to come out there and bail you out," he said, with a smile.

Suppressing the urge to hug him, I felt appreciated in a way that reminded me of Bill Rutherford. That thought, however, was immediately followed by another: Was it racist to equate the two men? Bob was su-premely well educated, and I didn't even know if Bill had graduated from high school. But like Bill, Bob hid his deepest pain from me just as I concealed my conflicted feelings from him, and both men had reason not to trust white people. Though it was unstated, Bob and I knew there was a lot roiling just below the surface of our relationship, even as he had begun to trust me. He sensed that something deep inside drove me to the work we were doing, and that it was something I had to do. Anyway, I thought, it was my feeling, connecting the two men, and for that matter a driving force in my passion for the work.

I needed one more thing to increase our chances of winning: permis-sion to drop Secretary Gardner from the case. Bob quickly assented, and so did McConnell.

I started putting together a trial plan. I decided that Bill Davis should take a more active role. It was crucial that Kinneary feel that the case rose out of a need of the black community in Columbus, and not because some white lawyer from the NAACP's national office in New York City thought it was a good opportunity to push a radical agenda. The more Davis participated in the hearing, the less likely that Judge Kinneary would be distracted by my role. In the days ahead McConnell, Bob, and I conferred about experts, pulling three into our case. I interviewed them and prepared their testimony over the phone.

At nine thirty in the morning on May 1, we entered the courtroom with our small group of supporters. Bill Davis made a brief opening statement and called our first expert, Walter Tarpley, the community relations director for the city of Columbus.

Tarpley set the stage for our other expert testimony, reciting evidence of all the available unemployed young black men available to do con-struction work.

Hoiles's cross-examination tried to weaken Tarpley's testimony. He asked:

"Does the Negro lad just graduated from college have at least an equal opportunity with the white college graduate of 1966 to gain em-ployment in almost any field he wants?" Hoiles asked.

"He does," Tarpley agreed. To me that answer was just plain wrong. I held my breath.

"What about Negro and white high school graduates," Hoiles pressed.

"No," Tarpley replied. "Family connections come into play at this level, placing Negroes at a disadvantage."

"How ready are Negro young people to work in the construction trades?" Hoiles asked.

"It's true many Negroes haven't spent much time training for jobs they didn't think they could get anyway," Tarpley answered, but "there are many already working in the more marginal craft jobs, and they can enter the field quickly."

Two professors from Ohio State University, Nason Hall, Jr., an urban sociologist, and Samuel Stellman, a consultant to the U.S. Office of Economic Opportunity, followed Tarpley. The testimony of both men established our psychological approach. They told the judge that black young men looking to enter the workforce knew the construction trades were closed to them and that had a heavy impact on them—that they lost hope, became hostile and even antisocial. Both also discussed the positive effect that the opening up of jobs would have in the black community, and how easily black workers could be trained.

Next I called Ohio Civil Rights Commission Director Ross to follow up on some questions I asked at the March hearing about discrimination among the craft unions.

Judge Kinneary quickly took over, however.

"Has a single individual ever gained admission to any craft union after having invoked the procedures of the Ohio Civil Rights Commission in the seven years you have worked for the agency?" he asked.

"Admission," Ross repeated. "I would be forced to say no."

As there had been about thirty cases involving racial discrimination brought against the craft unions, Judge Kinneary wanted to know what the results were.

"The object was to gain admission of qualified Negroes," Kinneary said. "Now, how many have gained admission as a result of the processes of the Ohio Civil Rights Commission?"

"How many have actually been admitted to the craft unions," Ross repeated.

"Yes," the judge replied impatiently.

"I know of no one," Ross answered.

"No one," Judge Kinneary repeated.

"No sir."

"What is the end result?" Judge Kinneary asked, after listening to a few minutes of evasive testimony. "Has your commission been effective? Has your commission been ineffective?"

"In the trades," Ross admitted, "we have not been effective."

While closing our case I placed into evidence the collective-bargaining agreements between the craft unions and the various contractors involved in the Ohio State bidding process. They didn't require workers to have any particular qualifications for particular jobs. The contracts also prohibited the unions from discriminating against workers who wanted to be referred out of the various hiring halls on the basis of race or union membership, allowing the contractors to hire nonunion workers if the craft unions couldn't provide qualified workers, which we claimed meant an integrated workforce.

Hoiles opened his defense by referring to a state legislative bill that would declare void any hiring hall agreements with a union that could not offer an integrated workforce on job referrals for public projects.

"Mr. Hoiles," the judge interrupted, "the court has gone along on the assumption that the state of Ohio does not want to practice—in any way, shape, or form—discrimination against any group. Am I correct in that?"

"You are," Hoiles replied.

"So why doesn't the state tell the contractors on the project to hire Negroes from other sources if they want to work on the project?"

Hoiles referred to a law requiring the state to accept the lowest bid, which prompted Judge Kinneary impatiently to direct Hoiles to call his witnesses. To my surprise he recalled Ellis Ross, who testified that, in a few cases before his commission, orders had been issued requiring minority complainants to be given admissions tests to craft unions, which accorded them equal treatment.

It was my turn to cross-examine.

"Many workers have never taken tests to gain admittance into the craft unions," I said. "Isn't it unfair to now require tests after the whites got in without them? In the father-son friends-and-family system that prevailed, didn't newcomers get trained on the job?"

"They do," Ross replied.

"So tell me, why should a Negro have to start a job and be able to perform it with no training when whites started out without training? Is that fair?"

"It is not fair to require that," Ross acknowledged. Sensing that Ross was tired of hedging, I took the chance I had avoided in March.

"You have no doubt in your mind, do you, that there has been racial discrimination in the craft unions?"

"Well, I'm pretty sure there has been, and this is based on twenty-six years of experience in the employment field," he replied.

"And you are pretty sure there has been in Columbus, Ohio, aren't you?"

"Yes," he agreed.

I had one last question—a little riskier.

"And you are pretty sure of the fact that no Negroes are in most of the craft unions in Columbus, Ohio, today based on those historic patterns of racial exclusion, aren't you?"

"Yes."

"If your commission got the electrical union to accept Mr. Ethridge under an agreement that didn't force the union to change its practices, would you be eliminating discrimination in the union?" I pressed.

"No," Ross acknowledged.

The judge picked up on the point, asking if that had happened on an individual person-by-person basis, and Ross said it had. Then he gave us a parting gift, adding, "It will probably take eons to complete the eradication of discrimination."

During my closing argument Judge Kinneary asked if he could stop the state of Ohio from entering into construction contracts for the project until it had a plan that would enable qualified Negroes to obtain employment. I said he could, explaining why and how he could make that happen. The logical follow-up question, "How many is enough?" wasn't asked. Perhaps the judge thought that when the number of blacks in a particular trade was zero, it was moot.

On May 17, the thirteenth anniversary of the Supreme Court's *Brown* decision, Judge Kinneary issued his ruling. As McConnell read it to me, tears of joy welled up in my eyes. We had won, totally and completely. Ethridge and Welch were qualified. The craft unions had discriminated against black workers, and the state officials were well aware that that meant an all-white workforce. No other effective remedy was available to the plaintiffs, except the intervention of the federal court. Especially satisfying was Judge Kinneary's finding on the psychological impact of workplace discrimination. "Discrimination in the area of employment stunts the educational and technical potential development of [Negroes] subject to such inequities," he wrote. "Injuries of this kind," he went on, "are not subject to any sort of monetary valuation."

Bob Carter hugged me. As word spread, a spontaneous celebration began. The following day I was part of a press conference presided over by Roy Wilkins and Bob. They introduced me as the lawyer who had won the case. Wilkins, Carter, and Herbert Hill, the NAACP's labor director, went on to announce a national campaign to duplicate and implement the decision across the entire country. Sitting at the press table with Bob, Wilkins, and Hill, the NAACP banner behind us, I finally had the win I wanted.

But staring out of my office window afterward, I became preoccupied by the air of unreality that prevailed during the press conference. A national campaign was wishful thinking. The NAACP barely had the staff and resources to handle the Columbus case, let alone mount a national effort. If openly imposed school segregation was still common thirteen years after the Supreme Court had condemned it, the decision of one district-court judge certainly was not going to bring about the collapse of black exclusion from the craft unions. I had begun to understand that civil rights lawyers were only effective when they were a part of a strong movement seeking change.

One other thing haunted me. For years American leaders had said the right words, but their deeds left blacks still struggling with exclusion, poverty, and the knowledge that they were barely tolerated by whites. They didn't need Judge Kinneary to tell them that discrimination stunted their lives. By inserting that concept into the case, I may have helped the judge to understand the destructive force of discrimination, but did the words "stunts" and "potential development," which I had helped to place in his mind, have a condescending ring? I wondered if that bothered Bob, and if he saw my victory as the price he had to pay for progress. I also wondered if my presence at the press table, a young white using the suffering of others to make his mark, was an affront on some level. The victory was Bob's, not mine. It was his theory that I had developed and executed, and I did not want to be seen as another Jack Greenberg in waiting. Quickly, however, I put such thoughts out of my mind. I knew that wasn't me. Sure, I wanted some glory. But Bob was both an intellectual giant and a leader. The achievement was his, just as the *Brown* victory was the product of black intellectual thought and lawyering that started with the great Charles Houston at Howard Law School and was passed along to Thurgood Marshall and Bob. While white lawyers helped, it was critical that both Bob's black world and my white world understood who the leaders were.

I think Bob could see how much I struggled to see the world through his eyes. My feelings for him transcended race, and I believe that his feelings for me did as well. There was something that reached across the space between us. Race was a barrier that could be broken and would not impede whatever bond was forming between us. I had been unable to overcome the barrier between Bill and me, which is how I became "Mr. Lewis." With Bob I was on my way.

12

Two Different Worlds

I volunteered at the NAACP a month after Janine was born and worked there until she was five. By that time, Brian and Patrick had come along.

The year before Janine went to kindergarten, Kitty and I had one of the very few conflicts we've had to weather as a couple. For me it was work-related. I wanted Janine at the local public school, and Kitty was adamantly opposed to the idea. Janine was going to private school, as far as Kitty was concerned, and that's all there was to it. I understood why she wanted it that way, but nevertheless I disagreed with her. My work almost demanded that she go to an integrated public school, but considerations of that variety had no bearing on Kitty's point of view on the matter. If you've been happily married with children for any amount of time, you can probably guess that the stronger conviction won out—which really says something about Kitty, and maybe about me as well.

While I was a civil rights attorney fighting to integrate northern public schools, Kitty was the daughter of a Pittsburgh cop. She grew up in a working-class Irish neighborhood. None of her fellow students from either the local public school or the Catholic high school she attended went to college. More than fifty years later, Kitty still reminds me about this smoldering recollection of her growing up.

"I took typing and home economics while you were reading Chaucer and Shakespeare in high school," the argument began. "I was taking a secretarial course. And while you went to Harvard, I was singing 'This Is My Beloved' while Slapsy Maxie Rosenbloom was holding a microphone to the bowl as he flushed a toilet offstage. You can talk all you want, but our children are going to private schools. I won't have your mother looking down her nose at our children the way she does at me."

"Half the kids who went to Harvard went to public schools," I replied, "and anyway if there are problems with the local public school, we can get involved and help make it better. Be a part of the change—"

"You won't do it," she said, cutting me off.

"I will."

"Not with your work schedule. You won't do it. I want our children to go to private school."

By the time Janine reached kindergarten age, the die had been cast. She went to the Ethical Culture School a few blocks down from our apartment building. "Ethical," as it was called by those who knew about the world of private schools in New York City, was known for being liberal and socially activist. It made an effort to have one or two black kids in each class. Beyond that, however, it was private and white and for the children of the ever-striving wealthy classes. I had surrendered, without much of a fight.

Our children all grew up well, mainly due to Kitty's caring. Their private school education taught them that they are members of an elite stratum of society, and the fallacy that they earned their place in that world by their own hard work. Although my children never said such things (or, as far as I know, thought such things), some of their schoolmates believed that the kids they saw who didn't make it out of the ghetto were lazy—and it was their fault that their possibilities seemed so rotten when the buses rolled through their neighborhoods on the way to Riverdale. While over the years our children have learned about the incredible difficulties of growing up in barely functional settings where young men dealt drugs or worked other hustles, always on one side or the other of prison's revolving door, it was only in an intellectual way, and with very little of the firsthand experience they would have had at a public school, where empathy could flow out of friendships. But what's done is done.

For me the regret for not sending our children to integrated public schools goes deeper. Although we never left New York City, my family and I engaged in a form of white flight. We withdrew, leaving it to other people who did not have our financial and social resources to make the public schools work and try to make integration a reality. Every time I say that I can understand the lawyers who fought against the NAACP's Northern school desegregation cases and the judges who did not comprehend what was at stake, or have the fortitude to make the hard decisions to go against their friends and neighbors, I think of myself because I gave them their excuse.

While Kitty was winning the private school war at home, I was fighting Northern campaign cases in Indiana—one in South Bend and the other in Kokomo. In both instances black children were assigned to broken-down, impoverished schools located in the spreading urban blight that was then an epidemic at precisely the same time those municipalities were building brand-new public schools for white middle-class families creating new, racially segregated suburbs on the outskirts of both cities.

Despite losses in Gary, Cleveland, and Cincinnati, Bob wanted the NAACP to take a leading role in South Bend and Kokomo. His assumption was that the local federal judges would rule against us, leaning on the other NAACP Northern campaign losses. However, Bob still believed that the Supreme Court would listen to his "impact," or de facto, argument.

Ground zero for the case in South Bend happened three days after we lost the Cincinnati appeal from Judge Peck's second-district court decision. A ceiling collapsed in South Bend's Linden Elementary School, which was 99 percent black. It was the third time. Fortunately the kids were on vacation. The local NAACP branch demanded that the South Bend school board close Linden Elementary and send the children to surrounding schools. I got the assignment to try to make that happen, and immediately asked for and got a hearing to achieve that goal.

Despite a local architect's unchallenged testimony in 1966 that South Bend's old, barely functional, wooden, and severely overcrowded 99 percent black Linden Elementary School was a dangerous firetrap, the local U.S. district-court judge, Robert A. Grant, denied my request for a preliminary injunction to close the building and assign the children to neighboring schools that had empty seats. I was stunned, as were the mothers sitting in the courtroom. Should I have sought out a highly credentialed Indianapolis or Chicago architect and paid any fees out of my own pocket?

I asked myself. The local guy maybe was not up to the judge's elitist standards. If my children were in that school I would have left no stone unturned to close the building. Now I would have to tell the mothers I would keep fighting. But that would not relieve their fears; I was just another white man in another white court who failed to protect their children. Later I tried to get Father Theodore Hesburgh, the president of Notre Dame and a South Bend power broker, to help me put some pressure on the school board. Although he was a member of the United States Commission on Civil Rights and an outspoken advocate of integration, I couldn't even get him on the telephone.

The following year a newly hired NAACP lawyer, Richard Bellman, joined me in South Bend to begin a full trial of the entire school system before Judge Grant. After some irate teachers testified about the horrible conditions in Linden, and my threats to call more to talk about the overcrowding, double sessions, outdated books, and lack of supplies in the other predominantly black schools, the school board threw in the towel. We worked out a settlement in which Linden would be closed and the administration would develop an integration plan for the other schools. At the end of the school year, however, when it was unclear whether Linden would reopen, the black community took to the streets. The cops were called. Rocks were thrown, shots were fired, and a demonstrator was wounded. Linden, however, was not reopened. But the administration reneged on its promise to integrate its schools, and Judge Grant warned me that if I tried to get him to enforce the settlement he would pay particular attention to the board's one black member. Overwhelmed with work, I put the case on the back burner, and it took another lawsuit brought by the U.S. Department of Justice years later to complete the job.

In the summer of 1967 I journeyed to Kokomo, Indiana, a relatively prosperous city of 55,000 (and growing, fueled by new industrial plants), to try a school case there. I wanted to spend a little time at home with Kitty, who was pregnant with our third child, and my growing family, and I needed some time to prepare the case. But the judge, Cale Holder, labeled me "Mr. Steel from New York," and gave me only one month. Somehow, with the help of Patrick Chavis, a fine local attorney and well-known African American state senator from Indianapolis, I managed to see Kitty give birth to Patrick and return a few days later, find expert witnesses at Indiana University, and put together our trial witnesses.

Virtually all of Kokomo's black community of three thousand lived in a small segregated area near the urban core of the city. In contrast to the much more prosperous white neighborhoods, the streets and sidewalks were either unpaved or crumbling, and lighting was nonexistent. "Ghetto" accurately described the area. Until the 1954 *Brown* decision the elementary schools were openly segregated. Thirteen years later the situation was not much improved. White teachers engaged in racial name-calling, and one-third of the city's black elementary schoolchildren were assigned to two paired old, run-down, almost 90 percent black, pathetically outdated buildings called Willard and Douglass. At the same time, in the all-white suburbs, the school board was planning a ten-million-dollar educational park, as well as a new junior high and elementary school. Our objective was to close Willard and Douglas and stop the new construction, which would segregate the schools even further.

Purely by luck the trial turned in our favor. The school board attorney, asking one of our witnesses about her complaints, caused her to blurt out a fact she had not told us—that a black first-grader had had her mouth taped shut by a teacher. A bored judge became interested. He inspected Willard and Douglass and listened intently to our educational experts explain why segregated schools damaged black children. Unlike Judge Peck in Cincinnati, he understood. Months later, long after the trial was over, Holder issued a ninety-four-page opinion. He ordered Willard and Douglass closed, but did not stop the construction of the educational park or the other new schools, as they had not been zoned yet. The following year both Patrick Chavis and I complained bitterly but to no avail, when the judge allowed all the Willard and Douglass children to be reassigned to neighboring schools, increasing their racial concentration.

Back in New York in the Hamptons, building sand castles at the beach with my children after that hearing, I thought about the mothers I met when we fought school cases, the children playing at their feet filled with energy but destined for a hard life where many doors would be closed. The black parents I met in Cincinnati, South Bend, Kokomo, and at least a dozen other cities and towns where the NAACP fought to obtain at least some semblance of integration, were trapped. Housing discrimination dictated where they lived, and employment discrimination further reduced their options. Black women raising their children alone were the most powerless, and their children were the ones who needed good public schools the most. Drugs were beginning to infiltrate the ghettos, and the menace of violence was hanging over the streets.

At Grandma Bessie's apartment after summer vacation was over, I sought out Lorraina in the kitchen and told her about my cases. If I asked about Duby and Sister Baby—I can't remember if I did—she would have said they were doing fine, but I certainly never ventured to ask about the schools they attended. I was afraid that if she needed help, I would fail her. Maybe she feared that also. As she showered me with warmth and affection I felt like a fraud—a champion of her people, so serious about things she knew about firsthand—the occasional visitor who disappeared out of the kitchen to take my place at the family table.

13

1968

Despite positive court decisions in the *Ethridge* case and in Kokomo, the Northern campaign yielded few meaningful results. The Supreme Court refused to review any of the federal court of appeals decisions that hinged on Bob's insistence that school segregation in the North was just as unconstitutional as the South's Jim Crow version.

Even the *Ethridge* case had stagnated. Moreover, Governor Rhodes didn't appeal the decision, which cut off the possibility of a higher-court ruling. As with most civil rights wins, the issue became enforcement, and not a single black in the all-white trades had gotten a job on the stalled Medical Science Building. Judge Kinneary had not set a hearing date to enforce the decision, and a second action that we filed, *Welsh v. Rhodes*, sat in front of him without any movement. In Kokomo, where again there had been no appeal, the school board was doing as little as possible to desegregate the schools, and Judge Holder had rubber-stamped whatever paltry actions the board had taken. In the area of protecting demonstrators, the Supreme Court and the lower federal courts had become hostile. As I saw it, we were in the midst of a judicial backlash.

In the larger civil rights arena, major problems eclipsed our court cases, prime among them America's war against the Viet Cong and Communist North Vietnam. While the more militant black leaders who were beginning to come to prominence in the mid- to late sixties dismissed him for preaching nonviolence, Martin Luther King, Jr., had tacked noticeably to the left. He took the SCLC to the North and planned the Poor People's Campaign. King also opposed the Vietnam War and argued that black youth were being used as cannon fodder. Meanwhile, the more-establishment-oriented Roy Wilkins insisted that military decisions lay beyond the purview of the civil rights movement. Ironically, Wilkins's position broadened the appeal of more forceful activists like Stokely Carmichael and H. Rap Brown, who had advocated black power and rejected nonviolence. As a result the possibility of a united movement was falling apart, with Wilkins getting pushed toward the sidelines. At the same time Bob Carter quietly began to act independently of Wilkins and the NAACP old guard that supported him. In the area of school desegregation, for example, Bob began supporting community control in the predominantly nonwhite schools of the North.

For Bob, however, segregation remained a critical issue. Having decided *Brown v. Board of Education*, the Supreme Court proceeded in a series of cases to strike down openly enforced Jim Crow segregation in public facilities, and to uphold the new provisions of the 1964 Civil Rights Act. But its failure to take meaningful action in the South, where for many years school segregation remained the norm, or to review any of Carter's Northern school cases, underscored the Court's avoidance of enforcement, leaving that issue to the next generation of justices. As a result Bob's Northern campaign had made little or no progress, not because it was ill conceived but because he was attacking deep-rooted prejudice supported by multiple components of the white power structure—from the politicians to the courts to the unions and the school boards—as well as white majority voters who felt they'd "given" enough.

As for me, I was battling burnout. We were running a footrace in a bog, and the NAACP legal department had developed a siege mentality. Younger activists began advocating more aggressive tactics. Roy Wilkins and the old guard on the NAACP board believed in the long view—that you push for change, and that meaningful reform took time. But what was writ large in the form of racial unease and uprisings across the nation was creeping into the fabric of the NAACP, where the board was divided between "young Turks" who said it was time to get tough and the old guard. Under Bob's leadership the legal department increasingly found itself aligned with the young Turks. It was a natural evolution: Bob wanted results. He wanted black kids to get educated, and black workers to get their fair share of the better-paying jobs. The cases that came our way reflected the change among Movement people, and the tension was palpable.

At black colleges and universities in the South, we were increasingly involved with aggressive student leaders at odds with administrators who were more interested in maintaining calm than promoting racial progress. In the cities there was an increasing number of uprisings, called riots by the media. The causes were different—ranging from poverty, joblessness, and disenfranchisement to the predatory draft that was sucking black youth into the war in Vietnam—but all boiled down to protest against the untenable existence to which the nation's black population was relegated. As the protests mounted and the NAACP scrambled to deal with one legal fire after another, the courts—including the nation's highest—became more and more hostile toward anything that did not involve some form of overt racism.

Fatigue, anger, and a sense of frustration were constants. Ironically, it was my work in the North that really focused these feelings for me. Nothing appeared to be changing in the North. The schools remained segregated. Construction sites swarmed with white workers—no blacks to be seen. I still had to hail taxis for Bob. Black unemployment was high, and the cities were exploding with racial violence. The police were engaging with trapped ghetto black youth as if they were the enemy—and in some instances that wasn't too far from reality. In the South, by contrast, there were signs of change in the cities. Hotels and restaurants were no longer enforcing Jim Crow, and blacks were beginning to vote. That said, the benchmark for social change in the South was low.

The Vietnam War started out as a tough issue for me. I was not like Major Warner, whose jingoism and hatred of the Soviet Union blurred his ability to see the issues around anything tinged red, but I had hawk-like reactions to what was called the "domino theory"—the idea that if all of Vietnam turned communist, other nations would follow. Perhaps it had been my Culver training. But the barbaric senselessness of the war eroded my views. Somewhere, too, I knew that the black waiters at Culver were now fighting for their lives in the jungles of Vietnam.

"It's a civil war," Kitty kept saying. "We've got no business being over there in the first place."

I equivocated for a while, but it wasn't long before I found myself following Kitty's lead. Saluting the flag was one thing I had been trained to do since I was thirteen, but killing all those poor peasants was something else, and when the marches started, we joined the thousands who were opposed to the war.

Roy Wilkins did his level best to contain the opposition to the war at the NAACP. The organization's official stance remained unchanged, but little by little, at the request of our more militant branches, Bob had started assigning his attorneys, who by then numbered six, to represent black students who were disciplined and/or arrested for antiwar activities. We tried to keep a low profile, but word circulated through the corridors. To say the least, Wilkins was not pleased.

Having joined the protest movement, I was rankled by the NAACP's nonposition toward the war. When Senator Robert F. Kennedy refused to challenge President Lyndon B. Johnson in the Democratic primaries in 1968, I despaired of a possible political opening to end the war.

That's why I watched with interest when Eugene McCarthy, a staunch opponent of the war, entered the New Hampshire primary and shocked the nation by winning almost half the vote. Friends quickly joined his campaign. I traveled to the Wisconsin primary to see for myself. Everything that was grinding me down at the NAACP fell away. I felt revived. Opposing the war seemed like the most useful thing I could do. I took a leave of absence from the NAACP and joined McCarthy's campaign to help with race-related issues. As a white guy, I knew I would have questionable standing, but the campaign had no black staffers as far as I knew, so I saw a real need there. Shortly after I joined the campaign, Robert F. Kennedy sensed that Johnson's poor showing in New Hampshire put the nomination within reach, and he announced his candidacy. Bob Carter was a Kennedy man, but that didn't worry me too much. I couldn't change horses in midstream, and Bob appeared to understand.

After President Johnson withdrew from the race, Vice President Hubert Humphrey joined Kennedy and McCarthy. Humphrey was the hands-down favorite of the NAACP establishment because of his strong support for the civil rights legislation of the sixties. When it came to the war, Humphrey and the NAACP were in complete alignment: Don't oppose and say as little as possible. Sensing an avoidable fracas, Humphrey chose to stay out of the Democratic primaries, believing he could win the nomination through backroom politics and avoid the furor over the war altogether.

I was in McCarthy's Indiana primary headquarters on April 4 when I learned of Martin Luther King, Jr.'s, assassination. That night the black areas of Washington, DC, were engulfed in flames, and President Johnson called out the National Guard to put the down the unrest. Bobby Kennedy rushed to Coretta Scott King's side, sealing his place in the hearts of black America.

Watching King's Atlanta funeral on television, I sensed a darkness descending on the nation. King was my generation's greatest American. There was a strong ring of truth in everything he said. The beauty of his voice and the purity of his expression inspired me and had sustained me many times when circumstance made me wonder if we could ever overcome the scourge of racism in America. After the funeral I went through the motions of working on the dispirited McCarthy campaign until primary day in Indiana, where Bobby Kennedy won both the black and the white working-class vote.

I returned to New York City feeling despondent, disappointed by McCarthy's inability to connect with black America. Also, the McCarthy campaign rejected my proposal to hire black staffers on the grounds that the staff was there on a volunteer basis. "We can't treat whites and blacks differently," one of the campaign higher-ups said, trying to appease me. It had zero effect on my thinking. I could afford the luxury of volunteering, and I knew from my work at the NAACP that very few black people were in a position to do that.

On balance, however, even with blacks working on his campaign, I viewed Kennedy as an opportunist. In his speeches he said little of importance about race issues, and when he did talk about race it was as a stepping-stone to something else. As for Humphrey, I was disgusted by his continued support of Johnson's war.

With no black leader able to pick up Martin Luther King, Jr.'s, mantle, I was not alone in thinking that the nation was drifting toward chaos and bloodshed.

As I faced the reality that spread out before me, I began reflecting on my experiences at the NAACP. It had become clear that the Supreme

Court would not open more doors to black Americans. Just as Wilkins wanted to stay out of war politics, most of the Supreme Court justices— as well as lower-court judges—wanted to steer clear of the politics and so- cial realities that allowed segregation to exist on a massive scale in Southern and Northern cities and schools. At the edges, here and there, a few judges from time to time challenged segregation's impact, but I sensed that the judiciary as a whole would uphold the established order. The Supreme Court justices had delivered a knockout blow to openly racist laws and opened the way to the passage of the far-reaching 1960s civil rights laws, which it upheld when challenged in court. But the Supreme Court turned its back on more subtle forms of racism and in my view would continue to do so at least until the pressure for change built up again. Someone had to pierce the thick hide of the Supreme Court's intransigence, and sound the alarm about the recidivism that was under way. And I was young and sufficiently filled with myself to think I could do that. So I began to write a critical analysis of the Supreme Court's decisions in race-related cases. A few weeks later I was finishing what would be the first draft when McCarthy campaign staffers got in touch and asked me to come to Los Angeles to help with the California pri- mary. I was skeptical, but Bobby Kennedy's campaign was still cautious on civil rights issues, and there was new energy in the McCarthy camp. I liked his continued call for nonmilitary projects for defense contractors that were designed to help create minority-friendly policies. The cam- paign even had a plan for low-income housing projects in the suburbs, which would allow job seekers—including blacks—to live where the job opportunities were. Compared with Kennedy, who was relying on emo- tion and his network of black support, McCarthy's campaign had more substance, even though it was still a virtually all-white operation. Again in Los Angeles, I was the white guy working with our limited black sup- port. At campaign headquarters, however, we expected that our black support would be minimal. I felt like an odd man out. But I figured that one way or the other, either McCarthy or Kennedy had to beat Hum- phrey for the Democratic nomination if we were going to end the war.

On the night of the primary Kitty and I watched the returns upstairs in the headquarters hotel. McCarthy was losing by a few percentage points, and the ballot count was winding down. From our perspective that was good news. Kennedy had threatened to withdraw from the race if he lost in California, but he was needed to neutralize Humphrey. The hope was that Kennedy and McCarthy together could prevent Humphrey from winning the nomination on the first ballot. If that happened, there was a chance that the Democratic Party might see the wisdom in choosing McCarthy, who was not as polarizing as the other two candidates. Perhaps he could heal the party, and provide a midcourse correction for the nation.

Then that fantasy exploded. On television, in front of our eyes, Robert F. Kennedy was shot. We stared at the screens in disbelief. Some of us cried. Some held each other silently. As minutes turned to hours and what had happened became clearer, we shuffled off into the night. Kennedy was not our candidate, but emotionally he had reached us. It wasn't too hard to forgive him for holding back from the real politics we thought would make a difference. As Kennedy died, I felt that part of my life was draining away with his. The McCarthy campaign was suspended. Kitty and I returned to New York. Over the next few days I watched the gathering of the pained and powerful on television. It felt as if I were in a trance. Familiar faces flickered on and off the screen. Their words seemed unreal. A second Kennedy's death, following King's assassination, was incomprehensible. But there it was.

Still on leave from the NAACP, I initially had nothing to do upon my return to New York. Gene McCarthy seemed like a shadow of himself, withdrawn and keeping his own counsel. The war in Vietnam continued. There were more protests. The Black Panthers were on the rise. I could relate to their armed militancy, but could not envision their liberating black America. Eventually the white legislatures and police would put down this openly armed show of power, I believed. Abbie Hoffman and Jerry Rubin, the clown princes of the youth rebellion, articulated my outrage, but I was removed from that scene with its drugs and pranks. White America was watching from the sidelines, and the NAACP seemed hobbled by Roy Wilkins and his narrow vision.

I went back to work on my first draft of the Supreme Court article. The more alone I felt, the stronger my prose became. School segregation was my first target; I attacked the Court for allowing it to fester in the North and the South alike. Other sections accused the Court of turning its back on peaceful civil rights demonstrators arrested by repressive police, and refusing to hear cases in which local officials had used federal urban renewal War on Poverty funds to engage in "Negro removal." The Court had retreated into conservatism, I charged, and would remain an obstacle to racial progress until a strong broad-based social movement emerged to demand equality.

Bob reviewed my drafts and encouraged me. In July, still on leave, I hosted with Herb Reid, a renowned Howard law professor and close friend of Bob's, a get-together for Senator McCarthy and NAACP delegates at the association's national convention in Atlantic City. In our hotel's presidential suite, Herb and I were delighted when scores of delegates—and of course Bob Carter—showed up to meet McCarthy.

We heard that Wilkins was not pleased.

In August I went to the Democratic National Convention in Chicago to participate in McCarthy's final futile struggle. There I witnessed Mayor Daley's slap across the face of an already horrific year, as his Chicago police and the National Guard crushed the rising tide of young Americans who flooded Grant Park and the streets to protest the war and the sure-thing nomination of Daley's candidate, Hubert Humphrey.

I left Chicago shaken and feeling cowardly for watching from the sidelines. As soon as I got back to New York from Chicago, I returned to the NAACP. While I worked on finishing up the Supreme Court article, I got back to my waiting cases. Besides the low hum of opposition between the young Turks and the old guard on the board, little had changed in the universe of the NAACP. The legal department was the same. But for me everything was different. King was dead, and his philosophy of nonviolence was dying as well. Angry voices rose from every quarter.

In Gary, Indiana, Cleveland and Cincinnati, South Bend and Kokomo, and many other small and midsize cities all around the United States, public school integration had remained a crucial and yet unattained goal throughout the 1960s. In large cities, however, the way community leaders approached school integration began to change radically. The war certainly had something to do with it. The disproportionate

John and me (ages 3 and 5) at
Albert (Major) and Bessie Warner's
Westchester County summer house
on the Long Island Sound.

Loraina and Bill Rutherford at
the second marriage ceremony at
Albert (Major) and Bessie Warner's
Miami Beach estate.

Bill Rutherford in the Miami Beach dining room.

Loraina and Bill.

Bessie and Albert (Major) Warner.

FROM LEFT TO RIGHT: Jack Warner, Rea Warner, Ann Page Warner (Jack's wife), Albert (Major) Warner, Jack Warner Jr. and his new wife Barbara, Bessie Warner, Harry Warner, Martin Rhodes (a Levy in-law), Irma Warner (Jack Warner's first wife and Jack Jr.'s mother), and Ruth Leeds and Al Leeds (who gave me the nickname "Blackie").

Spring 1941 at Crail Farm in North Carolina. FROM LEFT TO RIGHT: John, my father Arthur, and my mother Ruth. I'm sitting next to my mother.

Sitting with Bill and Loraina at a house we rented on Cobbosseecontee Lake in Maine in the summer of 1948, after I had rheumatic fever.

Cleaning bluegills with Loraina at the Cobbosseecontee house.

Posing for a picture on the set of *The West Point Story* in 1949. FROM LEFT TO RIGHT: John, Bessie, me, James Cagney, and Gordon MacRae. The photograph is autographed to my brother.

An autographed photo of my brother and me with Virginia Mayo on the set of *The West Point Story*.

Doris Day on the set of *The West Point Story*.

ABOVE: A plebe at Culver Military Academy in 1950.

ABOVE RIGHT: My senior photo from Culver.

Commissioned upon graduation from Harvard University as a second lieutenant in the United States Army Reserves.

The cast from Gore Vidal's *The Best Man* at the Morosco Theater meeting President-elect John F. Kennedy. Melvyn Douglas is the second from the left, next to Frank Lovejoy. Kennedy is talking to Lee Tracy and Gore Vidal. I can be seen in the background, second from the right.

My fiancée, Kitty Muldoon, and
Jimmy Durante at the Copacabana.

Posing for a snapshot with Patrick,
Janine, and Brian.

Walking to Freedom

Actor-theatrical agent William A. Maynard walks away
from the Criminal Courts Building with his sister, Valerie,
to enjoy his first taste of freedom after nearly seven
years behind bars for allegedly killing a Marine in 1967.
Maynard was freed on $5000 bail today after a hearing
that lasted only two minutes. Story on Page 23.

Tony Maynard walking away from the criminal courthouse with his sister Valerie and me after being freed from prison in 1974. (From *New York Post*, April 4, 1974.)

Tony in a kayak in 2013.

Tony visiting the office in 2014.

The Steel family at
Thanksgiving, 2005.

Kitty and me.

Kitty and me with Bob (Robert L.) Carter at the moment Barack Obama became president-elect.

Derrick Bell and me with Bob at his apartment.

number of black men who were being conscripted only to reappear in body bags highlighted how little things had changed.

The Movement's younger leaders started chanting "Black Power," and the result was predictable. Whites were scared, and Roy Wilkins voiced his opposition. As even the most liberal whites began to be forced out of, or to pull back from, active participation in the more confrontational groups such as SNCC under the leadership of its new chairs, Stokely Carmichael and H. Rap Brown, the struggle for racial equality took on a no-more-turn-the-other-cheek tone. In New York City the most visible conflict was over community control of the schools, as efforts to desegregate the schools had gone nowhere and the schools were miserably failing the children in nonwhite neighborhoods.

The effort to gain control of the public schools was a natural outgrowth of the lack of action by the highly centralized board of education. After years of promising the black community that it would devise a plan to integrate the city's schools, the board of education instead began a building program in predominantly black and Latino areas that would lock the children into their ghetto neighborhoods. As the building program went forward, administrators abandoned even the pretense that whites would attend these schools, and made no bones about the fact that it was designing these buildings especially for the local ghetto children. In East Harlem the construction of a windowless school as part of a new intermediate school complex called IS 201 particularly inflamed local residents and the local NAACP branch. When accused of creating a prisonlike structure for minority children, school administrators replied tersely that it was a sensible solution to avoid the constant repair of broken windows.

In response to pressure, the state legislature in 1968 passed a decentralization law that set up experimental boards in East Harlem and the mostly black Ocean Hill–Brownsville section of Brooklyn, as well as the relatively integrated Two Bridges section of Lower Manhattan. Under the new law, locally elected governing boards took over many of the central board's functions for the day-to-day management of certain schools, including IS 201, as well as for the elementary schools from which they drew their student bodies.

Both the IS 201 and Ocean Hill–Brownsville community boards

and their newly hired administrators quickly moved to rid their schools of teachers they believed had little interest in teaching their children. In doing so they followed the logic of Dr. Kenneth Clark, who had been the influential expert in the 1954 *Brown* case. In his book *Dark Ghetto*, Clark emphasized that one of the main reasons why ghetto children did so poorly was that too often the middle-class administrators and teachers who taught them held the opinion that they could not learn.

When the new community boards tried to transfer ineffectual teachers out of their schools, the United Federation of Teachers (UFT) resisted, denouncing the move as a breach of the union's contract and claiming that the move was racism against whites. Even after the community boards pointed to the many white teachers they had kept, the claims of racism mounted. Accusations of anti-Semitism also filled the air, as many white teachers were Jews. Nor did their young, enthusiastic replacements, many of whom were also Jews, quiet the charges.

Calling a strike, UFT president Albert Shanker closed down the system with the exception of the three experimental school districts. After two months the central board capitulated and ordered the community boards to take the "underperforming" teachers back. When the boards, with strong parental support, refused, the central board obtained court orders prohibiting further opposition, and forced the matter. A massive police presence both inside and outside the schools enforced the central board's edicts. If parents entered the school, they were subject to arrest.

NAACP branches in Harlem and Brooklyn asked Bob to send lawyers to defend the local leadership, and he assigned the job to me. But the state court judges who heard our cases were in no mood to listen to anything our side had to say. Despite my requests for hearings, one judge after another refused to allow the local community boards to call witnesses in defense of their position regarding the staff they had dismissed from their schools. To many in the black communities, and to me as well, it was a classic example of white man's justice.

Meanwhile, in September, I finished the Supreme Court article, and it was accepted for publication in the *New York Times Magazine*. I was ecstatic. Tormented by the indifference of judges and overwhelmed by my own feelings of ineffectiveness, I was now about to unleash a thun-

derbolt at the myth that the judiciary—especially the Warren Court—
had remained a great liberal bastion and a patron of black advancement.

Bob was pleased. When the advance copy arrived from the *Times,* set
in type and ready to go, he made arrangements with Henry Moon to run
off thousands of copies of my article so that he could publicize the militancy of his legal staff.

On Sunday, October 13, 1968, the *New York Times Magazine* pub-
lished my article. The editors titled it "Nine Men in Black Who Think
White." The title worried me a little, because they had lumped Thurgood
Marshall with the other justices, and I assumed that might anger him.
But it certainly was eye-catching.

The next day I went to work proud as a peacock. Bob met me for
lunch, after returning from court where he had defended a group of black
Columbia University students arrested during an antiwar sit-in. He left
to go to a NAACP semiannual board of directors meeting at the Hilton
Hotel, and I returned to the office.

There was a note on my chair when I arrived. It was from a colleague,
and it said I had been fired for writing the *Times* article. I thought it was
a joke. Then Bob called.

"I know you're not going to believe this," he said, "but the board fired
you.

"Don't worry," Bob reassured me. "I'll get them to reconsider and this
foolishness will blow over."

But I was worried. According to the NAACP press release, the board
disavowed my article because I had attacked the Supreme Court, which
had done so much for the civil rights movement.

I was stunned. For more than an hour, I hung out with the rest of the
legal staff, laughing at their kidding, but feeling like the world was upside down. Sure I had supported Gene McCarthy, but I had played by
the rules and taken a leave of absence, which was more than could be
said for some of the NAACP bigwigs who had openly supported Humphrey while they continued to work. Then Bob called to say that he tried
to have the board reconsider, but it refused to budge. "Just stay put," he
told me.

Waiting for him to return, I was filled with anxiety. The NAACP
had become my home, but now it was alien territory. Until a few hours

ago, as a staff attorney, I could fight for racial justice and confront my own personal demons at the same time. Now the NAACP was cutting me off and setting me adrift.

By discarding me so quickly, the NAACP leadership was telling me that no matter how hard I worked and no matter what I had achieved, I would always be a marginal person, an outsider, not "one of them." On one level I understood that just as white people had used and discarded black people all the time, so I was being tossed aside. But on an emotional level I was deeply wounded. I had given the NAACP my all.

Working for the NAACP, I had distanced myself on a deep psychological level from my own white world. Now I was being told to leave this sheltered place for reasons that were unclear to me.

Calling Kitty to tell her the news was difficult. When she asked how they could do that to me, I shrugged and said I didn't know why they had treated me so harshly. Back in the office, Bob was furious. The attack on me was the NAACP leadership's way of trying to control him, he explained. To fire me without consulting him first was an affront to his authority. Our staff who had gathered in Bob's office agreed that Wilkins and his supporters had used my article to weaken Bob for being too close with the more militant board members, the young Turks.

"I don't have to approve what my staff members write," Bob declared, "but everyone in the association knows I liked your article, and they know I hold you in high regard."

Listening to Bob, I felt even more conflicted. This fight about the direction and leadership of the NAACP had been brewing for a long time. It had been easier to attack me because I was white, but their target was a black man who had achieved so much and was the best civil rights lawyer in the country.

"You've done enough for them" was a common and profoundly discomfiting refrain I heard from acquaintances and family when they heard what happened. Others told me to get on with my life: Get another job, move on. Kitty, however, was my rock, and her support was a lifeline.

As for the article, some scolded me for it. Jack Greenberg wrote a highly critical letter to the *New York Times Magazine* in which he defended the Supreme Court and said I didn't understand how the law developed. When Bob read Jack's letter, he said it only showed how conservative Greenberg was. But to many in the legal profession the article marked me as a radical.

A few days later Bob told me that his friends and supporters wanted to use my termination as a way to challenge the leadership. "Do you want to stay?" he asked.

"Yes," I replied, unsure of my own feelings, but convinced that was the answer he wanted to hear.

"Well, just act like nothing has changed," he said. "Go back to work, and we will see what happens."

Back in the office, Deputy Executive Director John Morsell dropped by. "Don't take it personally," he said. "You've done a good job, and everyone likes you. You are welcome to stay as long as it takes you to make arrangements for other attorneys to handle your case. There is no rush."

That made me feel even more disoriented.

A few weeks passed. I continued working, and there had been plenty of discussion and internal politicking, but I was still fired. Bob and the rest of the legal staff announced that they would resign unless I was reinstated. The issues, they said at a press conference, involved both freedom of speech and due process, two rights that the association had long fought to uphold. When the board refused to reinstate me, Bob and the entire staff resigned.

In truly Kafkaesque fashion afterward, we all continued to show up to make whatever arrangements we could for others to take over our cases, and to find new jobs. But I couldn't shake the profound sense of loss. I kept circling back to the thought that I had disrupted and changed the course of my colleagues' lives, and threatened the viability of the legal program at the NAACP as well as helping the organization's conservatives to weaken the more effective members who still worked there.

I asked myself whether the article was worth it. Bob's legal program had suffered what appeared to be a mortal blow, and no one was burning the telephone wires to offer me another job. My fellow staff members would have to scramble to find work.

Bob quickly accepted a grant from Columbia University, and I left as soon as possible. I helped out on my cases where I could. In New York City the IS 201 and Ocean Hill–Brownsville community school boards had asked me to continue representing them, and I readily agreed. In the Cincinnati school case, I worked with Norris Muldrow to prepare another Supreme Court petition, which the Court refused to accept after I left when it arrived just one day late due to a snowstorm. But most of my cases fell helter-skelter into the laps of local NAACP or American civil liberties attorneys to handle as best they could. It was a terrible ending to my years at the NAACP, made tolerable only by Bob's support as well as the support and warm words of all our legal staff. You only wrote what we thought, they told me.

14

Bill Rutherford Dies and a New Beginning

While I was at the NAACP, Bill Rutherford died. I don't even know the date, but it must have been in the spring of 1967. Those were pressure-packed years at the NAACP. The Northern school cases were in full swing, with *Deal v. Cincinnati Board of Education* losing in the appellate court, but allowing both sides to add additional evidence to the record with regard to our intent claim back at the district-court level, and new school segregation cases starting in Kokomo and South Bend. Some of the big Northern demonstration cases, among them Hartford and Springfield, were tried during this time, as was *Ethridge v. Rhodes*. There were college demonstration cases, labor cases, and a housing case in 1968.

I think the real reason I don't remember exactly when Bill died is that it was such a complicated loss for me, and so much was going on in my life; what with endless cases and a new baby arriving every two years, I was able to blot out the hole his death left in my life. But that is no ex-cuse. I recently asked my brother, John, if he knew where Bill was buried or if we helped make the arrangements, and he didn't know either. What sticks in my memory is that I remember the pain of Bill slowly pulling back from the easy way we had when I was a child. I remember going from Skippy to Lewis to Mr. Lewis. I remember the hurt I felt when Bill seemed to decide that my metamorphosis was complete, and that I had emerged from the cocoon of Warner wealth as "one of them." Perhaps that was the way he expressed anger. Or was it just disappointment, or even just a fatalistic sense of the way things were? I was never sure.

In retrospect it all made perfect sense. Bill started calling me Mr. Lewis because he thought that's what I was becoming. For all the warmth between us, it was a one-way relationship. I never asked him about his personal life. It seemed as off-limits as that little house he inhabited in the dark copse behind our place at Crail Farm when the war started. I vaguely recall having brought up his time with the Seabees, and hearing about the endless drudgery and heat, but that conversation barely touched the surface.

Bill would always ask what I was doing, and I would tell him. He knew all about me, but I didn't even know the basics about him. Had he been married before? I have no idea. Nor did I know what his family was like or how he grew up or if he had any children. All I knew about him was the way he had looked out for me when I was a child, and that he lived with Lorraina in our maid's room and then at my grandparents', and that he was a kindly, gentle man.

I remember rushing to Mt. Sinai Hospital when I heard he had a terrible accident and was in critical condition. When I arrived my parents were already there. My father told me that Bill had died.

"He'd been drinking," my father said, "and fell down the back service stairs at the Hampshire House."

I had not faced death like that before, and I tried to hold back my tears. I don't remember what else we said. We didn't talk about where the funeral would be.

Although I loved Bill, I felt that neither of us knew how to handle my growing up. I certainly did not know how to keep alive my attachment to him. Instead I allowed the distance to grow between us. It was easier with Lorraina. She was a woman, and I could hug her. But he was a man, and we shook hands until he stopped doing that. For all my sense of what I wanted Bill to call me and how I wanted him to see me—as a civil rights lawyer fighting for him—I obsessed over the idea that I had treated him as if he didn't count, as if he were only a servant, and in part I did exactly that. But both of us had been prisoners of our generation. For my part I did not know how to treat him as a valued parent figure and show my concern for his welfare as he had shown for mine.

After Bill died, Lorraina worked for my grandparents for a few months, then returned to her family in North Carolina. I don't know whose idea that was, or whether she received any retirement money. I was more than content to hide behind my second-son status in the family and not ask those hard questions. That said, ours was an emotional good-bye. Kitty and I corresponded with her for a few years—again the flow of information was generally one-sided. We sent her pictures of our children, but there were never pictures of Duby and Sister Baby sent back. Nor did we ask for them. It was that tacit contract between the help and the helped. She didn't send them, and we didn't ask her to. Then Lorraina wrote to say she had remarried—a prosperous gentleman. She seemed content with her new life, volunteering at her church. When Grandma Bessie died a few years later, I was upset to find that she had left only a pittance to Lorraina in her will, so I engineered an improvement, but whatever the amount was, I knew it was not nearly enough for all that Bill and Lorraina had done for our family, much less for the love they had given me. But family loyalty—to my family—won out, and I was unwilling to make too much of a fuss about it. Lorraina wrote that she appreciated being considered in the will. Soon afterward our relationship slipped away.

"Don't take it personally." That's what John Morsell had said about my being fired.

It was hard not to take it personally. Not only was I cast out, I lost my opportunity to argue in the Supreme Court for the first time. The case was *Hunter v. Erickson.* I learned about it while preparing a school case for trial in Columbus, Ohio.

An Ohio supreme court seven-to-nothing decision had upheld an amendment to Akron's city charter requiring majority voter approval on any ordinance that regulated real estate transactions on the basis of race, religion, national origin, or ancestry. That meant that a 1964 local fair-housing ordinance was no longer effective, which was how a real estate agent felt safe refusing to show one of the plaintiffs a house the owners said they wouldn't sell to a black buyer. As I saw it, the Akron ordinance violated the Fourteenth Amendment's equal protection clause, because it only required voter approval of Akron's ordinances when fair housing was involved, making blacks face a double legislative process.

Bob Carter agreed when I told him about the case. He told me I could argue it if the Supreme Court decided to review the decision. After I got fired, Bob said there was no way the NAACP would allow me to argue *Hunter*. So in November 1968, we traveled to Washington, DC, together, and I sat next to Bob while he argued.

Mulling over my prospects, I wondered if I would ever again get the opportunity to argue before the Supreme Court. Two months later after the argument, on January 20, 1969, the Court announced its decision. We had won, eight to one.

In the weeks and months that followed my departure from the NAACP, I tried to write a book, working in a little former maid's room on the first floor of our apartment building, I wrote about my work at the NAACP. But my writing lacked distance, and was mostly an explosion of frustration at how judges treated our cases. At the same time I worked as a volunteer on a few cases. One involved the IS 201 complex of public schools. After the parents and administrators were ordered to stay out of the IS 201 schools, I had appealed. The appeal was heard in the court where I was sworn into the bar and where Bob had argued *Gaynor v. Rockefeller*. I had asked the court to rule that we were entitled to present witnesses at a court hearing before the judge had entered a final order locking my clients out. But at the argument the appellate judges made it clear that was not going to happen. The bored stares mixed with frowns among the five judges pushed me to escalate my complaints: "To accept the statements of white administrators without a hearing while refusing to listen to blacks is racist," I goaded them.

"What does race have to do with it?" one of the judges demanded.

"There is no other reason why the trial judge favored one side over the other without holding a hearing," I answered.

The judge responded with a dismissive shrug, and something snapped inside me. I pointed to the ceiling where Chief Justice Taney still floated above the proceedings: "In any courtroom that honors the man who wrote the Dred Scott decision, I am entitled to raise the issue of racism," I argued.

My sister-in-law Mary Duffy was in the courtroom.

"Does he always do that?" she asked Kitty.

Kitty knew this was not one of my better moments. She just smiled.

I was shaking as I walked out of the courtroom. I had acted badly and knew we were going to lose. Immediately I felt a wave of something like remorse overcome me. "They" were whites like me, and I had not helped the cause by allowing my emotions to control my tongue. A few weeks after the argument, the judges rejected my appeal in a five-to-nothing decision without writing a word of explanation. That same year, 1969, the state legislature passed new community-control legislation with the blessings of the UFT. The new law watered down the authority of the local school boards so drastically that meaningful community control became a dead issue in New York City for at least a decade.

In the fall Bob and his wife, Gloria, invited Kitty and me to a cocktail party at their co-op, which was in a middle-class Harlem development. There Bob introduced me to Henry diSuvero. Hank, as he was often called, was a civil liberties lawyer who had been butting heads with prosecutors in Newark following a massive explosion of black anger that erupted there in 1967, leaving scores dead and the city occupied by the National Guard.

Hank wanted to start a radical law firm, and we talked late into the night, drawn to each other. We decided to join forces. It all happened very fast. Two other recruits, Gretchen Oberman and Daniel Meyers, were ready to join. We would represent Vietnam draft resisters, take on the criminal defense of political demonstrators, war critics, draft dodgers, and anyone else who espoused our politics and was willing to pay a fee. Sometimes, we agreed, our clients would not need to pay a fee if they could not afford it.

The infant law firm of diSuvero Meyers Oberman & Steel set up shop in a cramped two-room suite a block west of the criminal courthouse. We agreed to allocate pay based on need—that is, if there was anything left after paying the rent and a shared secretary's salary.

This was precisely the change I needed. At the NAACP the cases generally dragged on and on; with the appeals, we often ended up on the losing side. Prior to taking the leap, I had not thought about what it meant to migrate from being a civil rights lawyer entirely focused on racial issues to becoming a criminal lawyer focused on war-related as well as racial issues, and other matters that might come in the door.

Little did I foresee where getting my feet wet in the criminal courts would lead me. Long after the utopian law firm of diSuvero Meyers Oberman & Steel was history, I would still be immersed in high-visibility criminal cases, many involving black defendants charged with murder.

Not that joining the di Suvero firm, however, meant abandoning a more traditional civil rights model based on trying to expand the equal protection clause of the Fourteenth Amendment in the field of housing. Far from it.

My NAACP colleague and close friend Dick Bellman had become general counsel to a nonprofit organization called the National Committee Against Discrimination in Housing (NCDH), which was set up by two friends of Bob Carter—Jack Woods and Ed Routledge—a black-white team with expertise in the field. Their mission was to open up the suburbs to African Americans. Dick's main job was to file lawsuits in the federal courts against municipalities that employed their authority over land use to block the construction of racially integrated subsidized-housing projects. Soon Dick had started lawsuits around the country, and he was desperate for help. I became his sidekick, working with him on cases from coast to coast, getting paid a nominal amount for each day I worked.

While working on Dick's housing cases, I was still functioning in a legal world I knew. Like most federal courts, whether tucked away in the upstairs floors of central city art deco post office buildings built as public works projects during the 1930s Depression years, or in newer stand-alone U.S. courthouses, all were well-appointed polished wood and gleaming marble temples to the dignified practice of law.

In the fall of 1969 the di Suvero firm opened its doors. Mary Kaufman, who ran the city National Lawyers Guild (NLG) mass defense office, which coordinated volunteers defending militant community groups, asked if we would represent a group called the Young Lords. The Lords were a newly formed militant Puerto Rican group taking a page from the Black Panther form of civil rights activism. They were using direct-action tactics, trying to organize East Harlem. One of their goals was to get the city's sanitation department to remove mountains of garbage that were often left to rot. The Young Lords also started a free breakfast program for local children. Needing a place to operate, they focused on the First Spanish Methodist Church on 111th Street. The minister who ran the church, however, objected, and when the Young Lords became insistent, he called the police. A short time later the Lords took over the church and started using it for its breakfast program as well as a day-care center, and a free clothing box. Again the minister called the police. When they surrounded the building, a standoff ensued.

In the winter of 1969 I went to the church with a small group of NLG lawyers, crossing the police lines. We met with the young leadership committee, which included two men who went on to notable careers in television—Felipe Luciano and Pablo Guzmán. Also present was another leader, Juan Gonzales. Because there had already been deadly cop shoot-outs with the Black Panthers and the place was surrounded, we warned the leadership that weapons possession risked the police attacking with overwhelming force. It was only a matter of time before the police would tire of the stalemate and take back the church, we said, and we hoped there would be no bloodshed.

Shortly after our visit the cops did retake the church. The Young Lords leadership was arrested and charged with assaults on the police and resisting arrest. Fulfilling our promise, we formed a team, including among others Jerry Rivera—later to become the TV personality Geraldo—to provide representation. Because I had trial experience as an NAACP lawyer, I played a principal role. As luck would have it, the case was assigned to a progressive Hispanic judge, who allowed us to engage in lengthy cross-examinations of the arresting police officers at what was called a preliminary hearing to determine whether there was enough evidence to hold any of the Young Lords on felony or misdemeanor charges.

The hearings took place in a dingy courtroom of the ground floor of the multistory Manhattan criminal courthouse at 100 Centre Street, which was swarming with people charged with crimes, their friends and families, cops, assistant district attorneys, as well as court personnel and other hangers-on. Almost everyone in the building who was not in uniform or wearing a suit was a person of color, either black or brown. They spilled into crowded bathrooms, grabbed a bite in a pathetic little alcove that served what passed for food, and mostly waited for their cases to be called.

The cops had done a lousy job of documenting whom they had arrested and why, and after a few days of our legal team questioning the arresting officers, the judge threw out most of the charges, allowing only low-level misdemeanors. A few plea bargains later all the cases were disposed of, with no one serving any jail time. As NLG lawyers we had done a fine job. From my perspective I had gotten my feet wet in New York's criminal courts and come away thinking I could handle its rough-and-tumble. As for the Young Lords, they were out on the streets again, but their movement had been weakened. Perhaps, however, that was not such a bad thing for its members, as the FBI and local police forces began to crack down and wipe out the Black Panthers. Like the Weather Underground and other more violence-prone organizations such as the Black Liberation Army—some of whose members engaged in open warfare with the police until they were killed or captured—they had utterly misjudged their ability either to gain widespread support or to withstand the power of the country's law enforcement agencies. In the end, therefore, the few lawyers representing the members of such groups could do little more than try to save or lessen the sentences of those that survived.

15

Tony Maynard

At around four in the morning of April 3, 1967, a white Marine sergeant, Michael Kroll, dressed in his uniform and recently back from the Vietnam War, sought to start a fight with a black man and his white companion in a seedy area of New York City's Greenwich Village. He was blown away by a shotgun blast and died instantly.

The killing was big news. Mayor John Lindsay latched on to the shooting. Kroll was a hero. New York was crime city. Lindsay had bad poll numbers and a reputation for being soft on crime. Voicing outrage, the mayor demanded that the police quickly apprehend the killer and bring him to justice.

That, however, was not so easy. The cops had no weapon, no fingerprints, and no suspects. Here is what they knew: A short time before Kroll was shot, a white navy boatswain's mate, Robert Crist, also in uniform, had a confrontation in Greenwich Village with a black man, John Barnhardt. According to Crist, who later described himself as intoxicated, Barnhardt propositioned him. Crist was outraged. Barnhardt attempted to get away. Crist chased him and knocked him down near the Blue Onion, a joint on West Third Street. As Crist walked away he was approached by another black man, who was with a white companion. The black man, whom Crist later described as being eighteen to twenty years old, of medium build, and five feet ten or eleven inches tall, berated him for striking an older and smaller man. Knoll drove up as the black and white men walked away. Crist got into Kroll's car, and the pair decided to seek out the black and white men and finish the argument. When they caught up to the two men, the Marine jumped out of the car and confronted the black man who had berated Crist, Kroll disregarded the black man's warning to stay away, and was hit by a shotgun blast to his face. The only other description of the black man who fired the shot by the Village nightlife characters in the area was that the killer looked like Martin Luther King, Jr.

William Anthony Maynard, Jr., was a fixture in Greenwich Village at the time that Kroll was killed. He and his brother-in-law, Michael Quinn, were partners in a soon-to-fail fancy Village clothing store. Tony was thirty-two years old, stood six feet one inch tall, had lean, movie-star features, and looked nothing like Martin Luther King, Jr.

Many months later, when he was arrested in Germany, charged with Kroll's homicide, and extradited back to New York, the newspapers referred to Tony as a theatrical agent and an actor. But Tony was more of an all-around-type guy who related to, and sometimes got things done for, people he thought mattered—a list that included James Baldwin, the author of *The Fire Next Time*; the jazz legend Charlie Mingus; and William Styron, the Pulitzer Prize–winning author of *The Confessions of Nat Turner*, which was published the same year that Kroll was killed. An aloof man, Tony was held in high regard by the people he deemed worthwhile—mostly people in the arts—to whom he was a helpful presence. The hoi polloi didn't exist for Tony. "He treated everyone not within his immediate entourage," Baldwin wrote, "with a bored, patient contempt." He was both street wise and worldly. He was well traveled and could get by in several different languages. He carried himself with the air of someone to the manner born. Tony had been in the army and done a short stint at the post office. He had also worked as "bodyguard and chauffeur and man Friday" for Baldwin, as the latter would write many years later in *No Name in the Street*. That's how he met Styron. The idea that Tony would have talked to a drunken sailor, let alone cared that he had harassed another black man on the street, much less carried an "inelegant weapon" like a sawed-off shotgun, was completely ludicrous to anyone who knew him.

Maynard's associations with jazz musicians and well-known authors, of course, had nothing to do with his becoming a suspect in the Kroll killing. And certainly he did not fit the description of a five-foot-eight-inch black man between the ages of eighteen and twenty-two, who looked like Martin Luther King, Jr.

Maybe being seen in the area with Michael Quinn, his white brother-in-law, as well as a beautiful white woman, had something to do with it. But Michael was never questioned or charged as an accomplice. And no one had even given the cops a description of the killer's white companion. It was as if the police did not care. They had a black guy and a couple of creepy Village late-night characters willing to finger him, and that was enough to satisfy them as well as the mayor. Probably the most obvious reason the cops focused on Maynard was his beautiful white wife, Mary Quinn, a model, who also worked in Tony's and her brother Michael's clothing store. Although Mary was in the process of divorcing Tony, as she had grown tired of his wandering ways, she still modeled in the store, and he still visited the Quinns in their Woodside, Queens, home, to which Mary had returned.

While New York City and particularly the Village were far more permissive than the rest of the country, interracial couples still turned heads, especially if the woman was beautiful. As a result it is inconceivable that the local cops had not seen the couple together on the streets and in the cafés.

As Baldwin wrote, Tony's "aggressively virile good looks" made him "particularly unattractive to the NYPD." Worse, Mary was Irish, as were many of the cops.

Arrested at the end of October in Germany, where he had traveled with a group of jazz musicians, Tony was held at Hamburg's Holstenglacis prison. There he wrote a letter to William Styron explaining his circumstances. Baldwin moved around a lot, and Tony knew it would be easier for Styron to get word to his former employer of the dire straits in which he found himself. Notified, Baldwin immediately traveled to Germany and pulled some strings through his publisher there to get in to see Tony.

The cops and district attorney's office would accuse Tony of running off to Europe to avoid prosecution. But like the false "stranger" eyewitness identifications by two unsavory street people who had never seen the killer before, which the police procured from witnesses who were in need of their goodwill when it came to their own activities, the flight claim was equally absurd, as Tony had gone to the American consulate in Hamburg, using his own name, to obtain a new passport.

After he was extradited to New York to stand trial, Tony was incarcerated in the Tombs, the vermin-infested, windowless jail attached to Manhattan's criminal courthouse. Assistant District Attorney Gino Gallina of the Manhattan DA's office was assigned to the case. Baldwin hired two defense attorneys who were well-known habitués of the New York criminal courts, first S. J. Seigel and then Selig Lenefsky, to represent Tony. Seigel and Lenefsky were typical lawyers who made their livings in the city's criminal courts—chummy with everyone and knowledgeable about how to game the system for the best possible plea bargain. Because the lawyers were looking for a plea, which was their usual practice, even though Tony said he would never take one, little in the way of actual lawyering took place. Both men had a reputation for doing things in a seat-of-the-pants manner, and Baldwin's retelling of his meetings with Tony's sister Valerie and the eighty-year-old cigar-chomping Seigel creates the feeling of their totally superficial defense.

Baldwin describes Seigel's song and dance upon learning that the trial had been postponed. "This might be all to the good," the aging lawyer explained, "because it meant that Judge So-and-So instead of Judge What-not would be sitting. He, Seigel, was on friendly terms with Judge What-not, he'd call him in the evening." The reality was simple. Tony was just another modestly-paying client in a world where the big spenders got the best shot at a fair trial.

"What in the world were we to say to this terrifying old man?," Baldwin wrote about Seigel. "How could we ever know whether he had spoken to a single person, or made the remotest phone call on Tony's behalf?"

Meanwhile, Tony's alibi witnesses—his ex-brother-in-law Michael Quinn and Mary, as well as their brother, Patrick, and Mama Quinn— were being strong-armed into disavowing their recollection of Tony in the Quinn apartment at the time of the crime. To achieve that result Gallina had Michael and his wife thrown in jail as material witnesses, and threatened to have the latter deported, as she had overstayed her visa. And just like that, Tony's alibi was running on empty.

With even a little engagement Tony's first lawyers could have fought to protect the Quinns and their testimony. Instead they allowed the Quinns' alibi testimony to evaporate.

And that was just the beginning of what Tony's lawyers did not do. They made no effort to track down any of the witnesses who were on the Village streets the night Kroll was shot. Nor did they obtain a lighting expert to explain why an eyewitness identification, especially by strangers who had been out in the streets all night (more than likely drinking, buying or selling dope, or cruising for a pickup like Barnhardt), was virtually impossible, especially given where the witnesses said they were located and where the lighting was coming from. That said, Gallina still could not get a conviction. One juror held out and saved Tony—at least temporarily, as the whole trial would have to be done all over again.

With a new trial on the horizon, Seigel was out of the picture, and Lenefsky, who had handled the first trial, had no interest unless he got paid handsomely to do it. Shortly afterward Gallina, who had left the DA's office, became Lenefsky's partner. Years later I would learn that Gallina represented mobsters—specifically the Genovese family—which was strongly suggested by the gangland-style way he died—shot seven times on a Greenwich Village street.

To represent Tony, the court appointed Gussie Kleinman, a lawyer who was famous for making plea deals, and getting good ones because she was on cozy terms with the judge who assigned the case to her. With Gussie known for her inability to try cases, Tony saw the disaster coming and threw her off the case, deciding that he was better off representing himself. Once the second trial started, however, he thought better of that decision. When he informed the judge that he would not be able to represent himself adequately, the result was a mistrial.

A few weeks before his third trial was to begin, Tony's sister Valerie was still looking for a new attorney to represent her brother. Baldwin had been unreachable since the end of the first trial and was, according to Valerie, on the verge of a nervous breakdown. A struggling artist without any funds for a fee, she was at her wits' end.

Valerie came to our little office below Canal Street on Broadway and asked me to become Tony's unpaid attorney. After being turned down by a dozen criminal lawyers, she found our law firm because Hank diSuvero, also as a pro bono attorney, was representing the prisoners involved in an uprising in the Tombs. Hank told her he couldn't take on any more clients and referred her to me. Valerie told me the story of her brother's arrest and the struggle to free him. Interested, I went to see Tony in the Tombs. It was a hot summer day, and the jail still seethed with tension from the recent uprising. I waited for at least an hour in a large, cubicle-lined room for lawyers and their clients. Prisoners were released into the room one at a time amid the slamming of steel-barred gates and barked commands. Most prisoners slunk in, slovenly dressed, shoulders hunched, with angry or sullen looks on their faces. Because of the uprising, all razors had been forbidden, so they were unshaven and looked the worse for wear. Not so with Tony Maynard, despite the shaving ban. Striding through the gate, he stood erect, well dressed, and sharp-eyed, looking for me—the lawyer his sister had sent him.

Brought up for many years by a doting, status-conscious grandmother, who was a churchwoman and allowed him to run free much of the time in Florida, Tony seemed like the last person who would commit such a street crime. His father had been many things, including a New York City police officer, a bartender, and a jack of all trades. Like his dad, Tony did not like to be tied down. He came across as his own man, and had traveled with Baldwin and participated in the civil rights demonstrations with him. Tony had also spent time in Europe and North Africa with jazz musicians, as sort of a manager and guide. He had returned to New York only a year or so before Kroll was shot, but managed to get situated as a student of one of New York City's more prominent acting coaches and had been cast in a black-exploitation movie, according to a trade-paper clipping he showed me.

As Tony talked about his life, I puzzled over how much was puffery and how much real, and what he had really done to keep himself so well turned out. As improbable as some of his story seemed, I tended to think that most of what he told me was true. Whatever he did to further his own ambitions or feed his fanciful illusions, there was something genuine about him. As Baldwin later wrote, Tony seemed like the last person in the world to walk the streets with a sawed-off shotgun stuffed under his jacket.

The more Tony talked, the more he pulled me in. I was the one who could come and go; he was confined, but he seemed to exude a kind of freedom that was both unfamiliar to me—and attractive. As much as clothes and outer appearances mattered to him, he appeared to be a man who could live within the confines of his own mind. By contrast, I couldn't have cared less about the way I dressed, but I needed to prove myself and gain approval. I think he intuited there would be nothing seat-of-the-pants about my efforts on his behalf, and that I was the right lawyer to defend him. For my part, Tony came into my life not long after Bill Rutherford died. He spoke Bill's perfect English and had a similar sort of proud bearing. That said, Bill didn't come to mind when I met Tony. It wasn't until much later that the possible connection suggested itself, perhaps to answer the question of why I was so willing to give over a part of my life—hundreds of hours—to Tony after just an hour or two of talking.

Thinking about the two men, I saw Bill as a person who had been trapped in a job he couldn't easily quit, and a life that forced him to say, "Anything you say, sir." For his part, Tony was trapped in a criminal court system run by white men who cared no more about his guilt or innocence than Major Warner cared about what Bill truly felt. But there was something else. Like Bill, Tony did not seem to have that deep well of anger I had come to recognize in some black men who had been exposed to the endless discrimination heaped upon them by whites all through their lives. Perhaps, as I would later learn, that had to do with Tony's family's West Indian island past. Then again, it was possible that both Tony and Bill had developed the ability to suppress outward expressions of anger when it was in their interest to do so. Thinking about us, I felt that Tony and I seemed to share similar impulses related to our pasts. Although we came from completely different backgrounds, we were the same age, and both of us appeared to be seeking a measure of freedom from our beginnings. I had veered off the accepted pathways accorded to the progeny of the wealthier classes, and Tony had disdained the working-class life that awaited black men of his generation. Our tangents closed the distance between us and allowed us to relate to each other in the Tombs as we sat together talking about the effort it would require to set him free.

The more I came to believe in Tony's innocence, and felt myself developing a bond with him, the more I worried about taking his case.

I had spent my career fighting cases that would, if won, change lives in a long-term way, but it was only recently that I found myself working in the criminal court system, where decisions had such an immediate concrete effect on my clients' lives. Concerned, I told Tony that I had never handled a murder trial.

"That woman Gussie is a joke," he said handing me an article that ridiculed Kleinman. "I know you will do your best."

Tony's case was a crash course in the difference between criminal and civil trials. At the NAACP my trials rarely lasted a week. Certainly they were intense and all-consuming as long as they lasted, but as an NAACP lawyer I was always on the attack. My job was to put public officials on trial for breaking the law. In virtually all my cases, judges rather than jurors were the deciders. And no matter how resistant this or that judge was to the arguments I made, the jurists before whom I tried cases accorded me a reasonable level of civility. Win or lose, my NAACP clients had their day in court and were generally appreciative. They would sit next to me or in the front row of the courtroom. There were no corrections officers standing right behind them with handcuffs at the ready. There were no prison bars a door away from the proceedings, and no possibility of a life sentence.

By contrast, criminal trials were often marathons that lasted weeks or months in hostile settings, with judges smiling benignly at the jurors, all the while ruling time and time again in favor of prosecutors who enjoyed every advantage of their office and a staff of detectives with whom to obtain convictions. In a poorly funded criminal defense, preparation for the next day took place late at night, and it took endless adrenaline to stave off exhaustion and remain ready to take on whatever the prosecutor threw at you in court. A skilled criminal lawyer, or even one like me, who was adapting his style from a civil-oriented practice, could attack with his cross-examination. But even there he was hampered by his inability to investigate his case fully, and he had to be careful. Jurors were predisposed to believe cops, who protected them from the very people a criminal lawyer was defending.

Then there was the theater of the thing. Challenge the prosecutor or the judge too much and you risked turning off the jury. If you challenged them too little, you got steamrollered. Day after day you had to walk that line, always in an atmosphere that presumed your client was guilty and that you were just some slick lawyer trying to trick the jury by feeding them stories designed to confuse or clutter what would otherwise be clear and straightforward, all in the service of getting an acquittal by spouting spurious paeans about the presumption of innocence and reasonable doubt.

Advised by an experienced colleague before the trial began to ask the new assistant district attorney assigned to the case, Stephen Sawyer, not to choose Irwin Davidson as the trial judge—as he was what defense lawyers called a hanging judge—I did that. In those days the prosecutor could choose the trial judge in a murder trial, so I spoke to Sawyer and told him I thought there was a strong possibility Maynard might not be guilty. Sawyer, however, must have taken that as a signal I would fight hard to gain an acquittal. So he promptly placed the Kroll homicide before Davidson.

My experienced colleague was right with regard to Davidson. As James Wechsler would later write of Tony's trial, "There were too many crucial interludes in the trial when it seemed impossible to differentiate the presiding judge—Irwin D. Davidson—from the prosecutor."

Showing his colors immediately when I asked for more time to prepare, Davidson paid no heed to my total inexperience in representing a defendant accused of murder. When another outbreak of prisoner discontent in the Tombs once again stopped deliveries of razors and clean clothes to prisoners, Davidson made Maynard, looking rumpled and unshaven, appear in front of the jury we had started to choose. It wasn't until my partner, Danny Meyers, filed a federal lawsuit shaming the district attorney's office that Davidson allowed Tony to shave and change clothes in a holding cell behind the courtroom.

During the two-month trial I was home only long enough to eat and sleep. I might have prevailed with a different judge, but as Wechsler pointed out in the many columns he wrote after the trial was over, Davidson sided with the assistant district attorney at every turn. Some of the rulings were truly bizarre, such as the one that prohibited me from calling a lighting expert to challenge the testimony of a prosecution expert, the deputy director in charge of the engineering division of the New York City Bureau of Gas and Electricity, who claimed that the backlighting from the bank's plate-glass window on the dark, shadowy side street where the crime occurred was sufficiently bright for the purposes of identifying the shooter. By contrast, my expert, a Broadway lighting designer, would have testified that the killer's face would have been in a shadow, making his features indistinguishable.

Equally outrageous, not until twenty-two days after the start of Tony's third trial did Sawyer produce the names and interviews of a number of witnesses who talked to the police during the 1967 investigation, some of whom told different stories about what happened. One witness, according to a police report, said that someone else killed Sergeant Kroll. Another person confessed to the crime. Barely able to prepare for each successive day of the trial, Dan Meyers and I didn't have the time or the resources to chase down any of the people on that list. The prosecutor said in a pat way that his office and the police had checked out everyone and everything on the list and there was nothing of merit for the court to consider, which Davidson quickly accepted as conclusive enough to rule that what the authorities had done was sufficient.

To defend Tony, before the trial Dan and I had tried to revive the alibis that had been disavowed after Michael Quinn and his wife were thrown in jail as material witnesses. To do that we visited the Quinns at home in Woodside, Queens, and at brother Patrick's bar to see if they would consider testifying that Tony was at their apartment on the night of the crime, and explain why they disavowed their statements. Concerned that their silence would lead to Tony's conviction, the Quinns agreed to risk the prosecutor's ire. Davidson, however, did what he could to frustrate us. He cleared the courtroom the moment I called Michael Quinn to the witness stand, and announced that he would not allow Quinn's testimony if it included an admission that he'd committed perjury—even if, as we claimed, he had been forced to disavow the alibi by an assistant district attorney. Davidson reacted immediately. He sent for another assistant district attorney to open a prosecution investigation against Michael. I objected, and the colloquy that resulted was typical of our dynamic:

MR. STEEL: Your Honor, may I state that, for the record, we have other witnesses whose testimony you are affecting by this procedure.

THE COURT: Will you sit down or I'll have you thrown out of this courtroom.

MR. STEEL: That is an open threat to every other member of the Quinn family who wants to testify in this case. You are threatening them all. It is the most outrageous thing I have ever heard.

THE COURT: Do you think it might be necessary for this screaming person to be put in restraint?

MR. STEEL: Do that, Your Honor. Do that.

THE COURT: I have never heard anything like that.

MR. STEEL: I have never heard anything like you, Your Honor. In a murder trial, you are threatening the witnesses of the defense openly in court. I have never heard of a thing like that.

THE COURT: Why don't you behave yourself? You will have a stroke. Everybody is gathered around you; they are afraid you are going to come up and attack me.

MR. MEYERS: There is nobody afraid.

MR. STEEL: Nobody is going to attack Your Honor. You attack the dignity of this court by being in court.

And with that Judge Davidson held me in summary contempt.

Looking back now at what I said, I can see that I had crossed that invisible line between rational advocacy and an emotional response to outrageous provocation. The Quinns were deeply shaken, and I was beside myself. Nonetheless the Quinns decided not to back down. They courageously testified that Tony was at their apartment on the night of the crime, and withstood the pounding on cross-examination from Sawyer, delivered with Davidson's full approval.

Even so, despite Davidson's hounding our every move, I sensed the warmth in some of the jurors' eyes, and that some were rooting for us. Also some of the jurors appeared impressed that William Styron testified for Tony as a character witness, as did Tony's grandmother. Tony also testified in his own behalf, withstanding not only Sawyer's cross-examination but Davidson's endlessly biased rulings in favor of the prosecution.

To undercut the Quinns' alibi testimony further after I rested our defense, Davidson allowed Gino Gallina to testify that he had broken no laws or rules by imprisoning the Quinns until they renounced their alibis because he had an immigration officer threaten to deport Michael's wife, Giselle. Adding insult to injury, Davidson protected Gallina from cross-examination with regard to his blatant wrongdoing.

After both sides rested and Sawyer and I summed up, Davidson gave a one-sided version of what the witnesses had testified to. After his jury charge, the jurors debated for three days, evenly split between guilty and not guilty. When the courtroom door was open to the back area where the jury room was, we could hear the jurors' raised, sometimes angry voices. Prodded by Davidson, after the all-white jury reported it was hung, the jurors finally compromised on a manslaughter verdict. Apparently satisfied, Davidson shortly afterward released me from contempt.

When I saw Tony in the Tombs that evening after the verdict, he gave me a big hug and assured me that we would overcome what had happened to both of us: "No injustice this great can stand."

"I'll do whatever it takes to get this overturned," I said.

"I know you will," Tony replied. "I'll stay strong."

Two months later Davidson sentenced Tony to the maximum ten-to-twenty years. On his way upstate to prison, he remained unshaken.

I couldn't say the same for myself. I had come a long way from that ceremonial courtroom eight years earlier with the visage of Chief Justice Taney and the legacy of *Dred Scott* bearing down on me. But in that time I had learned that it did not take a ruling that blacks would be forever slaves for other judges to let them know that their status still remained in slavery's shadow.

16

Auburn Prison and Life in the Hamptons

"You don't catch hell because you're a Democrat or a Republican," Malcolm X said in his 1963 speech "Message to the Grassroots." "You don't catch hell because you're a Mason or an Elk, and you sure don't catch hell because you're an American; because if you were an American, you wouldn't catch hell. You catch hell because you're a Black man."

That speech was well known among the black activists of the 1960s. I doubt there was anyone among the African American leaders of the Attica uprising who hadn't read it. "Message to the Grassroots" was about the race problem in America. It referred to what Malcolm X deemed the white co-opting of the 1963 March on Washington. More generally the speech argued that there had been a failure in the fight against racism. Malcolm X claimed that the rhetoric of nonviolence hadn't worked, and that it never would. He said push had come to shove and it was time to paint the streets red. "Revolution is bloody," he told the parishioners of Detroit's King Solomon Baptist Church. "Revolution is hostile, revolution knows no compromise, revolution overturns and destroys everything that gets in its way."

This is the same speech in which Malcolm X juxtaposed the figures of the "house Negro" and the "field Negro." He jabbed a linguistic finger at the former, explaining that when the house Negro talked about America, he used the words "we," "us," and "our." The house Negro was oblivious to the blunt fact that he neither was nor ever would be invited to participate in the great American dream. Meanwhile the field Negro was just looking for a way out. For some that meant drugs and for others, revolution. Malcolm X went further in his taxonomy of racism, talking about Uncle Toms and the way Movement people patted themselves on the back for the so-called victories of the civil rights struggles while the house and field Negroes alike got no relief. The triumphs of the Movement were legal half measures called coups, according to Malcolm X.

"Uncle Tom" was never a term I used, but Attica for sure was not taken over by the spirit of complacency ascribed to the house Negro in "Message to the Grassroots." The sentiment there was decidedly militant, which among some prisoners translated into anti-white. I didn't personally experience it that way, because the leadership saw the observers as coming to their aid. I thought about Malcolm X in the Attica yard one night during the takeover, when the place seemed to be vibrating with danger. Maynard had not reappeared to stay with me and a small group of observers had remained at the negotiating table while the rest of the group had retreated to safety with William Kunstler and Bobby Seale, who had joined the observers that day and talked to the inmates without making any concrete suggestions. Quickly Seale left the prison, saying he had to talk to his Panther comrades to get instructions, never to return. To fill the void left by Seale's departure, one of our observers took the mike and told the prisoners about the twenty-eight points we had negotiated. But when he added that the local prosecutor planned to charge those who had committed crimes to the full extent of the law, a cry of rage rose up. I shuddered as a wave of panic swept over me. Would we become hostages ourselves for being such miserable failures on the key issue of amnesty? But no. Kunstler, who returned after escorting Seale out, soothed the milling crowd. As quickly as we could, we left the yard to rejoin the other observers, most of us never to return again.

Thinking about that night later, I told myself that I was not a radical, contrary to the way some of my friends, family, and even Tom Wicker viewed me. To them I had gone beyond mainstream advocacy for an oppressed minority to justifying their militant rebellion. The reality, however, was different. Certainly I reached the point of understanding that the prison authorities had pushed the inmates past the breaking point and were responsible for what had occurred. But I had never advocated rebellion or armed resistance. I thought rebellion and armed resistance were bound to fail with America's large and relatively satisfied middle and working classes, virtually all of whom viewed blacks and white radicals as a danger to their way of life. Nor, in my mind, were understanding violence and justifying it the same thing. There was no justifying taking guards prisoners, as they were already trapped in the same oppressive system themselves. I may have lived, at least in my mind, on both sides of the racial divide, but in actuality on these issues I lived on one side only. While I supported civil disobedience as a form of militant nonviolence, I was not willing to take hostages or bomb buildings, and wasn't willing to say that those who did such things stood on firm moral ground. I wasn't willing to give up my class prerogatives either. I liked going to the theater, and I liked having a weekend place at the beach. So while I was willing to put myself in harm's way, if I thought it would make a difference, or to work endless hours to try for a particular outcome in a case that would matter in the bigger picture of racial injustice, it was easier for me to do that than it was for most. I could step out of the struggle into the comfort of a bourgeois life, as I did almost every night. I didn't have to worry about how I was going to pay the bills. I worked like a dog, but having Bessie Warner as a grandmother smoothed the way. I opposed the status quo but was unwilling to burn the house down to try to create a new world.

Several months before Attica, I hit a wall. I was in dire need of a break. It was January 1971. Kitty and I both needed to get away. The time had come, and we were going no matter how tight my work schedule. Puerto Rico was our chosen destination, and we had planned to fly down and check out a little resort that a friend had recommended, a quiet place off the beaten path. Then events already in motion got in the way. On November 4, 1970, there had been an uprising at the state prison in Auburn, New York. Like Attica, it was called a "correctional facility," but that was and remains a misnomer since no one was getting corrected there. Auburn was severely overcrowded. The prisoners were paid pennies for their work. The food was inedible. Medical care was virtually nonexistent, as were the programs that prisons were supposed to offer by way of rehabilitation. During the uprising thirty hostages—all of them prison employees—were taken and then released, completely unharmed, in return for a pledge that there would be no administrative or physical retaliation against the leadership of the uprising. That pledge was immediately broken by the prison administration.

By the time I was contacted about the situation at Auburn, the prisoners who had taken part in the uprising were in desperate need of help. After being moved out of Auburn, the six key leaders had been indicted for a long list of felonies and then returned to the prison where the alleged crimes took place to await trial. The venue for the trial was Auburn's courthouse—not a particularly inmate-friendly venue. A young lawyer named Jeffrey Glen, from Mobilization for Legal Services, had been trying to put together a legal team to help the Auburn Six, who were not only segregated from the rest of the prison population but placed in "the Tank," where they reported continuous abuse at the hands of guards in retaliation for the uprising. Glen initiated a federal case against the then newly minted state commissioner of correctional services, Russell Oswald, who was either unaware of the torture being inflicted on the Auburn Six or didn't care.

"It isn't only that they're not going to be able to participate in their own defense," Glen told me. "They may not survive what's happening to them in the Tank."

What came next I knew all too well from my time at the NAACP. The lawyers had a lot of heart, but they didn't have much trial experience. Without a Movement lawyer, they were in over their heads. Meanwhile, lives were in danger.

The judge who would try the case upstate was Edmund Port, a former United States attorney. It wasn't his job to protect criminals from the penal system. In general judges were not very friendly to prisoners. When inmates took over the prisons selected to punish them, they couldn't expect much relief from the court. Asked to come and try the case, I found it impossible to refuse. That said, I definitely felt as if I was betraying a loyalty—namely mine to Kitty. I tried my best to wriggle out of it.

"You can squeeze it in," Glen said. "Once you get us up and going and we see what the drill is, we'll be fine."

I couldn't say no.

On March 9 we started the nonjury trial before Judge Port. On the first day Glen and another lawyer, Elizabeth Fisher, called to the stand three of the Auburn Six, all of them named as plaintiffs against Commissioner Oswald. After brief testimony on the conditions in the Tank, the deputy state attorneys drilled into the prisoners, subjecting them to long cross-examinations. While this was happening, I managed to talk by telephone to a psychiatrist, William Tucker, who had seen our lead plaintiff, Robert Clark, on a few occasions and had inspected conditions in the Tank himself. Despite Tucker's strong reluctance to testify against the state, he agreed to come to the courthouse, and I put him on the stand.

"Did you treat Robert Clark?" I asked Tucker.

"Yes, I treated Clark a few times after the uprising and before he was shipped to Attica."

Then, in a sideways retreat, if there can be such a thing, Tucker lurched into a sort of bureaucratic avoidance, explaining that the guards were having a hard time carrying out the prison rules, and that, to compound matters, there was a great deal of revolutionary activity on the part of the prisoners. I let him talk it out before confronting him: "Didn't you tell me yesterday that an atmosphere of terror prevailed?"

"Yes," he admitted.

The otherwise impassive judge peered down from the bench, clearly taking that statement in—it had left a mark.

The Auburn Six had been brought into court in shackles, but there was nothing unusual about that or the fact that we only had time to prepare them to testify in a holding cell behind the courtroom and then, one by one, hustled them to the stand to tell their stories about being stripped naked twenty-four hours a day and locked in freezing cells, and how the windows were left open twenty-four hours a day. It was the middle of winter in upstate New York. We got them to talk about the near-starvation rations they were offered under the glare of lights that were never turned off. On and on it went. It was a bleak story—guards banging their sticks on the bars to wake them at all hours, unnecessary "cavity" searches, and other acts of savagery. They were even tear-gassed. It wasn't an easy litany to hear—not for those of us who believed the prisoners. It wasn't easy for the assistant state attorneys to hear either; they didn't want the vile truth of what had happened aired in court.

"In that environment," Tucker said, "the prisoners can't participate in their defense. Forget about criminal trials. We're dealing with people who aren't sure they're going to survive."

I could sense that the judge knew which way the wind was blowing after he heard Tucker's testimony, so I tried to plant the idea that the Auburn Six should be transferred to prisons closer to New York City. The attorneys working on their cases had a lot to do, and limited budgets. If the six were nearby, and not shuttled to prisons around the state, we could better prepare them for trial.

Judge Port cut me off: "We are not in the horse-and-buggy era. You got up to Auburn all right. Proceed."

While it's impossible to know how things would have turned out, I often wonder what would have happened at Attica in the fall of 1971 if Port had listened to reason regarding the transfer of prisoners. Perhaps that might have altered the events at Attica, because as it turns out, Port's decision had its repercussions. A big part of the problem during the uprising at Attica, and one of the reasons we could get no traction between the inmates and prison authorities, was that the inmates were convinced that Commissioner Oswald's word was worthless. Partly they came to believe that based on his failure to take any steps to alleviate their misery, and partly because members of the Auburn Six were transferred there to tell the tale.

When I left for my vacation, it still felt like ten degrees outside up there. There were still prisoners in limbo confined to the Tank with the windows open, stripped bare of clothing and bedding.

"You did more than you said you would," Glen said as I was leaving. "We can handle it." I still felt terrible.

By the time Kitty and I got to Puerto Rico, I was stiffened by feelings of remorse and guilt for leaving. I knew how hard the situation was going to be to resolve, and I wasn't sure if Glen and his friends could pull it off. If they failed, lives were on the line. Death from exposure or being driven to suicide—it all swam around in my mind.

These thoughts turned me into a complete wreck. We rented a car and drove out to the resort. The place was west of San Juan. When we got there and saw the room and the loud earth-moving machines outside that were digging a hole for a swimming pool, something inside me snapped: "We gotta get out of here," I told Kitty.

I wanted to go straight back to New York, but we drove around the end of the island and through Ponce before deciding to go back to San Juan. Panic and the growing sense that I had done something immoral by leaving things unfinished at Auburn were eating away at me. "We gotta get off this island," I said.

In my mind I was already on the train back to Auburn, but as we looked at the departures board at the airport, we got on a puddle jumper to St. John in the Virgin Islands, where we got a room in a little hotel. During the two or three days we were there, I never stopped thinking about the six men in upstate New York. Meanwhile, almost despite my obsessive thinking, I repaired myself a bit. On the first day I was in a thick fog. The next day we went to an underwater park and snorkeled. Simple stuff. It was nice. I felt calmer. Auburn, however, was ever present. The first thing I did when we got near a phone back in New York was to find out what was happening. Jeffrey Glen told me that to cut the trial short and avoid having to issue a ruling, Judge Port did the expedient thing; he persuaded the prison administration to split up and transfer the Auburn Six to different prisons. All still faced criminal charges, but at least the physical abuse stopped.

Most people didn't think much about how prisoners really live. Few cared if inmates lived in constant fear of physical or sexual attacks. It didn't matter if they got showers once a day or once a week, and not many people in the mainstream really cared if they were fed edible food or paid only pennies for their labor. Most law-abiding citizens didn't lose much sleep wondering if the nation's criminals and the unlucky jailed innocents had access to a library or to decent medical care. If anything, the public believed that prisons mollycoddled inmates, letting them sit around watching television all day: "Jail shouldn't be a picnic." I heard that chestnut far too many times.

New York's prisons were not as bad as the chain-gang hellholes scattered around the South and depicted in Hollywood movies like *The*

Shawshank Redemption. Life was cheap in the New York system, but not as cheap as that of the prisoners who poured boiling tar on rural roads in the sweltering heat of a Mississippi summer. In New York death and mayhem were more often the result of the system's indifference. Guards did nothing to protect the weak from the predators, leaving each man to fend for himself.

When it came to the prison population, there was no appealing to reason. There was no room for commonsense arguments, even ones that hinged on fiscal soundness, given the public disdain for the nation's prisoners. It did not matter that it cost more to send a person to prison than to Harvard. It didn't matter if prison taught people how to become better criminals.

I saw it differently. The black and Latino inmates who imported the rhetoric of revolution from Karl Marx and the radical protests against the Vietnam War were trying to take charge of lives that no longer belonged to them, and often never really had. They were not educated. Life was hard. Many had gone from being wards of the state to being the property of the state. So when that vocabulary of the various revolutionaries found its way into the nation's prisons, I thought it was a good thing. Rather than passively riding out their prison sentences or participating in nefarious activities, a growing number of prisoners were reading and writing and trying to think through exactly how so many of them wound up incarcerated. They traced their evolution from underdog to nameless number. And with that knowledge, coupled with a new way of looking at their situation in the American prison system, there was room for real change. Whatever their crimes had been and however uncertain their motivations, this new kind of prisoner had a shot at bringing about real reform. He pressured the corrections department to treat him more like a human being. He wrote articles and books, and he disseminated information. Not much changed, but it was a step in the right direction. Caged in a rigid world that was all about dog-eat-dog survival, some prisoners were trying to bend the story.

Those thoughts rattled around in my brain when I was at home in my Central Park West apartment or on the weekends as I strolled down the beach a stone's throw from our house in the Hamptons. That was the other side—my life as a privileged person. Our house in Bridgehampton was on the other side of a semiprivate street that ran parallel to the

Atlantic Ocean, situated on the gold coast of Long Island's playground communities.

In the spring of 1969, my brother John's second wife, Bette-Ann, had read an article about a young architect named Charles Gwathmey, and became obsessed with the idea of getting him to build her a house. He had built a stunning house for his parents—Robert Gwathmey, the social realist painter, and Rosalie, who was a celebrated photographer. The ultramodern-looking structure was in Amagansett, one village east of the Hamptons. Bette-Ann was bowled over. She had to have a Gwathmey house. I'm not sure exactly how it came about, but either Bette-Ann or John proposed the idea of a three-house Steel compound on the ocean, to be designed by Gwathmey and to be paid for, of course, by our Grandma Bessie. Major had died two years earlier, so a large part of the estate was hers to do with as she pleased. Land was purchased, and Gwathmey got the commission to create the compound.

"Charlie Boy," as we came to call him, was about my age. He was a charismatic and athletic guy with movie-star good looks and the talent and drive of someone you could tell was going places. By the time he died in 2009, his portfolio included the Guggenheim Museum's expansion, celebrated buildings on major university campuses, office towers and condos, and many homes for the rich and famous. Back then in our planning process, Gwathmey became an ever-present character. Meanwhile, I was recovering from the fallout from my *New York Times* article and was moving on to starting a law firm with Hank di Suvero.

Hank, Dan, Gretchen, and I crammed ourselves into a two-room office we opened near the courthouses on Centre Street below Franklin. It was long before TriBeCa became a trendy neighborhood for Manhattan's cultural elite. Back then it sat at the shank end of SoHo—long before that was developed—and near Chinatown. So the rent was cheap. We worked on criminal cases, helped Vietnam War resisters fight the FBI or dodge the draft, and I began to work with Dick Bellman on his housing discrimination cases.

One case in particular would have greatly upset Grandfather Warner. The Catholic left, with Father Berrigan in the forefront, was mounting its own form of nonviolent protest against the Vietnam War by breaking into government buildings and spilling blood over draft records. When an FBI office was raided in Glen Cove, Long Island, and the intruders made off with some FBI documents, the U.S. attorney's office tried to force a nun, Sister Carol Vericker, to testify about the break-in.

The Center for Constitutional Rights (CCR), a progressive nonprofit law center, was asked to quash the subpoena requiring her to testify after the government had granted her immunity to overcome her Fifth Amendment rights to remain silent. After losing before a federal district-court judge, CCR asked our firm to join its lawyer, Jim Reif, on the appeal. Within days we came up with a series of legal arguments, and I joined Jim to argue before the circuit court. To my surprise, given the political climate, we won on our technical interpretation of the key federal statute.

I never met Sister Carol, but I did have a fine dinner with Father William Cunningham, S.J., who was also a lawyer and whose name appeared on our appeal brief. Major would have turned in the slot he occupied deep inside the Warner mausoleum, high on a hill straddling the border between Queens and Brooklyn. I went home from my dinner pleased as punch. Father Canninghorn was a fine companion, and his politics were probably to the left of mine.

Back in Bridgehampton, I was presented with the plans Gwathmey had drawn up for the Steel compound. I blanched at the size of the house he proposed to build for Kitty and me. It had five bathrooms. Kitty looked too, but I don't know what she thought because, male chauvinist that I was, I didn't give her a vote.

"It's too big!" I howled. "And it has too many bathrooms!"

Funny to say, but I didn't have a problem with the location or the way the project was being financed. My issue was the idea of the thing. I did civil rights work; for a Movement lawyer the house was simply unthinkable. Movement people didn't have houses like that. Period.

After my final rant on the subject, Kitty gave me one of those whatever-you-say looks, and that was that. The three Gwathmey houses became two, and we moved into the more modest house across the street.

By the summer of 1970 the houses were completed. Hank had taken on a few cases connected with members of the Weather Underground, and so it was that I found myself filling in for Hank one day. My foster client was Dionne Donghi, a member of the Cincinnati collective who, having dodged gun-related charges earlier in the year, was arrested for forging checks. An undercover FBI agent named Larry Grathwohl collared her along with another member of her collective. As if that weren't complicated enough, Grathwohl had gotten Donghi pregnant. The assistant U.S. attorney prosecuting her case persuaded a federal judge to deny her bail, but after some wrangling I got her out in time for her to have an abortion. We were front-page tabloid news the next day. After the abortion she often wound up cooling her heels in a house Hank and his wife, Ramona Ripston, had rented in Sag Harbor, about seven miles down the road from mine in Bridgehampton.

On the weekends Hank, Ramona, and Dionne, and her friends sometimes came over to our house to swim in the ocean. One evening Bette-Ann and John were having a party in their new Gwathmey house across the street. Bette-Ann invited all of us over after dinner. Kitty and I wanted to stay home with our children, and Hank and Ramona had gone off somewhere, so Bette-Ann suggested that our guests come anyway.

"I wouldn't have them over," I warned her. "They don't like rich people."

"Don't worry," Bette-Ann responded. "We'll be fine."

At some point during the party Dionne and her friends slipped downstairs to the master bedroom and started rummaging among Bette-Ann's clothes. They spread an array of designer T-shirts—all the same brand but different colors—on my brother and sister-in-law's king-size bed to chortle at the excess. Wondering where they'd gone, either John or Bette-Ann discovered the scornful revelers and kicked them out.

"Some nerve," my brother said. "They're not Movement people. They're just pigs."

That's what they think about you, I was tempted to say. But I bit my tongue and said, "I warned you!" instead.

The most interesting thing about all this was that I didn't spend much time thinking about the possibility that Dionne and her friends saw Kitty and me the same way. But of course they probably thought we were pigs too. While I may have been selectively blind to the reality of the situation,

Kitty saw it. Still, I managed to keep things separate. I do remember all too well when they derided something Kitty had said: "She's just a housewife."

Kitty was furious. Even after I asked Hank to keep the Weather Underground people away from our place, the lines Donghi and her crowd almost certainly drew between them and us weren't always clear to me. To me she and her comrades were products of the time, fledgling adults who allowed their anger, and maybe some guilt, to take over their lives. A lot of them came from privileged backgrounds—like mine, or similar enough. Unlike me, however, some of them were destined to spend years in prison. Unlike them, I straddled both worlds. As for Kitty, she had working-class roots and zero patience for the sense of entitlement or the terrible attitudes that could only belong to people who were born and raised to believe they had the world on a string.

The Weather Underground people, however, did have a refrain that got to me: "Which side are you on, boys, which side are you on?"

To this day I don't know the answer to that question. I wasn't on their side, but I wasn't on whatever was the other side either. And that was the backdrop for a dinner at John and Bette-Ann's where I did make an appearance and actually outdid Donghi and her friends.

Kitty and I were invited to join a few friends of my brother and Bette-Ann. It was a mix of people, but some of the guests worked in high finance and, I assumed, the making and spending of piles of money. We gathered in the living room with its gentle Gwathmey curve, its soaring ceilings, and its dramatic ocean views. The living room opened out to a deck with a bridge that spanned the dunes before turning into stairs that touched down on a wide expanse of beach. Behind the living room with its long built-in couch and matching chairs, nestled below the overhanging third floor, was the dining area where we all repaired for dinner.

The table was alive with the usual Hamptons house talk—tennis and parties and gossip—and then somehow I became the topic of conversation. Who knows, maybe I started it. It could have happened that way; I don't remember. But I do remember that the conversation turned to racial unrest, and no one who was there that night will ever forget that at some point things turned mean.

"Why are they so violent?" one of the money guys asked me. "Why do they have to burn their own neighborhoods down? We passed their Civil Rights Act. We gave them what they wanted."

The more I said by way of answering the questions that came at me like the mosquitoes out there on a windless night, the more the others turned on me. And then, all of a sudden, I was the enemy. And that did not sit well with me. But then I embraced it. I'm not sure what actually triggered my outburst, but I remember what I said as if it were yesterday: "They're going to come down from Harlem, and they're going to line you all up against the wall, and then they're going to machine-gun you down!"

There was silence.

"What a way to go!" someone quipped after a few beats.

No one laughed.

After dinner Kitty and I retreated across the street to our house, followed by staring eyes. Not a word was uttered. Soon afterward headlights traced our yard, and the dinner guests disappeared down the road.

Afterward I wondered if there was any projection in my outburst, if maybe I was acting out my own fears when I sentenced my brother's dinner guests to summary execution. When I was a child attending Riverdale Country School, Harlem had seemed like a sort of no-man's-land—a nonspace we traversed to get where we were going. But that was not the reality. Harlem was another country, separate and filled with a very particular variety of anger and despair and, at the same time and despite all that, very much filled with itself. The "collective" known as Harlem was based on shared experience that was stronger than whatever tied Dionne Donghi to the other Weather Underground people she ran with, having its roots in slavery. And if the people did decide to come down from Harlem to find a pound of flesh, I'd be thrown against the wall too.

17

The Harlem Four

Following Tony Maynard's trial and shortly after returning from Attica, I was asked to take part in the defense of the Harlem Four, who were accused of a long-ago murder of a white storekeeper and stabbing of her husband in their 125th Street clothing store in 1964. Six boys, including the present four, then in their late teens, had been accused of that crime during a robbery attempt. The black-on-white crime would have been sensational enough, as it occurred on Harlem's main white-dominated business street, but it had been blown way out of proportion by a later completely debunked *New York Times* story that claimed there was a group called the Blood Brothers that required the killing of a white for admission to membership, and that the killing of Margit Sugar had been for that purpose.

The defense team, I was told, would be supported by an interracial group called the Charter for a Pledge of Conscience, which included the actors Ossie Davis and Ruby Dee as well as Manhattan Borough president Percy Sutton, an old friend of Bob Carter from his NAACP days. As with Tony's case, I could expect no fee, but the group had worked hard in support of the boys' mothers, and many people in Harlem considered the case a racist prosecution.

The boys, originally called the Harlem Six, had been arrested quickly after the killing, and the evidence against them seemed compelling. A seventh boy, who became a prosecution witness, said he was involved in the plot to rob the store, but his mother had kept him at home when the crime was committed. By the time he got out of his apartment and ran to the meeting place, the crime had already occurred, and the others told him what went down. A young black girl told the police she was near the store when she saw the boys run out and down the street. There was a fingerprint of one of the boys on the store door. Finally, two of the boys confessed while in custody. Trying all six boys together, with the later recanted confessions of the two boys put into evidence, the 1965 trial was a slam dunk. The convictions, however, were thrown out on appeal, the court ruling that the two who had confessed had to be tried separately. In the following trial one of the defendants was convicted of murder, and the other pled to manslaughter. That left the Harlem Four. Even though they had spent seven years in prison and none of them was accused of being the actual killer, and despite the fact that the Blood Brothers story had evaporated, the legendary District Attorney Frank Hogan demanded a plea to murder if the young men wanted to escape a trial.

I joined Bill Kunstler and a much-older and ready-to-retire local civil rights lawyer, Conrad Lynn, to defend the first-named defendant, Wallace Baker, which would require me to go first in all the arguments, presentations of evidence, and summations. Why did I join the defense when there was so much evidence against the defendants and did I think they were guilty became recurring questions. I have always answered that the boys denied their guilt, and there were serious concerns about how the cops went about developing their evidence. None of the four was accused of the actual killing of Mrs. Sugar or the knifing of her husband, and forcing them to take a plea to a life sentence made no sense after they had served seven years in prison. Also, and central to my thinking, I was convinced that it was only because the four were black that the prosecution demanded a plea to felony murder, which required a life sentence for all who participated during the commission of a felony.

It was my second long murder trial. Bill and I endlessly attacked the prosecution case and hit pay dirt enough times to seriously weaken it. At the end of the trial I gave a summation that lasted all day, harping on flaws of the prosecution's evidence. Bill followed the next day, his blue eyes flashing and his deep baritone voice hitting all the right notes. By the time the assistant district attorney got his turn, we sensed that a conviction was far from a sure thing. After he summed up and the judge charged the jury, the jurors deliberated for three days, then declared that they were hung.

Two weeks after the judge had dismissed the jury, which told the press that its last vote had been seven to five for acquittal, and with Bill already traveling to his next case, I negotiated, with the approval of the young men and their mothers, a manslaughter plea with a sentence of time served. The four were released immediately. Afterward they held a press conference on the courthouse steps declaring their innocence. One of the New York tabloids ran a front-page headline: "Harlem Four Plead Guilty and Go Free."

Years later I checked with the charter support group and was told that only one of the four had run afoul of the law, and that was for a drug-related nonviolent crime. Credit for their crime-free lives, of course, goes to their mothers and the good people of the support group, who stood by them throughout their long years in prison and helped them reenter, and integrate themselves into, civil society. No matter how the four lived out their freedom, however, and no matter whether they were guilty or innocent, our team of civil rights lawyers had served not only them but the people of Harlem, who were fed up with mass imprisonments of their young boys. At least for a tiny moment, we had held "the Man" downtown in check.

Stop-and-frisk programs come and go, but racial profiling seems to be a permanent fixture in America. No matter the progress we've seen in race relations, police and residents of white neighborhoods still eye African Americans with suspicion if not open hostility. And while the old "There goes the neighborhood" refrain can nowadays refer to gentrification— the occasional incursions of middle-class whites into all-black neighborhoods, bringing with them higher property values and rents and pushing the nonwhite residents farther away from where the jobs are and redeveloped city centers—we still live in a highly segregated nation.

When I ventured up to Harlem as a college student, going there seemed like the height of cool. I used to drive up on double dates, and go to one of the jazz clubs on what is now Adam Clayton Powell Boulevard. We pretended that Harlem was no different from Fifty-Second Street, where jazz blared out of the bars, but despite the friendly atmosphere in the clubs, we were always careful. On the way back downtown, car doors locked, we would scan the streets for trouble until we hit the border where white people lived.

Years later when I was working for the NAACP, I spent time in black neighborhoods. Usually I was with an African American with roots in the community. Alone, I always made a beeline for my destination. Often I thought people were looking at me. Maybe, but I was certainly looking at them. My fear, I sensed, had to do with feeling that if I were black, I might want revenge for the indignities they suffered in white areas of the city. Sometimes I had seen these affronts—the difficulty in getting cabs, the rudeness in department stores, the bad tables in restaurants, the stares and under-the-breath slurs directed at African American men accompanying white women, and the hassles young black men endured from white cops. Almost always remaining passive when I observed these incidents, I tried not to look, embarrassed about whatever it was inside me that made me hesitate to intervene. If I were black, I was sure, watching whites look on and do nothing would infuriate me all the more.

After the NAACP, when I started working on criminal cases that were assigned to me by the courts to defend indigent defendants accused of homicide, all my clients were African Americans or Hispanics, who were accused of crimes that took place in black or Latino residential areas.

As a court-assigned lawyer I had access to private investigators, but they could not bill the city more than five hundred dollars to interview witnesses and check out my clients' alibis and other defenses. They invariably did a superficial job, filing reports that would sometimes simply repeat the prosecution's case against a defendant, with the only addition being that they were unable to verify an alibi or interview eyewitnesses. In almost all these assigned cases, the evidence against my clients seemed strong, as they were often caught at the scene, ratted out by a codefendant, or identified by witnesses who knew the clients. But the fact remained that the investigator hadn't really looked, which is why I would sometimes try to locate witnesses myself when the prosecution case was not airtight, walking the streets of Harlem, or riding the elevators and edging down the corridors of dimly lit public housing projects. On these missions I could barely conceal my fear. With openly expressed anger directed toward whites on the increase since my NAACP days, I could feel the hostility in people's eyes.

As I came to see how futile it was for me to try to do my own investigations, I decided that this type of defense work was not for me. Given my lack of resources, there was no way for me to weed out the few who may have been innocent from the guilty. In reality I was playing little more than a clerical role for the court system, receiving a few dollars to make it look as if it was about innocence and justice.

Tom Wolfe, a novelist I read despite myself, as he had a satirist's way of sticking it to white liberals, painted the picture neatly in his bestseller, *The Bonfire of the Vanities*. I especially fixated on the scene where the white bond trader and his woman friend strayed into a black ghetto in the Bronx. There he accidentally ran over and killed a black teenager while escaping from a blocked roadway and what he believed to be a gang getting ready to pounce upon him. I could understand only too well the white guy's fear. *Bonfire* spun a tale of the city's criminal justice system, even when dealing with a wealthy white person it had ensnared.

Fortunately, unlike Tom Wolfe's *Bonfire* character, I never encountered a gang of young black men whom I thought were preparing to attack me. But I was frightened out of my skin by a single young black man.

One evening I jumped on a completely empty uptown local at a New York City subway station. A young white woman came on the train and sat down. Before the doors shut, a black youth entered from the door connecting us to the next car. I looked him over carefully. He appeared vaguely on edge. I sensed that he was high. He walked the length of the car, passed me, and headed toward the front car. He hesitated and looked around. I followed him with my eyes, hoping he would soon disappear. Suddenly he turned toward me and snarled, "Why the fuck are you looking at me?" I answered as mildly as I could that I was not looking at him, my eyes dropping down to the *New York Times Book Review* I was clutching in my hands. "Don't give me that shit," he said. I kept my eyes down and thought about getting off before the doors closed. But the young woman was still the only other person in the car, and I could not leave her alone.

The doors closed, and the train slowly moved into the dark tunnel. The youth stood by the door to the next car, muttering. He was no more than fifteen feet away. I pretended to read, fearful that if I looked at him, even out of the corners of my eyes, I might be "dissing" him. A sense of foreboding enveloped me.

For one fleeting moment the tables were turned. My world of authority, security, and comfort was far, far away. I had watched this black youth as if he were a dangerous bug, and now I was the bug, frozen under a microscope. The young woman got out at the next stop. We were alone.

The youth kept staring at me, waiting for me to look at him. I tried to read my article, my eyes missing sentences and jumping paragraphs. The words had no meaning. As we approached the next station, I decided to sit tight. If he hasn't come after me so far, I am probably okay, I thought.

I was right. He had made his point. When we stopped, the youth moved on to the next car. A sigh escaped my lips. I was free.

But what about him? Had he achieved his own instant of freedom before the pain of leading the life of an alien in the only world he knew closed back in on him? Or was he beyond pain and beyond release, inhabiting a universe beyond the outer reaches of my understanding? Or did I have it all wrong? Was he just some irresponsible kid on a power trip?

As my pulse slowed, I pondered thoughts I have reflected upon many times. What if I was killed by a young black man, and the newspapers had a field day with the story? What would my family say about the killer? And what would I say if a black man killed my Kitty? Would I mumble about societal causes and racism? Or would I scream ugly, vengeful thoughts? And why did I not think about a white man being the killer?

I left the subway at Grand Central to join my wife and another couple at an upscale seafood restaurant. On the way I passed assorted panhandlers, each ready with a line. The subway incident flew out of my head as if I had amnesia. Over dinner the conversation was warm. A waiter hovered in the background. Order had been restored.

Prior to Martin Luther King, Jr.'s, death, the failure to address the staggering problems of the nation's ghettos had led to mounting disaffection. After his death some African Americans, and especially the young civil rights leadership, openly turned away from King's philosophy of nonviolence.

Many of the new voices, such as H. Rap Brown and Stokely Carmichael, were themselves branded as outlaws by law enforcement authorities, alienating greater and greater numbers of black youth. The escalating efforts of the police and FBI to destroy the Black Panthers, coupled with years of race-baiting by national politicians like George Wallace, the election of Richard Nixon, the end of the War on Poverty, the large numbers of African American Vietnam War casualties, and returning veterans who had been exposed to drug-infested Saigon and the butchery of the jungles, facing a lack of decent jobs at home or any sign that the American people appreciated their service—all of it took a toll. White soldiers returning home confronted many of the same problems as well, but their communities were often better equipped to deal with them.

To me the racial boundary lines that divide America are a curse and a major cause of black poverty, education, and unemployment. Ghetto schools are by and large inferior. People are packed into overcrowded housing. Nearby jobs are often unavailable as manufacturing has generally fled core cities. Drug use is a persistent problem, black youth are targeted by the police, and black men fill the prisons. No more need be said. The facts are known. Because of those boundary lines, the few mixed neighborhoods that sometimes exist often become black as they are the only places most African Americans can afford outside the ghettos. If blacks have the financial ability to look for housing in white areas, they have to await anxiously the reception they will receive. Even now their children live in fear of the local police and vigilantes, as the killing of Trayvon Martin illustrates.

The struggle to open up white Northern neighborhoods has gone on since the Great Migration of blacks moving North began. Bowing to the pressure exerted by civil rights organizations, and hoping to head off further nationwide racial disturbances triggered by Martin Luther King, Jr.'s, death, Congress in 1968 enacted the theoretically far-reaching Fair Housing Act. It outlawed almost all racial discrimination in housing and gave the federal courts jurisdiction to hear cases involving violations.

The first case I worked on with Dick took place in California shortly after our new firm opened, where we represented a Chicano community group, the Southern Alameda Spanish Speaking Organization (SASSO), which wanted to build a federally subsidized apartment development in Union City, an old agricultural area situated halfway between San Jose and Oakland. The area was fast becoming a bedroom suburb for the rapidly expanding industrial areas to the north and south. Chicanos, who had long farmed the land, were being pushed out of the area by whites moving into new residential developments.

In 1969, while the city council still had a Latino majority, SASSO obtained approval to rezone a tract of land for a project designed to fit in with other garden-apartment developments in the area. Whites in neighboring tracts, however, petitioned for a referendum. The vote went 1,149 to 845 against SASSO. As a result the land was returned to its old agricultural designation, and the city council was barred from rezoning the tract for a year, by which time the new white voting majority would command a council majority.

We claimed that the referendum was discriminatory. Four years later, after losing before a federal district-court judge, we persuaded the circuit court in San Francisco to rule that the referendum had an arbitrary and therefore unconstitutional impact on the Latinos who lived there. To avoid further court proceedings and blocking tactics, SASSO agreed to scale down its project, and the new complex eventually took its place alongside other higher-rent, overwhelmingly white developments.

Dick and I hoped the SASSO precedent would help other nonprofit housing organizations and private builders to overcome white resistance, but our adversaries came to realize that they could defeat fair-housing groups through foot-dragging tactics. Even more ominous, the U.S. Supreme Court, in another housing decision a few years later, wrote a footnote in its opinion, knocking out our SASSO case as precedent in similar cases. An arbitrary decision by a public body was not enough, the Supreme Court announced, to prevail. Instead a builder protesting racial exclusion would have to prove that the public body, whether the zoning authority or town council, was intentionally discriminating. That ruling was sure to scare off potential builders, as they would not want to lay out the start-up money.

Meanwhile, back in New York, my partners and I had begun a long and intense struggle to overturn Tony Maynard's conviction. While I could have walked away after he was sentenced, as I had not agreed to represent him on appeal or to continue searching for additional witnesses to establish his innocence, I had committed myself immediately after the verdict was rendered to freeing him. The Legal Aid Society had a competent, if understaffed and underpaid, attorneys' appeals bureau that handled post-trial proceedings for indigent defendants, but that thought never entered my mind. Instead I was determined to do whatever I could, using my own resources and those of my struggling law firm to get Maynard out of prison, no matter how long it took and no matter the cost. My partners, of course, could have said, We can't do this. Our firm is skating on thin ice financially without this added burden. You can go it alone if you want, but we just don't have the resources. Instead they said just the opposite. "We are with you all the way." My partner Gretchen Oberman was one of the city's best criminal appeals lawyers, and she would handle the appeal. As Gretchen worked to get the appeal ready, Dan and I would continue to investigate the reports that had been turned over to us during the trial.

Tony had become more than a case. He was a cause.

I had never helped anyone, black or white, who needed the kind of help Tony did. Certainly I had never intervened to protest the condescending way in which Bill was treated. Nor had I tried to see if Lorraina's family could do anything to ensure that Duby or Sister Baby received an education. At the NAACP the school cases asked a lot of me. I had done whatever I could do to represent the mothers and fathers of the children whose desegregation cases I had fought. But I barely knew any of their names. I had developed a meaningful relationship with Bob Carter, but he had been my mentor, teacher, father figure, and a friend. By contrast Tony needed me to do what few lawyers do for their indigent clients: He needed me to make his case a paramount concern in my life, always on my mind, always looking for ways to achieve his exoneration. There would be no underpaid Legal Aid attorney doing what little could be done with scant resources and a huge workload. Now I would do for Tony what I had been unable to do for Bill and for Lorraina.

Perhaps I was being naive in believing I could succeed. I didn't know how unbending the criminal justice system was. I did not know then that once a defendant had been convicted, especially of a violent crime, and the prisoner was packed away somewhere upstate, the chances of overturning that conviction were minimal. Appeals courts rarely upset jury verdicts, and judges as a rule turned a deaf ear to claims of new evidence. Even so, I believed we would prevail. There had been two mistrials and a long train of prosecutorial mistakes. And I had Jimmy Wechsler on my side. The *New York Post* packed a lot of punch, and Wechsler was publicizing the injustice that had been done to Tony. Writing column after column, he excoriated both Judge Irwin Davidson and the prosecutor, Stephen Sawyer. Gretchen Oberman also gave me hope that relief was within reach. In our talks together she pointed to Davidson's many rulings that were contrary to the decisions of the appeals courts.

However, it took Gretchen many long months to get the record together and write her brief. During the oral argument in the appellate division, I was hopeful (even with Chief Justice Taney peering down from the ceiling). Of the five judges hearing the appeal, Gretchen told me two were fair minded, and two virtually always favored the prosecution. That left Theodore Kupferman, a former moderate Republican congressman from the "silk stocking" Upper East Side, as the swing vote. I had reason to think he might go our way: My dad had supported him financially in his election campaigns. Kupferman, however, sided with the two "law and order" judges, and we lost three to two. Courthouse scuttlebutt had it that the district attorney's office had spread the word far and wide that Maynard was guilty and clever lawyers were trying to get him off. Perhaps that had swayed Kupferman. Or maybe Wechsler's solid support of the Democratic Party turned him against us. It was impossible to know. Certainly it was not that the law was against us as the three-man majority literally wrote nothing to justify their votes, and Chief Judge Murphy wrote a powerful dissent that was joined by the same Harold Stevens who had written the *Gaynor* opinion.

Even with the loss, there was still hope. Gretchen would appeal to the state's highest court, and the judges there would all read Murphy's dissent. At the same time, events on the local front were promising. I had received a jumbled, semicoherent letter from a prisoner in which he said that he had killed the Marine. As the letter contained facts that had not been reported in the press, and the man had had no contact with Maynard, I was hopeful this could be our break.

I called Sawyer and asked him to investigate. He turned me down flat. As Davidson was still the judge on the case, I filed a motion with him and attached the letter, but when the Legal Aid Society attorney counseled the prisoner to take the Fifth Amendment, Davidson sent the man back to his upstate prison and denied my motion. There had been no investigation, no court hearing. No nothing.

Then I got word that Sawyer had a man held in civil jail before and during the trial as a material witness. According to a psychiatrist friend who had access through his work to the jail's medical records, this man was kept in a near-catatonic state with massive doses of drugs. Sawyer's plan was to have this man, despite his altered state, testify that Tony had confessed to him. During the trial, however, Sawyer decided not to risk calling him. After Maynard was convicted, the man was released, despite the fact that he would need his drugs on the outside and had committed a homicide. Again I sought a hearing to prove to what lengths Sawyer was willing to go to manufacture a case against Maynard. But Judge Irving Lang, who was filling in for an ailing Davidson, denied my motion.

Finally in 1974, before Tony's appeal was argued in the court of appeals, I struck gold. A reader of Jimmy Wechsler's called him up to tell him that a key prosecution witness, Michael Febles, had a criminal record. As Febles had identified Maynard as the killer, Sawyer was bound to turn over information about him—such as prior arrests—but, despite my request, had failed to do so. When I obtained the court transcript of Febles's guilty plea for what turned out to be a Peeping Tom crime, I found out he had a long and severe psychological history that I could have used to show that his testimony was untrustworthy. That got Judge Lang's attention. He held a hearing and determined that this evidence could well have changed the verdict. As a result the conviction was vacated and Tony was released on bail, which was posted by William Styron. He had spent seven years in prison.

Tony was euphoric. He ran down the steps of the courthouse and up the street away from the Tombs. Kitty, Valerie, and I ran with him. It was as if we were fleeing from the possibility that the court might suddenly decide that there had been a mistake, and drag him back. But that didn't happen. Tony was free.

That evening Kitty and I took Tony to a restaurant that he picked out called Nirvana. It was on the top floor of the Essex House Hotel on Central Park South, a high-class place next to the Hampshire House, where my Warner grandparents had lived along with Bill and Lorraina. Tony was delighted, but the space and the lights and Central Park shimmering below were almost too much for him.

"I feel the walls closing in on me," he said. Then he smiled and said over and over as if it were a mantra, "Yes."

The next day Tony came down from Harlem, where he was staying in Valerie's work space, to our apartment on Central Park West. He came bearing something that was new and fantastical to me, but is now fairly commonplace: a bird-of-paradise flower for Kitty.

Later, on the street, Tony picked Patrick up high above his head. Patrick shrieked with delight. Thinking back, I remembered Bill Rutherford picking me up like that. That memory, in all probability, tied me even closer to Tony.

In the days that followed, on the weekends sometimes I would take long walks with Tony and a stray dog that he adopted, having to double-step from time to time trying to keep up with his long strides. There was no talk of what Tony would do with his newfound freedom, which in any event was not complete, since the district attorney's office could still decide to retry him. To persuade District Attorney Richard H. Kuh, who had replaced Hogan, to drop the charges once and for all, I hired a polygraph expert—one the district attorney had also used—who submitted a report that concluded there was a high likelihood that Tony was not involved in the killing of Sergeant Kroll. Still we waited, Tony walking the city, trying to get the bleak walls and steel bars of prison life out of his head.

Finally word came. There would be no retrial. Tony was free.

Winter approached, and Tony asked if he could live in our Bridge-hampton house until we started going out there again in the spring, which was fine with Kitty and me. I alerted the person who watched our house, but still I received a few calls asking about a black man being there. Tony came back to the city refreshed, but still unable to think about what to do with his life or about working. By then I had begun to give him some spending money.

Worried, I wondered what would become of Tony. I did not want him as a dependent. In my mind I had enough on my plate already. I had three children to support and a law practice that barely paid the rent of our office. Yet I could not say good-bye to Tony. So I tried to motivate him.

"I got you out of prison, and you have two sisters to help get you on your feet. You have got to start taking care of yourself," I thought about telling him. However, something told me that would not work. Still, I felt responsible, perhaps because I lost his trial and he had spent all those years in prison, or perhaps deep down because I had been unable to set things right with Bill, or maybe just because Tony had my number. He had that quick intelligence and saw right through all the bullshit.

In desperation I came up with the idea of persuading James Baldwin to write a book about Tony. But Jimmy always seemed to be traveling or away, and I did not really know what their relationship had been.

Finally I got through to Baldwin through his brother who had a brownstone in the city, and he agreed to meet Tony and me at a popular restaurant called the Ginger Man, which was near Lincoln Center. The three of us met there in midafternoon sitting at the bar, Tony to my left, looking young and handsome, dapper as ever, and the famous writer to my right—smaller and older than I would have thought from pictures I had seen, looking alternately with his large bulging eyes at Tony and me. How the two men greeted each other I have forgotten, but I remember that Baldwin was noticeably wary.

Tony was hungry, so he ordered oysters, and we each had a glass of wine. Then I made the pitch.

"Tony can't take care of himself," I said. "He won't work or can't work, and Valerie is tired of taking care of him. There is a great story in what happened to him, and only you can tell it. Both of us would cooperate, helping in any way we could, and a book could open doors for Tony."

Baldwin said their relationship had been over for years and that he had no intention of it starting up again. He was in a different place now and didn't want Tony coming around. He asked Tony if he understood that, and Tony said yes, he would do whatever Baldwin wanted.

"I'll do the book," Baldwin said, "but our relationship is long over. If I need to talk to you," he said, eyeing Tony, "Lewis will arrange it. And you are not going to like the book I will write about you. I will say you were guilty, not of the crime, but of being an arrogant black man who didn't know his place and who thought he was free to do whatever he pleased."

Tony shrugged, and picked at his oysters.

A few months later Baldwin received a big advance for the project. Tony got a substantial check out of it and immediately purchased a car. When I saw him next, he was wearing fancy fingerless driving gloves. Then Tony disappeared for a while. When he reappeared back in my office, it was to tell me how he had crashed the car in Central Park and walked away from it.

I hoped there would be more money when Baldwin finished the book, and maybe a movie, but it was not to be.

"You have to keep Tony away from Baldwin," Jimmy's literary agent told me, "or Jimmy won't write the book."

"It's my story," Tony said when I talked to him about it. "I want to see that Jimmy gets it right."

"Leave him alone," I told him, "or the deal will be off." And that's what happened. Baldwin backed out. So there was Tony again, needing rescue.

For quite a few years he found white women—there was a series of them—to take him in. I remember one in particular, a very attractive Canadian, who appeared to have money and seemed really to care for and understand him, but that relationship also came to an end.

Somewhere in the middle of these adventures, I persuaded one of the city's finest negligence lawyers, Alfred Julien of the Julien & Schlesinger law firm to bring a case against the city for wrongful imprisonment. Julien turned the case over to his partner, who did a great job, finally settling the case for $250,000. Tony got two-thirds of the proceeds. Again he went off with his stash of money, and once again I was hopeful. For months I did not hear from him, but then he showed up, this time telling me about a sailboat he had purchased that had sunk in the so-called Bermuda triangle during a storm.

18

Rubin "Hurricane" Carter and John Artis

The battle to free Rubin "Hurricane" Carter and John Artis was unavoidable for me. Tony Maynard's case revealed the desperate situation blacks confronted every time they were hauled into criminal court to defend themselves in a world dominated by white people. Having experienced "white man's justice" firsthand, I knew guilt or innocence didn't matter much once someone was in the system. You could see it any day of the week in Manhattan's massive criminal courthouse, one African American or Latino after another represented by lawyers who maybe knew their names—or not—facing cynical, indifferent, bored, or hostile white judges. Most of them were guilty of crimes, some of them heinous, but the process assumed they were all wild animals, black beasts, the scum of the earth—and of course guilty. You could see it in the faces of the people whose daily life involved pushing defendants into the prison system. Contempt permeated the air.

The exception that proved the rule was one of the Manhattan court's few black judges, Bruce Wright. Turned down as an undergraduate by Princeton and Notre Dame in 1939 because of his race, he had served in the army in World War II and afterward had become a lawyer and then a judge who wrote books telling it like it was. At bail hearings before most judges, it was a foregone conclusion that most poor and black defendants could not come close to raising the money needed to obtain their freedom. Not so with Judge Wright. He treated every bail hearing with the seriousness it deserved, and often would find drug programs or even jobs so that he could release a defendant rather than have him languish many months in jail without a trial, unless he agreed to a plea bargain to shorten his possible sentence and obtain his release. For his diligence and concern the press anointed Wright with the sobriquet "Turn 'Em Loose Bruce." That intimidated the other judges into sticking to the high-bail protocol or seeing their prospects for long careers on the bench, let alone promotions, greatly diminished. So when the question of fairness arose in cases involving black defendants, I had a ready ear.

That Harlem Four case was a good example. With Bill Kunstler I also represented two black prisoners who had been awaiting trial in the Brooklyn House of Detention charged with killing an inmate who broke ranks with prisoners who were refusing to go to court on the grounds that they couldn't get a fair trial. After they were acquitted, Bill asked me to join him on cases all over the country.

"That's the way you make your name," he told me. "When the newspaper stories start coming in about you from everywhere, people take notice."

There was enough work for me in New York, I had told Bill. But the real reason was that I couldn't bear the prospect of spending months on the road away from Kitty and my children. Not that I would take just any work offered to me in the city: I turned down an attaché case lined with hundred-dollar bills the day Roy Cohn visited our little office on Broadway to see if I would consider a federal criminal case involving mobsters. A big-time lawyer, former counsel to Senator Joe McCarthy, and friend of New York's Cardinal Francis Spellman, Cohn was smooth. While I enjoyed the spectacle of him sitting in my straight-backed metal chair trying to hide his disdain for my cramped office that looked out on the tar roof of the local United Auto Workers' second-floor office right below us, I knew it was the most paltry of Faustian bargains that he was offering.

Having followed Selwyn Raab's 1975 coverage of the *Carter* case in the *New York Times*, I felt the case's pull, so I called him. Raab had written that the prosecution's two key witnesses had recanted their testimony that they had seen Hurricane Carter and John Artis leaving the scene of a 1966 triple murder at a bar in Paterson, New Jersey. Raab didn't say Carter and Artis were innocent, just that nothing he'd seen or heard established their guilt, and the more he looked into the state prosecutor's case, the more questions arose.

For instance, the Paterson police said that one 12-gauge shotgun shell and one .32-caliber bullet had been found in the car that Carter had rented and Artis was driving after the triple murder they were accused of committing. The only problem, Raab noted, was that the shotgun shell was older, had a different casing, and contained smaller pellets than the spent shells and pellets found at the crime scene. Also, all the recovered bullet fragments from the .32 were copper coated, but the bullet supposedly found in Carter's car was unjacketed lead—typical ammunition for police officers' backup weapons, which were often .32s. In addition there was another murder that same night—it would become central to the prosecutor's case—committed by a white man named Frank Conforti, who had used a 12-gauge shotgun to kill a black man at the nearby Waltz Inn. Both the weapon and unfired shells had been seized when Conforti was arrested. Those shells matched the one the cops said was found in Carter's car. The Conforti arresting officer's report listed two "Westerns," but there was only one such shell in the police property envelope that the department still kept. If that weren't enough, it took five days for the bullet and shell that were allegedly found in Carter's car to be vouchered into the police property book.

After a stop at the crime scene, the car and Carter and Artis were taken to the police station, where they were interrogated separately. Their hands were not checked for traces of gunpowder, and there were no weapons in the car. One was shown the bullet, the other the shell. Both men said they had nothing to do with the crime and had not seen any bullets or shells. Still in custody, Carter and Artis were then taken to local hospitals and shown to two survivors from the bar. After neither victim identified them as the killers, they were taken back to police headquarters and again placed in separate rooms. Both agreed to take lie detector tests, which were administered by a police sergeant. A few hours later they were released.

According to Raab, there was a dispute as to whether Carter and Artis had passed the lie detector tests, which wasn't going to be resolved because the Paterson police department claimed that the tapes were destroyed in a flood. But the fact that two black murder suspects were released in an investigation of a triple homicide where all the victims were white was pretty good proof that Carter and Artis passed the tests. Had a matching bullet and shell actually been found in the car, and/or if either man had failed the lie detector tests, the police would have found some way to keep them in custody.

There were many other discrepancies. The white car that left the crime scene had out-of-state plates, as did Carter's car, but only two black men fled, speeding off in the getaway vehicle. In the Carter car, however, a third black man, John Royster, was sitting in the front passenger seat, next to Artis, who was driving normally and immediately pulled over when flagged down by a police cruiser. Carter was in the back when they were stopped. Seeing three men inside, all acting calmly, the officer asked Carter, whom he recognized, where they were going. Satisfied with Carter's answer, the cop resumed his search. After dropping off Royster, Carter and Artis were stopped a second time by the same officer in the same squad car—only this time he called for backup and drove Carter and Artis to the crime scene so that a young woman named Patricia Valentine, who lived above the Lafayette Bar and Grill, where the crime occurred, could identify them. Valentine said she went to her window after hearing the gunshots. There she saw two black men wearing sports jackets run out of the bar and jump into a white car with out-of-state plates.

When Carter and Artis, neither of whom was wearing a sports jacket, were put in front of her, Valentine didn't recognize them as the men she had seen from her window, but she said that the car looked similar to the one that sped away. As time passed, the differences between the car that Valentine had seen speeding away after the shooting and Carter's car dwindled. Also, the two survivors of the shooting said both the killers were about six feet tall, light skinned, and one had a mustache, but neither Carter nor Artis had a mustache and their height disparity—one short and the other tall—was striking. Equally telling, Carter was a well-known middleweight contender who lived in a white Paterson residential neighborhood. With three hometown witnesses, it seems unlikely that no one would have recognized him. But even if they hadn't, Carter's baldness, his very dark skin, and his prominent goatee were standout features. At police headquarters neither Carter, who knew the value of lawyers from his past street crimes, or Artis, asked for an attorney. Instead they had continued to cooperate with the police. Finally Hurricane left the country for a boxing match, returning afterward.

Four months later two small-time criminals named Al Bello and Arthur Bradley claimed they had been outside the Lafayette Bar. After they heard shots, they saw two black men run out, and they ran inside where they saw the dead and wounded sprawled all over the place.

Bello and Bradley had burglarized a building down the street from the bar just before the shooting. Arrested for the burglary, they fingered Carter and Artis and went free. Based on their say-so, the Passaic County prosecutor made his move. On October 14, 1966, Rubin Carter and John Artis were arrested and charged with triple homicide.

Raymond Brown represented Carter at the first trial. He was one of the best criminal lawyers in New Jersey, and I had worked with him at the NAACP. It was clear that Brown believed Carter was innocent. It was equally clear from conversations I had with various people who knew that Brown had had earlier unpleasant experiences with the first trial judge, Samuel Larner—when the latter was also a criminal defense attorney— that his courtroom would be an inhospitable place.

During a time of race riots occurring in New Jersey and all over the country, Carter and Artis had no chance at their trial. Even with all the prosecution's evidence problems, and without any explanation as to why Carter and Artis would murder complete strangers in a neighborhood bar, they were convicted of the triple murders. Escaping the death penalty, they were sentenced to life.

Years later, after Raab and a public television reporter, Hal Levinson, had obtained sworn recantations from Bello and Bradley, local New Jersey lawyers and the public defender's office represented Carter and Artis at a hearing before Judge Larner that sought to set aside their guilty verdicts. After taking testimony, Judge Larner rejected the postconviction recantations of Bello and Bradley, but something surprising had emerged at the hearing: a tape recording of Bello's interrogation by the police. On the tape the chief investigator, Lt. Vincent DeSimone, could be heard telling Bello he would make sure nothing happened to him for breaking into a building on the night of the murders if he testified against Carter and Artis. It was as clear as day. DeSimone told Bello he'd be performing an important service because black people were "strictly for the colored." Later on the same tape, DeSimone could be heard coaching Bello on how to identify Carter and Artis, as well as the white car.

After Larner's ruling, Carter said he would never rely on a New Jersey lawyer again. He asked Raab for help, and Raab suggested Myron Beldock, whom he knew from another wrong-man murder case. After speaking to Raab, I reached out to Myron, who assured me he thought the two men were innocent and would welcome my participation.

Then I took the next step, which was to speak to Artis, who was attending Glassboro State College on a daytime prison-release program.

Traveling down to Glassboro, I met with Artis in the college's student center. We met at the information desk and spent the afternoon together. Dressed casually like the other students, but a little bit older, John looked like the least likely murderer you could imagine. He was tall and lean, with short-cropped black hair, an easy laugh, and a ready smile. What was he doing there, a convicted killer, going from class to class unguarded? I asked him. He told me how he helped some guards escape after a prison uprising. They knew he could not have killed anyone, he said. So they moved him downstate to a minimum-security prison and let him attend Glassboro. A guard picked him up in the morning and drove him there and picked him up at the end of the day and drove him back. They were after Rubin and not him, he added. He felt that if he had gotten out of the car before Royster, he would have been the second man.

Most of the time John and I talked about witnesses who could track his every move the night of the murders, and possible character witnesses. John told me he had never been in trouble, was a star athlete in high school, had always worked afterward, and had many white friends. At the time of his arrest he had been contemplating either joining the army or trying to get an athletic scholarship to college. His thing back then was dancing away the night, and that was what he was doing in a club called the Nite Spot when Rubin, who had a table and knew he was a local athlete, asked John to drive him home. At the end of our conversation I was convinced he was innocent and said I would represent him.

Driving back to New York City, I thought of Tony Maynard, whose freedom I had won two years earlier. The similarities were striking. Tony and John were about the same age when I first met them. Both were tall, lean, and good looking. Both were black, accused of killing whites in hyperpublicized crimes. Both had been fingered by lowlifes. Both were articulate and thoughtful. Both were without funds to counter powerful prosecutors. And, most important, I thought both were innocent after one long afternoon meeting. There were differences, of course. Tony had an ethereal, free-floating quality even when imprisoned. John, although convicted, was "free" when I met him, and was much more down to earth. What was was, and he was making the best of it until somehow the truth would emerge, and he would be free. Until then, however, he would do things their way if that would make life more tolerable. Maynard, on the other hand, much like Rubin Carter, I later learned, wanted things his way, and had no give no matter what the consequences. At least with John, I thought, I would not have to worry about him in prison, and I could just concentrate on getting him out. As with Maynard, I knew a tough struggle lay ahead. The authorities needed a black killer behind bars when the victim was white in a highly publicized crime. The public demanded it. Someone had to pay to calm the fears of white people who lived way too close to the ever-invading and -expanding black masses.

Myron Beldock and I meshed immediately. Like me, Myron was a sucker for near-hopeless cases. A balding, work-addicted man fighting a middle-age bulge, Myron was the kind of lawyer who followed every strand of evidence to its most obscure conclusion, and that quality garnered the respect of his colleagues and adversaries alike.

Getting to work, first we checked the 1967 trial transcript to follow up on the revelation that DeSimone made Bello and Bradley a promise in return for their testimony.

During that trial Bello had denied that anyone in law enforcement had made him any promises in exchange for his testimony. Contrary to their obligations, the prosecutors never told the defense about De-Simone's promises, and they didn't turn over the tape recording as a prior statement of one of their witnesses. The value of the tape should not have escaped Judge Larner, but instead Larner's opinion justified the prosecutor's failure to turn it over.

Appeals courts don't go out of their way to do favors for prisoners who accuse a prosecutor of failing to disclose evidence, especially when it comes to a street crime. Their rulings generally say something to the effect that this or that undisclosed evidence would have been unlikely to change the verdict. But most appeals happen with zero outside interest, so judges need not concern themselves with public oversight. However, when the press is skeptical about the guilt of someone doing hard time, the *New York Times* runs a front-page story, and famous people start taking an interest, judges sometimes evaluate cases more carefully. Fueling the controversy in this case, Carter had just published a book, *The Sixteenth Round*, about his life, the trial, and his years in prison. Not since Claude Brown's *Manchild in the Promised Land*, an acclaimed autobiographical coming-of-age story about life in Harlem during the sixties, had anyone written so powerfully about ghetto life and the struggle to survive in prison. Also, a defense committee was organized by George Lois—a well-known art director, mover and shaker, and man-about-town. Bob Dylan wrote a hit song, performing "The Hurricane" at a fund-raiser at Madison Square Garden, as part of his Rolling Thunder Revue tour, which included Joan Baez. Another concert at the Houston Astrodome featured Stevie Wonder, Ringo Starr, and Dr. John. At the Garden concert, Carter rallied the crowd by a telephone hookup from prison.

Asked to pardon Carter and Artis, New Jersey governor Brendan Byrne tapped a black state assemblyman, Eldridge Hawkins, who had a foot in both camps and was not trusted by our black contacts, to look into the case. Soon we got word that Bello had concocted a brand-new story— that he and Bradley were actually inside the Lafayette when the shootings occurred, instead of walking toward it when they heard the shots, as they testified in 1967. In the new story Bello and Bradley went outside after the shots were fired and saw Carter and Artis with no firearms standing near the tavern door. Bello told Hawkins he thought they were involved, but that others he didn't see had committed the murders.

Hawkins visited John Artis with an offer of freedom if he admitted to being an accomplice. Artis declined. A few months later Bello testified before a grand jury in Newark, where he recited an expanded version of his "I was in the bar" story, but in this version Carter and Artis were outside the bar with weapons.

Meanwhile Myron and I argued the case before the New Jersey Supreme Court. On May 17, 1976, the convictions of both Carter and Artis were vacated in a unanimous decision that hinged on the prosecution's failure to turn over the tape recording of Bello and DeSimone. But Judge Larner's rejection of the postconviction Bello and Bradley recantations was not overturned, which would allow them to testify again if another trial was held.

With Bello's and Bradley's stories in such disarray, Myron and I hoped the newly appointed Passaic County prosecutor, Burrell Ives Humphreys, would drop the case. The retrial would cost millions of dollars and further destabilize the powder keg of racial tension between the black community and law enforcement in Passaic County. The black community was already up in arms that Frank Conforti, the white man who had killed a black man on the same night, had been allowed to plead to manslaughter and had already been released from prison after serving his time. Humphreys was supposed to be a good liberal—a card-carrying member of both the ACLU and the NAACP. Before we could test his sincerity, however, we had to get Rubin and John released from prison.

For Myron and me, the bail hearing was our first appearance on the Passaic County prosecutor's home turf. The courthouse in Paterson was a ponderous Victorian structure attached to a modern utilitarian wing where the criminal trials took place. We had been apprehensive about one of Carter's supporters, Muhammad Ali, coming to the proceedings, but Rubin and George Lois wanted him there.

Inside the county courthouse we were greeted with hostility. When Myron and I tried to work out seating arrangements for Rubin and John's family and Ali, a court officer growled at us: "What do you think this is, a celebrity show? They're no celebrities. They're killers. No one gets any favors here."

Ali arrived shortly after us, emerging from a limousine to tell the press he was there to see that justice was done and to help out with bail money. He was quickly ushered to the front row. The other spectators were searched one by one and told to keep quiet. Humphreys hunkered down behind his table with a handful of assistants sitting behind him. Vincent DeSimone, heavyset and graying, occupied a rear seat in the spectator section. The scene seemed set for warfare rather than accommodation. When we approached our counsel table a few short feet away from Humphreys, there was only the curtest, most perfunctory of nods. Normally my practice was at least to start out with a handshake, but the chill was so intense that it seemed to create a barrier between our tables.

Before the hearing Myron and I went to see John and Rubin in the holding cell. Rubin was anxious: "Bad vibes, man. I felt safer in the state pen. These Passaic County cops could kill us," he said.

"Nothing's going to happen," we told him. "Just be cool, and let us get you out." As we worked our way back through the narrow passageways to the courtroom, I wondered who was right. Fake accidents and jailbreaks did happen. A few minutes after we returned to the courtoom, Rubin and John appeared at the side door, court officers holding each by the arm. We rose as the judge slipped into his bench and then made brief arguments. The evidence of guilt was substantial, the judge said, but he would release the defendants for modest amounts, twenty thousand dollars for Rubin and fifteen thousand for John. Bail was posted, and after nine years in prison they were released. Rubin was right. The vibes were bad, and we got out of Paterson as quickly as we could.

Within days Humphreys announced that he was forming a special team to reinvestigate the case. He said he was going to let the chips fall where they would, and DeSimone, who had recently become Passaic County's chief of detectives, would have nothing to do with the case.

We would learn later that this was a lie. The Carter-Artis Task Force was supported by a special million-dollar appropriation from the county, and DeSimone was in charge. While Myron and I played catch-up, trying to learn all we could about the cast of characters involved in the case, DeSimone and his team prepared for round two, scripting their witnesses and intimidating ours. Al Bello was once again going to tell his original outside-the-bar story. Humphreys claimed that Selwyn Raab and Hal Levinson had confused Bello and tricked him into recanting. As for the entirely different story that Bello told Assemblyman Hawkins, Humphreys waved it off as yet another conspiracy, this time led by Myron, who supposedly wanted to peddle a "tell-all" book. It was a rubber reality. Under the leadership of Humphreys and DeSimone, alibi witnesses were harassed, including one from Washington, DC, who was brought to Paterson and kept in custody until his memory faded. Meanwhile, one of Humphreys's top assistants, Ronald Marmo, oversaw a Passaic County grand jury that started issuing subpoenas to everyone who had any dealings with Bello, something Myron and I were able to stop, but not before the grand jury madness had the desired effect of frightening off witnesses.

At the same time, Carter was making our coming courtroom battle much more difficult to win. A married man, he started seeing Carolyn Kelley, one of the "Free Hurricane Carter" organizers, and led a high-profile existence. Rubin's actions were at odds with our attempts to portray him as a family man whose wife had stuck with him, but there was no telling Rubin what to do. Then it happened: a disaster. Rubin and Kelley had attended a boxing match together in Atlantic City and then went to a party at a Delaware hotel. Before the night was over Kelley was in a local hospital, claiming that Rubin beat her up. The local prosecutor investigated and decided not to charge Carter. Even so, a Passaic County judge, William Marchese, let Humphreys hold an unheard-of nine-day bail-revocation hearing. The ensuing media circus was deadly. Rubin remained free, but public support evaporated. The Houston fund-raiser that occurred after the Kelley incident was a flop, and even the Madison Square Garden event raised only small change for the defense committee. Myron and I got jury selection moved out of Paterson, but the new location was only twenty miles down the road to Hudson County, where the publicity had been just as bad and the potential jurors were just as white working class, the very types of jurors we were most worried about. Meanwhile Judge Marchese excused himself as the trial judge.

As crime increased in the sixties and cities were abandoned for the suburbs, white attitudes had hardened. Myron and I stayed focused on how to persuade what would almost certainly be an overwhelmingly white working-class jury to put aside whatever racial attitudes they had and focus on the lack of any hard evidence linking Rubin and John to the triple murders.

After the Carolyn Kelley fiasco, I received word through a back channel that if John sought to have his case severed from Rubin's, Humphreys would not object, and Rubin would be tried first. If he won, John's charges would be dropped. If Rubin lost, John would be allowed to plead guilty to a lesser charge, receive a time-served sentence, and remain free. Without any hesitation John said he was innocent and would never plead guilty to anything. To win at trial Rubin, John, Myron, and I agreed that we needed the jury to hear both Rubin and John testify that they were innocent and would never commit such a crime. We also agreed that both John and Rubin would be far better off with Myron and me working together rather than Myron facing multiple prosecutors and their lineup of witnesses alone. That decision made, we moved on.

The new trial judge was a man named Bruno Leopizzi. Initially we thought that was a good omen, as Leopizzi had a reputation for being fair, but that reputation would soon be tested. When Bradley balked at testifying again, Humphreys's case was in serious trouble. To resurrect it he decided to supply a motive for what until then had been a motiveless crime. To do that he would play the race card. Humphreys would argue that the motive for the triple murder at the Lafayette Bar and Grill was racial revenge. Carter and Artis, Humphrey claimed, went on a killing spree to avenge the murder of Roy Holloway, the black man shot by Frank Conforti in the Waltz Inn earlier on the night of the Lafayette shootings.

Leopizzi agreed to instruct Humphreys not to mention his motive theory in his opening statement. But Leopizzi said he would allow Humphreys the opportunity to revisit the issue during the trial if there was sufficient evidence. That put us on high alert to do more research. The good news was that motive evidence had to make sense, like buying life insurance on a spouse before killing him or her. But the bad news was that a judge had lots of discretion. We would argue that there was simply no connection other than race between the two crimes. But we had no idea how Leopizzi would eventually rule. A former well-connected local defense attorney, the graying middle-aged jurist was clearly a "work with me and we'll get along just fine" type of judge. To rule against Humphreys, however—who worked out of the same courthouse as he did and shared its clubby atmosphere—would be much harder than to rule against us, two outsiders from New York. Leopizzi's background was also worrisome.

Like other former defense attorneys who had become judges, Leopizzi had represented a lot of guilty clients. He didn't become a judge by offending prosecutors and the other powers that control judicial appointments. He knew how to toe the line, and he expected us to do the same. In our early discussions with him he gave the impression that part of his job was maintaining appearances. We weren't supposed to make the prosecutor or the police look bad. If you play hardball, I can play hardball too, was Leopizzi's subliminal message. The subtext seemed to be, We all know the truth, so don't rock the boat. The rules, however, were different for the two sides, beyond the assumption of guilt presupposed by that stance. Humphreys and his assistants made up their own rules. They threatened witnesses, allowed or encouraged police officers to make up testimony, accused us of engaging in a gigantic conspiracy, and even commandeered a grand jury. When we fought back, Humphreys and his assistants replied with sanctimony.

Our intensity was another problem. Both Myron and I were fervent in different ways, he more courtly and diffident and I more direct, but it amounted to the same thing. It didn't matter if we were in court, having a casual chat in the judge's chambers, or talking to the press, our message was the same: Rubin and John are innocent. The more the judge tried to get us to loosen up and act like members of the old boys' club, the more Myron and I dug in our heels, which drove Leopizzi batty. In Leopizzi's eyes we were the cliché moral-high-ground types; overwrought in manner, overworried about abstractions like justice, hypervigilant, and dogmatic. Save it for the jury, was the message we got: With me, just be straight. We know what happened.

Early on, once the trial started, Humphreys raised his racial revenge theory again. We were in chambers, and Myron and I said we wanted the argument to take place in open court. Leopizzi was not pleased, saying it would be taken care of the next morning.

Our objection to the racial revenge theory was straightforward. It had no connection to our clients, it appealed only to racial prejudice, and it would force us to try two cases instead of one. But before Myron and I could state our positions the next morning, Leopizzi announced that he was going to allow the racial revenge evidence. I was shocked: We had been denied our right to argue.

"You are turning this trial into a racial nightmare," I blurted, rising to confront him. "That is what you're doing, and you should know it."

"I'm not even going to respond to that idiotic accusation, because that's all it is." Leopizzi glared down at me.

"It's the truth." I defied him, my voice resonating with all the strength I could summon.

"Mr. Steel," Leopizzi replied, "you should learn to keep your mouth shut at the proper times and choose your words, and you should think before you speak."

Seeing that this ruling could likely determine the outcome of the trial, I was beyond being silenced. Rubin and John looked on intently. Tension etched both their faces as I dug deep inside myself to keep this judge from using their blackness as the measure of whether they would spend the rest of their lives in prison.

"For two hundred years of trials in the country," I shot back at him, "courts have been trying blacks for no other crime than the color of their skin."

"You just accused the court of turning this case into a racial nightmare," he growled, "and for this I will cite you for contempt and take care of it at the end of the trial."

The threat of sending me to the county jail for up to six months served only to provoke me more. The first two rows of the spectators' gallery were filled with press people who were following the showdown. As I continued to argue, it seemed to me that Leopizzi realized he could be the target of some fairly damaging news stories. Whether or not that was true, he loosened the reins. For the next two hours, while the jury remained tucked away in its little back room, Myron and I took turns hammering away at the prosecution's theory.

"Stop double-talking," Leopizzi commanded us every now and then. Other times he tried to reason. "Let's assume it's a tavern where black people go and they did become completely enraged over the type of homicide that Conforti committed. What's wrong with that?"

"You honestly believe that each of the blacks felt the same way, that each and every one of them—"

"Let's assume," Leopizzi cut me off, "that maybe five or six felt that way out of a crowd and say—"

"I'm sorry, Your Honor, but that's the nightmare," I said, interrupting him.

It really was unthinkable. Our clients were up against the "fact" of angry black patrons from a different bar where a white-on-black murder had occurred the same night as the shooting at the Lafayette. Turning that into Rubin and John gunning down four people was madness.

"When people are not treated as individuals and are lumped together and called 'angry blacks,'" I told Leopizzi, "that triggers an emotional response."

"Is that evidential?" Leopizzi asked. "Talk from a lawyer's standpoint and not from not any other standpoint."

"We are talking about stereotypes," I said, almost begging the man to understand what was at stake.

Amazingly, Leopizzi seemed to weaken.

"How can these defendants who allegedly knew nothing about an angry black mob be bound by what it did?" Leopizzi, visibly irritated now, asked Humphreys.

It was not the right question, but it illustrated the situation. Leopizzi didn't get that the angry black man was a stereotype. It was a cipher, interchangeable with vague racial fear. Humphreys's vision was of a universal black mob. It presupposed that black anger toward whites was everywhere, like oxygen. That Leopizzi formulated any question at all, however, signified a willingness at least to give us a foothold—not much of one, but better than nothing.

"Without that," Humphreys replied, "Carter and Artis—both of them guilty men—stand a good chance of being acquitted."

When Myron and I attacked Humphreys's reply, Leopizzi became enraged. His moment of weakness behind him, he shot us an "I see through you shysters" sneer: "Be lawyers!" he barked. "And stop pretending you don't understand why the racial motive theory makes sense!"

He was going to allow it. It didn't matter that the killings could have been a robbery gone awry. Or that they could have been the result of a mob hit on a numbers bar that had withheld the take. Of all the possible explanations, racial revenge was the most far-fetched, especially as Humphreys had no evidence that either Carter or Artis had ever been in the bar or even knew it was there.

I had to fight the impulse to sag a little when the jury reappeared after lunch. Leopizzi apologized for the delay, explaining to the jury that that was how the system worked to ensure that both sides got a fair trial. It was an ironic thing to say given the situation he was describing. The system needed no advocate—it needed a watchdog. Rubin and John had just forfeited their presumed innocence to a cultural stereotype.

And so it began. A cop who was on duty when Waltz Inn owner Roy Holloway was killed talked about the outpouring of anger among the bar's black patrons. Humphreys drew out all the frightening details of the bloodthirsty black mob. Myron and I were dead in the water. We used our cross-examinations to establish that Rubin and John were not a part of the crowd, and to insert the shadow of a doubt in the form of a suggestion that perhaps not everyone there was angry, or even black. It was useless. The die was cast, and the vibrations of black rage had infiltrated the courtroom. We could nibble away at the edges at best.

It got worse. Two more police officers testified that some people from the Waltz Inn went down to the police station to demand action. Ed Rawls, a bartender who worked at the Nite Spot, where Rubin and John had been that same night, was part of the crowd. It was his stepfather who had been killed, and he had yelled at the desk sergeant.

"If you don't take care of him," Ed Rawls said, speaking of the gunman, "we will."

The jurors listened with rapt attention as they were told about this other case of white-on-black murder, with its threat of black street justice. Critically, however, there was no connection to the murders at the Lafayette. After leaving the police station, Rawls went back to work at the Nite Spot. Rubin was at his special table, called "the Champion's Corner." John was dancing in the back room. The jury heard testimony that when Rubin and John learned about the shooting, both men gave Rawls their condolences. In Humphreys's mind, and apparently in Leopizzi's as well, that was enough of a connection.

Had Rawls been on trial for the Lafayette murders, motive might been established, but the only connection between Rubin and John and Rawls's warring words at the police station was in the imaginations of white people who had seen too many news stories about angry black men, black people running wild through streets, black kids smashing anything in sight, black women carrying looted merchandise, cars over-turned, shattered store windows, firebombs exploding, burned-out build-ings, and everything else associated with urban blight. Too many movies, including Warner Bros. pictures, featured ink-black bodies, eyes flashing, drums beating, spears in flight.

The jurors were accustomed to this sort of cultural junk food, and they gobbled up Humphreys's feast of racial stereotypes. Rawls had threat-ened revenge, and Carter and Artis gave him their condolences, but in Humphreys's way of framing the information, it sounded like a scene from *The Godfather*—slick innuendo and polish. The jurors were sup-posed to know that condolences meant "I'll kill those white devils." It was a nasty strategy, but effective. Just look at that shiny-shaved bald black head and those staring eyes, Humphreys might as well have said of Rubin. Look at that frown. Look at that tense, wiry body ready to spring. This man did not have the capacity to feel sorry for another human being. He was barely human. He was an animal. He didn't care about anything.

Then there was more.

Another witness produced by DeSimone's Carter-Artis Task Force testified that on the same night—it was unclear if before or after Hollo-way was shot—Rubin had visited a woman's apartment looking for a shotgun that had been stolen while he was at training camp. So there was Rubin looking for the same sort of weapon used on the very night a white man had gunned down a black man and around the time two blacks had gunned down four white people. The evil aspect of the racial revenge theory was clearly visible; Humphreys didn't need to connect the dots. If Rubin didn't find his own gun, weren't there lots of shotguns floating around in the black part of town available just for the asking? Of course there were: Black people always have guns.

Next came the bullet-and-shell testimony. Paterson police detective Emil DiRobbio testified that he was given the keys to Carter's car and con-ducted a search. Consistent with his 1967 testimony, he said he found a 12-gauge shotgun shell under some boxing equipment in the trunk and a bullet near the right front seat, both of which he placed in his pocket. This time around, however, DiRobbio tried to cover up the weakness caused by the mismatches. He added that three people saw him with the bullet and shell around the time he found them: Paul Alberta, a police reporter who worked for a proprosecution Paterson daily newspaper, another detective, and Patricia Valentine, who happened to be standing nearby at a watercooler in the police garage.

Myron and I would have been conceding way too much of this testimony if we did not go on the attack, so we took on all four witnesses, and according to many press reports we did brilliantly. It wasn't hard. The police reports were at odds with DiRobbio's story. Another problem for Humphreys was the fact that Valentine never testified during the first trial about seeing the bullet and shell in the police garage after the crime. As for Paul Alberta, who didn't testify in 1967, none of his many trial stories back then mentioned the discovery of the bullet and shell. Yet now he remembered DiRobbio's claimed exclamation, "Holy cow, look what I found!" When Alberta admitted that DiRobbio was his personal friend, I could hear the press corps snickering.

Patricia Valentine's eagerness to add to her prior testimony also made her an easy target. What she had to say about the car's taillights in particular should have undermined her testimony. From her window above the bar, she said the taillights lit up almost all the way across the back of the car when the fleeing driver hit the brakes at the end of the street. The lights looked like butterflies, she claimed, forming triangles at the outer edges of both sides of the back of the car, with the triangles at their widest at the car's sides and narrowing toward the center as they ran along the trunk to within a foot or so of each other.

The more expensive version of the 1966 Dodge Monaco did have taillights that matched this description, but Carter's rented car was the cheaper model. The taillights on that model were different—chrome replaced the horizontal lights. In daylight, with the sun glinting off the detailing, someone might get confused, but at night, if you hit the brakes of the model Carter rented, as Valentine said the driver did, there would be no butterfly taillights, just the vertical lights of the cheaper model.

My cross-examination of Valentine made her cry, but she defiantly stuck with her story. The car she saw leaving the scene was Carter's, not merely a similar one as she testified in 1967. And the lights did light up almost all the way across the rear end, she was sure. At the trial's end Leopizzi refused to let me place into evidence photographs of the two models, showing their taillights.

Looking and talking every bit like the bloated thug he was, Alfred Bello told the jury his 1967 story. Myron and I kept Bello on the stand for days, drawing out his life of crime, the many favors DeSimone had done for him since he had become a prosecution witness, and asking him to help us understand the two or three different versions of what he claimed to have seen. That's when Humphreys surprised us in the judge's chambers. His office had used a lie detector expert to get Bello to tell the truth, he said. If we cross-examined him on why he returned to his original story, Humphreys wanted Judge Leopizzi's permission to call the polygrapher as a witness and enter the lie detector test into evidence.

Lie detector tests are not admissible evidence because their reliability is questionable. When we pointed that out, Leopizzi quickly agreed. But this was different, he ruled. The prosecution only wanted the jury to learn about the test to explain why Bello had once again changed his story, not to prove the truth of the original story. Myron and I were boxed into a corner. We knew the jury would not make Humphreys's and Leopizzi's distinction. Ignoring our objections, Leopizzi warned us that if we questioned Bello about why he made the final switch, that would "open the door" to the lie detector testimony. We had no choice: It was better to hope that the jury would discount Bello's testimony.

Rubin was another matter. In *The Sixteenth Round* he laid bare his early life of street crime. Escaping from a juvenile detention center, Rubin had joined the army, where he became its European Theater boxing champion. After receiving an honorable discharge, he returned to New Jersey, thinking that the past would be forgotten. Instead the authorities found him and locked him up again. Angry at the world, he returned to his old ways and ended up back in prison. Eventually, however, he came to his senses, put his street life behind him, and turned to boxing to make his living. But the past still trailed him like a ghost.

By 1964 Rubin had become a middleweight contender. In what was supposed to be a curtain-raiser article for his middleweight championship challenge against the champ, Joey Giardello, Rubin said some things to the sportswriter Milton Gross that could hurt him at trial.

According to James Hirsch, the author of a book on Rubin, there were a few things that were left out of Gross's *Saturday Evening Post* article that provided context, including Rubin's opinion that "blacks were living in a dream world if they thought equality was around the corner, that reality was trigger-happy cops and redneck judges."

What got quoted, however, was far more incendiary: "We used to get up and put our guns in our pockets like you put your wallet in your pocket. Then we got out in the streets and start[ed] shooting—anybody, everybody. We used to shoot folks." According to Hirsch this was sheer bluster intended to rattle Rubin's opponents. The article also brought up an incident in Harlem where a group of bottle-wielding boys got into it with a building superintendent, which ended with one of the boys, a fifteen-year-old, getting shot and killed by an off-duty police lieutenant. A friend told Gross that Rubin had said at the time, "Let's get guns and go up there and get us some of those police. I know I can get four or five before they get me. How many can you get?" That sealed Rubin's image as the face of black militancy in America, two years before the triple murder at the Lafayette.

Rubin knew Humphreys would cross-examine him relentlessly about his criminal record and the outlandish things he said to the press and in his own book. But Myron and I were convinced that not only could Rubin survive his cross-examination, but it would give him the opportunity to show the jury that he was a person of real substance, a writer as well as a boxer, a self-educated thinker, and street philosopher rather than a racist killer, and that writing and doing were two totally different things.

"You have left the prosecution case in tatters," Rubin said by way of explaining why he saw no reason to take the stand. "If the jury sees Humphreys cross-examine me, they will see a white man and a black man going toe-to-toe, and they will convict me."

No matter what Myron and I said, Carter held firm. "Racial revenge is the problem," he said. "Without me, Humphreys has nothing to go on. If I take the stand, he will try to use me to make up what he doesn't have."

"You won't let him," I argued. "It's our only chance."

Rubin sidestepped my frustration with him. "It's their system," he said. "They were supposed to prove me guilty beyond a reasonable doubt, and they haven't proved me guilty at all."

Myron and I each had two hours for our summations. We divided up the areas of proof and methodically led the jury through the weaknesses of the state's case, how witnesses had been manipulated along with evidence, and still the prosecution's case was implausible. We attacked the racial revenge theory and asked the jurors not to use it as a substitute for hard evidence.

Burrell Ives Humphreys took only two hours to sum up. Race was his trump card, and he played it with abandon.

"None of us like to admit that things like race prejudice and anger and hate for people because of the different color of their skin exist in this world," he slyly told the jury. "We teach our children the contrary. We support civil rights. We bear in mind the words of Reverend King, in which he had a dream of a day where people would judge his children by the quality of their character, not the color of their skin.

"But, ladies and gentlemen," Humphreys warned, having thus affirmed for the jurors their inherent goodness, "we didn't live in that world in 1966. It was a world filled with people who hate. As much as you might want to look away, as much as you might want to say it couldn't have happened for that reason, it did happen for that reason. What other reason could it have happened for? Coincidence?" Humphreys asked, again reminding the jury about the supposed link between the Waltz Inn and Lafayette Bar and Grill killings. "We like to think so, but the facts don't add up to a coincidence. They don't add up to a coincidence at all."

Humphreys continued, pandering to individual members of the jury. To our Greek juror's prejudices, he dangled the image of Greeks and Turks massacring one another. Leopizzi rebuked me for objecting to that. Eyeing our Irish immigrant juror, Humphreys said, "We see hate and anger and revenge, and we see people fighting in Ireland because of religion." Then Humphreys went in for the kill. Adopting Bello's discarded "in the bar" four-man version of the crime, ignoring the two-man version he told the jury, Humphreys implicated the third man who had been in the car with Rubin and John—John Royster—and the Nite Spot bartender, Ed Rawls, saying that they may have been in on the killings. Without a shred of proof, he spun a tale of Rubin and John stopping off at Rawls's house after the crime, dropping off their guns, and changing clothes. Out of nowhere there appeared a cabal of four black men looking for blood and vengeance. It was the racial nightmare white America feared most—the image that Leopizzi had condoned.

As I looked at Humphreys's bloated, self-satisfied face, my stomach knotted in disgust. He had unleashed evil spirits. Tomorrow Humphreys might become the cautious, petty bureaucrat again, but today he had been a malevolent monster.

We asked for a mistrial the minute the jurors left the courtroom, on the grounds that the racism and pure speculation the jurors had been fed were way over the line of what could be permitted in a summation. Leopizzi gave us that now-familiar twisted smile and denied our motions.

The next day the judge charged the jury and sent it out to deliberate. It was December 22, 1976. We had been in court constantly since the Tuesday after Labor Day, when we started arguing pretrial motions, and had been presenting evidence for six weeks, six days a week. Myron and I were exhausted, hoping against hope that our worst fears would not be realized.

We had barely had time for lunch when we were told the jury had reached a verdict. Rubin and John were surrounded by armed court officers before the foreperson of the jury read the guilty verdicts, which came like stabs to the heart.

19

A Racist Court

Rubin and John's sentencing hearing did not take place for six weeks. While we waited, I escaped to Duck Key in Florida with Kitty and our children. I had been missing in action as far as my family went, but it was hard to slip back into their simpler rhythm of meals, bedtimes, and play. I worked at it, though. We caught fish on an excursion boat, watched dolphins do tricks at a local aquarium, and did other stuff that should have occupied me entirely but didn't. Instead I struggled to escape the cloud that followed me after the conviction. There was no pleasure unattended by flashbacks. I dreaded the loop of nightmares about the trial. The anxiety was there before I awoke in the morning. I was irritable and hard on the kids, picking on every little thing they did. Kitty only looked at me with sidelong glances, knowing I was in one of my states of obsession.

Somehow the convictions had happened to me, even though I wasn't going to be doing hard time, and everything else faded into the background. No matter how Kitty tried to empathize with me, she could do little more than observe and perhaps steady me as I remained consumed by the warfare that engulfed me. She protected the children from my moods, found her own direction, and integrated me back into the family's life. Somehow, even in my least likable mode, Kitty was there for me.

When I got back Myron was fixated on Bello's lie detector test, which Humphreys used to block a crucial part of our cross-examination. He had been in touch with the polygrapher, Leonard Harrelson, at his office, and was surprised to learn that Harrelson believed Bello was telling the truth when he said that he was inside the Lafayette at the time of the shootings. Asked why he submitted a report that said Bello's testimony at the first trial had been truthful, Harrelson replied that that was his understanding of Bello's testimony. Informed that Bello had testified in the first trial that he'd been walking on the sidewalk toward the bar when he heard the shots, Harrelson said he would check his notes and call back. After that he ducked Myron's calls.

Prior to the sentencing, we read in the newspaper that Vincent DeSimone had been the acting chief of detectives during the trial, and was only sworn in as chief after the jury verdict. By presenting him to the jurors as the chief, Humphreys had prevented us from suggesting to them that DeSimone needed a guilty verdict to get his promotion. Judge Leopizzi, who gave a glowing speech at DeSimone's swearing-in ceremony, had to have known and should have set the record straight. Instead he had ignored DeSimone's false testimony.

Leopizzi's failure to maintain even the appearance of neutrality signaled how confident he was that the state appellate court system would stand behind the guilty verdicts this time. The more we challenged him, Leopizzi must have figured, the more we would look like nitpickers looking for a loophole.

The sentencing hearing took place on a bleak winter morning. Leopizzi swallowed a derisive chuckle when we asked him to disqualify himself for being biased. We also asked for a hearing based on what Myron learned about Harrelson's report on Bello's lie detector test. Leopizzi swatted us away: "Let's get to the sentencing and stop all this nonsense," he said.

At every sentencing hearing, the defendant can say whatever he wants before the judge renders his or her decision. We decided to use the opportunity to plant the seeds of our appeals by talking about the racist underpinnings of Humphreys case against Rubin and John. All four of us would have a say.

Rubin cut straight to the bone. He and John were condemned on the basis of their race, plain and simple. What happened to them was no different from what had happened to the Jews in Germany. That could be trouble, I thought. He was going too far, and might harm our chances with Jewish judges down the line. But Rubin's analogy was no surprise.

The millions who died under slavery and the millions more who have led stunted lives under the American version of apartheid are sometimes equated with the Holocaust by African Americans. I have tried to be open to these claims, but when I think about the Holocaust I see slavery and the American postslavery experience as different. Despite their horrible cruelty, the plantation owners needed their slaves alive. After the Civil War, the Ku Klux Klan, although a brutal terrorist organization that penetrated every level of society and functioned above the law, like Hitler's SS, did not advocate a "Final Solution" as far as I knew. Blacks had not only survived the Klan's one hundred years of terror, they had created their own institutions in the South; hundreds of thousands had migrated to the North, and the progress of the civil rights movement gave hope that the nation could at least reduce the racism and prejudice that Rubin was talking about. After his final words Rubin would once again be alone in a world that demanded obedience. Imagining Rubin as he would be in only a few short minutes, I understood he was announcing his defiance.

"You executed three people without a trial, so you have no right to bring up Nazi Germany," Judge Leopizzi shot back after Rubin sat down.

Then he turned to John, whose remarks were less provocative yet equally pointed. The case required two black men as defendants, and if John Royster hadn't gotten out of the car first, he would be going to prison, he told the judge.

When John talked about himself in more general terms, Leopizzi interrupted him to acknowledge that he had risked his life to rescue a group of trapped prison guards during a riot, and that he had also almost completed a four-year college program while in prison: "You have been rehabilitated," Leopizzi told him.

But John would have none of it. So the judge and the wrongfully convicted man stood there hashing out their mutually exclusive versions of a story that was ruining John's life. When it came time to close, John took on the racial revenge theory.

"If I wanted a racist motivation," John said, "four hundred years of my great-grandfather's ancestry is enough motivation for what we blacks have suffered here in this country, not the mere fact that one white man—no disrespect—killed one black here in Paterson."

When it was my turn, I stood, tongue-tied.

"I couldn't do it," I managed to say. "I couldn't sentence this man." My words seemed to take Leopizzi aback. It was obvious that he was deeply ambivalent about John.

"I beg you not to ask how many days you need to be punished," Leopizzi said, his voice a little shaky. "If you do," he continued, "I will ask you about the persons who are buried beneath the ground."

Imposing the same judgment that Judge Larner had pronounced after the first trial, Leopizzi directed that both John and Rubin serve three life sentences, with the proviso that John serve his sentences simultaneously while Rubin would have to serve two out of his three life sentences, one after the other consecutively. John and Rubin were credited with the 3,497 days they had already spent in prison. John would be eligible for parole in 1981, and Rubin fifteen years later. The "Sixteenth Round" was over.

In the dog days after John and Rubin were sentenced, the state court system gave every indication of closing ranks. It took more than a year to get a copy of the trial transcript, and what the court sent was incomplete. Legal papers we filed with the clerk got lost, and court employees were unhelpful—perhaps even hostile.

A clutch of New Jersey attorneys, including Ronald Busch, Harold Cassidy, Jeff Fogel, and Lou Raveson, as well as a young attorney in Beldock's office, Ed Graves, enabled us to keep our sanity. I also enlisted NAACP assistant counsel Jimmy Meyerson to help us get organizational support. The NAACP's history of using the legal process to achieve racial justice might influence some appeals judges to view our arguments more seriously, I thought. Jimmy also came to our posttrial court sessions, until he tangled with Judge Leopizzi while we were seeking a hearing on one of our many posttrial motions. Enraged by his obvious hostility toward Myron and me, Jimmy gave Leopizzi a piece of his mind, only to be run out of court and warned never to come back again. To this day Jimmy remains a close friend and a fine, no-holds-barred civil rights lawyer who says what is on his mind.

Needing brief-writing help, we enlisted Leon Friedman, who

would be a key player in the hearings to come. Leon was an expert in constitutional appeals. Like Myron and me, he was attracted to underdog cases. Fitting in perfectly, he signed on without the expectation of a payday.

Leon took the lead on our legal briefs. He also presented the appellate court arguments on Rubin's behalf while I argued for John. Myron and I remained responsible for developing new evidence, preparing motions, and examining witnesses at posttrial hearings. As time went on, the three of us melded our styles and approaches in total harmony.

Rubin's ability to keep fighting had a lot to do with a group of Canadian citizens who adopted him as their cause. "The Canadians," as Myron and I came to call them, lived together as an extended family in Toronto—a tight community that dated back to the 1960s. On a trip to study an Environmental Protection Agency project in Brooklyn, they had "adopted" a black youth named Lesra Martin, who had a summer job working for the project. With the family's permission, the Canadians took Lesra to Toronto. Showered with caring, Lesra made great strides in school and read *The Sixteenth Round*. He began writing to Rubin in prison. Visits to Rubin followed, first by Lesra and then the Canadians. Soon the Canadians took up Rubin's cause.

When the Canadians started to show up at Myron's office wanting to help with our ongoing investigations and legal strategy, I suspiciously asked Myron what they were really up to. Myron answered, "Who cares? They are keeping Rubin alive."

Shortly after Rubin and John were sentenced, a friend, Seymour Wishman, told me that the Passaic County prosecutor had misled us about the Bello lie detector test results. He couldn't tell me much more than that without his source's authorization. Seymour circled back about a month later to tell me that his confidant, whose credentials were impeccable, said the lie detector test results had been "unfavorable to the state's position and inconsistent with their theory of guilt." The source was not willing to go public, so the moves open to us were limited.

Excited, I called Myron. A friend of his knew the polygrapher, and called him. Harrelson said he would see us. We flew to Chicago and met with him in his suburban office. After a few beers at lunch, Harrelson explained how he worked. First he asked a witness for a narrative of whatever events were being tested. From that story he developed four specific questions.

Bello had told him that as he was approaching the Lafayette he saw a black car and a white car parked outside. Going inside, he ordered a beer. While he was sitting at the bar, a black woman came in, and the bartender handed her something. The woman left, and shortly afterward, as Bello was about to leave, the killers arrived. They didn't see Bello. After they shot up the bar, Bello said he went outside. He said he saw a woman and a white man before turning to his right, where he saw two men he had not seen in the bar. He later learned they were Rubin and John.

After hearing this narrative Harrelson worked out his four questions and attached his electronic sensors to Bello. One of the questions was whether Bello was in the bar when the shooting occurred. Bello said he was. After checking the moving paper strip that recorded pulse rate, blood pressure, and breathing indicators, Harrelson concluded that Bello was telling the truth. Immediately afterward he told DeSimone and Martin Kayne, the assistant prosecutor working with him on the reinvestigation. Harrelson recalled that DeSimone was upset. Bello could not have been in the bar during the shooting, DeSimone argued. Reviewing his chart in front of DeSimone, Harrelson reiterated his opinion. Other polygraphers from New Jersey were present during the discussions. After reviewing his chart, they agreed. All the while, Harrelson added, other members of the prosecutor's staff wandered in and out.

Asked why he wrote a report three weeks later stating that Bello's testimony at the first trial was true, Harrelson said that that was what he'd been told regarding Bello's testimony at the first trial. He explained that the three-week delay between the test and the report came about because either DeSimone or Kayne had asked Harrelson to talk to Humphreys before he wrote the report. A few weeks later he talked by phone with Humphreys and told him that the story Bello recounted was true. But what else was said in that lengthy conversation, Harrelson told us he could not remember.

We asked Harrelson if he had ever told anyone that his initial chart reading was only preliminary, as Humphreys was now claiming, and that he would study his charts further before writing his report.

"Absolutely not," he replied. "It doesn't work that way. You read your charts immediately, and that's it."

Letting us copy his files, Harrelson agreed to put what he told us in writing and testify at a hearing about what had happened. Even if Harrelson had avoided telling us how the report's duplicitous wording was worked out, Myron and I were euphoric. Trapped in our plane on an O'Hare Airport runway for three hours during a tornado warning, we were oblivious to our fellow passengers' complaints as we plotted our next moves.

Back in New York we filed a motion for a new trial based on Harrelson's disclosures. After Judge Leopizzi sent us packing, we asked New Jersey's intermediate appeals court to intervene. But its three judges were equally unmoved. Finally, in 1981, the New Jersey Supreme Court ordered a hearing.

Despite breaking the judicial logjam, the supreme court denied our request that a disinterested judge determine the motion. Instead it referred the case back to Judge Leopizzi, whom we knew from a previous hearing on another issue would twist and turn to rule against us.

Three years earlier the judge held a hearing closed to the public and press in which he asked all the questions. The hearing involved evidence that one of the jurors and the court officers who were supposed to stay with the jurors to see that they did not talk or read about the case had engaged in flagrant misconduct. Barbara Hoekja, a National Jury Project researcher, who had worked with us on jury selection, spoke to John Adamo, a juror, who had been picked out of the jury wheel to be one of the alternates right before the remaining twelve jurors began their deliberations. Adamo told Hoekja he had been very disturbed by his experience as a juror. However, he refused to say why, because he thought Rubin and John were guilty. Later he relented and told Hoekja in confidence that another juror had told him that Rubin Carter had failed a lie detector test and that colored the entire trial experience for him.

Adamo also told Hoekja that during a bus ride to the motel where the jurors were staying, a juror had joked with the court officers about the "melanzans" they were passing along the way. Among Italians the term *melanzan*—a corruption of the word for "eggplant"—was a racial slur. Adamo also said that the court officers who ate dinner with the jurors to make sure they didn't discuss the case told them about two black men who committed a heinous street crime and got off on a technicality the same way "those bastards" were going to get off on a technicality.

To persuade Adamo to go public, Hoekja showed him an excerpt from DeSimone's testimony before a Passaic County grand jury in the summer of 1966, shortly after the shootings occurred. In the transcript DeSimone discussed the lie detector tests administered to Rubin and John on the night of the crime. DeSimone had testified that the police polygrapher told him he believed Artis was truthful when he said he had no direct knowledge of the shooting but had suspicions regarding who was involved. Likewise, the polygrapher concluded that Rubin was not a participant, but thought he knew who was responsible.

Hoekja also showed Adamo a local newspaper story, written at the time Bello's and Bradley's recantations were first made public in 1975, which stated that, according to "authoritative sources," Carter and Artis had "failed" their lie detector tests. As a result Adamo felt that if the authorities were willing to leak false stories, their case must have been shaky. Before he agreed to come forward, however, Adamo decided to talk to the juror who had told him about the lie detector results. When the other juror admitted that the conversation took place, that juror also expressed fear that he and his wife, who had told him about the test results, could be held in contempt for talking about the case. At that Adamo also got cold feet. Even after a second conversation in which the juror hesitantly agreed to back him up, Adamo held back—that is, until Hoekja said she could no longer keep silent.

Hoekja didn't have to force the matter. Adamo contacted Judge Leopizzi himself. After questioning Adamo, Leopizzi called Myron and me, as well as Humphreys, and ordered all of us to come to court on October 5, 1978. After giving us a transcript of Adamo's remarks, Leopizzi told us that because our appeal from the convictions was pending before the appellate division, we could make any applications we wanted to that court. In the meanwhile he sealed Adamo's charges and said he would do nothing further unless instructed to do so.

As the misconduct Adamo brought to Leopizzi's attention was grounds for a new trial, we asked the appellate division to order a hearing. When the court turned us down, we asked the New Jersey Supreme Court to allow us to appeal the issue immediately. On November 21, 1978, the supreme court denied our request. Frustrated, we turned to the U.S. district court for relief under the age-old legal principle that persons convicted in state courts were entitled to seek a federal review of their constitutional claims after they had exhausted their state appeals. Initially the federal judge assigned to our case, Herbert Stern, was concerned because the state courts still had not decided our main appeal from the trial. After some back-and-forth regarding the need for a hearing on Adamo's charges sooner rather than later, Stern suggested to Deputy Prosecutor John Goceljak that he voluntarily agree to a hearing in front of Judge Leopizzi. The other option was a hearing in front of Stern himself.

h"Make up your mind," Judge Stern said, knowing full well that the prosecutors would choose Leopizzi.

Judge Leopizzi held closed hearings for three days. At the hearing Myron and I were little more than disheartened observers. Far from commending Adamo for coming forward about the misconduct he had observed, Leopizzi treated him with contempt. But with the other four jurors, he transformed himself into a kindly, understanding father figure.

Sadly, the juror Adamo had named as his informant was less than forthcoming. He no longer remembered the lie detector conversation, but admitted that he had asked his wife if she had ever told him that Carter had failed a lie detector test. That was all Leopizzi needed. He ruled that Adamo was so emotionally disturbed about becoming an alternate right before the jury deliberated that he made up the lie detector story.

As for the "melanzan" remarks that the jurors had been exposed to on the bus rides to and from their sequestered motel rooms, the juror who used the epithet readily agreed that it was a word he used from time to time. The problem was that he didn't recall doing so on the bus trips to and from court, but even if he did, it would have been in reference to the black population of Paterson, and not the defendants.

"*Melanzana* means nothing else than 'eggplant,'" the juror testified. It could not be equated with any derogatory term, he claimed.

Leopizzi had heard enough. In his fifty-page opinion he ruled that the "melanzan" comment had no racial undertones, and went the extra mile by singling out Barbara Hoekja for being a troublemaker: "It is certainly regrettable that Adamo's vulnerability arising from his deflated ego permitted him to be manipulated by Hoekja," Leopizzi wrote.

The message was clear: Attack this conviction at your peril, which was why we were so distressed by the news that the New Jersey Supreme Court assigned Leopizzi the task of holding the Harrelson lie-detector-test hearing. Four years had passed since Harrelson's original revelations, but at least we had immeasurably strengthened our ability to expose Humphreys's deceptions, as we had developed additional evidence.

My friend Seymour Wishman had convinced his source on the prosecution's team, Richard Thayer, that he had an ethical obligation to come forward. We also had two other surprise witnesses. One was Richard Caruso, who had been an investigator on the million-dollar Humphreys/DeSimone reinvestigation team. The other witness was Michael Pollack, a *Bergen Record* reporter who had spoken to Harrelson the day after the New Jersey Supreme Court had ordered the lie detector hearing. Harrelson told Pollack that he was sure Bello was inside the bar during the shootings, and that there had been an effort to get him to change the results.

When I called Pollack about the story he wrote, he told me it was clear from the context of his interview with Harrelson that the pressure came from the prosecutor's office. I asked him to testify. After checking with his editors, he told me that he was willing if I subpoenaed him.

At the hearing ordered by the state supreme court, under Judge Leopizzi, Harrelson told his story as he had told it to Myron and me, carefully forgetting his long conversation with Humphreys during that three-week period between when he tested Bello and finally wrote his report. But that was enough: The story spoke for itself.

Thayer, who had been an assistant prosecutor in Humphreys's office when Harrelson tested Bello, testified that he was aware of the prosecutor's deception, and was relentlessly cross-examined.

The prosecutor's attack: Thayer had wanted to handle a certain case for the office, and it had been assigned to another assistant prosecutor. Ridiculous, I thought. Now in private practice, he would lie and damage his career to get revenge? Absurd. Little did I realize the extent of Leopizzi's mendacity. When he eventually wrote his one-hundred page decision, that is exactly how he discounted Thayer.

Richard Caruso, the former Passaic County police department investigator who had been assigned to the reinvestigation, was tagged as a traitor when he testified. On the polygraph issue Caruso had not actually been present when Harrelson discussed his results with the prosecutors. He had only heard reports about what was said. Hearsay, the judge ruled; there was nothing for him to consider. But there was more. Caruso had his investigative file with him, which we had subpoenaed because he had told Myron about the damning evidence it contained, including notes about how a cop at the crime scene had fed Valentine the description of the Carter car.

If you saw the movie *The Hurricane*, you might think that the Canadians had succeeded where Myron and I had failed, specifically when it came to the file that Caruso kept after leaving the police department. Untrue. We had known about the Caruso file for a long time. While the Canadians helped in immeasurable ways, providing hours and hours of paralegal work that we simply could not afford or fund, the Hollywood moment had not occurred. Myron had tracked down Caruso after he revealed the file's contents and persuaded him he had a duty to make it available. Caruso promised to turn it over if he and the file were subpoenaed.

In court Caruso testified that in the beginning, as a task force investigator, he was able to talk to witnesses and do his job. But at some point in the reinvestigation his findings started to undermine the prosecution's case, and that's when things turned sour. When Caruso got wind of Valentine's taillight testimony, which a cop on the scene bragged he had fed her, he was told she was off limits to everyone except DeSimone. After other details of the prosecution's case didn't jibe with what was actually being said by witnesses, Caruso and his boss advised Humphreys not to retry the case. Caruso's boss was replaced, and DeSimone openly took charge of the investigation. The final straws were Harrelson's lie detector test and hearing about DeSimone's efforts to get the polygrapher to change his opinion. Caruso resigned. Even so, he was still a cop and had observed the code of silence.

Leopizzi was not impressed. Caruso's story added nothing, he said, and he told Caruso he was no longer needed in the courtroom.

Certain that we would never see the notes if they left the courtroom, I asked Leopizzi to have the clerk hold them as an exhibit.

"There is no reason to do that," the judge replied as he signaled Caruso to leave.

"We have never read them, and they should be impounded and sealed," I argued. Picking up on the prosecutor's opposition, Leopizzi asked Caruso if he had talked to our team with the file in front of him.

"I did," Caruso acknowledged.

"You're excused," Leopizzi intoned.

As Caruso rose to leave, I felt my anger rising. We had labored for years to get our hands on Caruso's notes but had never read them. Now, I was sure, the prosecutor's men would ensure that we were going to lose them forever, and I said as much.

"Let's not make a charade here. You know what's in the file," Leopizzi admonished me, motioning Caruso out of the courtroom a third time.

Barely in control, I restrained myself from charging the bench, moving so close that I was only a short distance away, its height between us. A few steps away, I stopped, my arms waving, overwhelmed by what was happening.

Leopizzi must have seen the "madness" in my eyes. Relenting, he placed the notes in a large envelope.

"I will seal it nice and tight," he twitted me. "It will be a pot of gold."

I was still shaking when I started walking out of the courtroom. Seymour Wishman, who had been watching from the front row, placed his arm around me: "You had me worried there," he said, trying to comfort me.

"He finally got to me," I said.

"I know. I know," Seymour calmed me, "but you have to hang on. You have a long way to go." He was right. I had more work to do. We had one more witness to call.

I called the reporter who told the judge the Harrison story he had written about.

Leopizzi would have a hard time creating a reason why he would make up a story, I thought. He had his notes to back up his testimony.

But the wagons were circled. Leopizzi remained impassive. The reporter did not even rate a mention in his decision. Instead Leopizzi endorsed the ethics of Burrell Ives Humphreys, who had long since left the prosecutor's office to become a superior court judge.

After Rubin and John's second conviction, the New Jersey Supreme Court engaged in a slow-motion dance before resolving all our challenges.

Leon Friedman was the principal author of our New Jersey Supreme Court briefs, pulling together all our arguments, highlighting the ways in which the case got stranded at the intersection of criminal and constitutional law.

Back in 1980, before the lie detector hearing, Chief Justice Robert Wilentz had signaled his intense interest by setting aside the entire morning to hear the issues. At noon Wilentz canceled the court's afternoon schedule to give us the full day.

"Wasn't the theory based on a concept of group guilt that was intolerable?" Wilentz pressed Deputy Prosecutor Goceljak, shaking his head in disbelief each time he heard an evasion. There was still more pressure from the other justices when Goceljak discussed whether we were entitled to a hearing about Harrelson's lie-detector-test report. We were heartened, but as the days dragged on after the argument, we began to sweat. Almost six months went by before the justices ordered Judge Leopizzi to hold the lie-detector-test hearing. They would not reconsider the case until that happened.

By the time we returned to the state supreme court with Leopizzi's one-hundred-page lie detector ruling, which concluded that there had been nothing more than an inconsequential misunderstanding between Harrelson and the prosecutor's office, it was March 1982. John watched the proceedings from the gallery, having been released from prison in December the year before, although remaining on probation until his second life sentence expired in 1991. The justices, who focused the argument on the lie detector issues only, now seemed more evenly split. Wilentz appeared to favor our camp, and we figured that the court's longtime liberal, Morris Pashman, would side with us. That meant we needed two more votes. If the justices' questions to the attorneys signaled their proclivities, at least two or three of them seemed close to joining what we perceived to be the Wilentz-Pashman camp.

We waited another five months. Leon was on vacation in his Cape Cod house when I reached him to tell him the terrible news.

"Lewis, you must have heard it wrong," he said. "We won." "No, no," I told him. The vote was four to three.

To our amazement Justice Pashman sided with the prosecution. Justice Sidney Schreiber's opinion upheld the racial revenge motive because Carter and Artis knew someone connected to the earlier murder at the Waltz Inn. Schreiber wrote that meant "they were members of the particular local community involved," and "fueled by the racial overtone, the defendants may have been motivated to avenge the death of Rawls' stepfather." By that logic any black man who knew Rawls and had heard about the earlier homicide could have been tagged with that motive. The majority opinion also decided that Humphreys had done nothing wrong in his summation when he referred to warring ethnicities—the Irish and Turks and Greeks—regardless of their correspondence to the ethnicities of jurors hearing the case. The four justices also accepted Leopizzi's jury misconduct and lie detector findings.

Justice Robert Clifford's dissent, written on the behalf of Chief Justice Wilentz and Justice Mark Sullivan, concentrated on the Harrelson lie detector hearing, and how we were denied key information that could have been used to discredit Bello and seriously undermine the credibility of the police investigation.

I was not surprised at Clifford's limited dissent, which did not discuss the racial revenge theory. But Chief Justice Wilentz's silence galled me. Wilentz knew better: He had said so from the bench himself.

The supreme court's four-to-three decision hit Carter hard. It was starting to look as if he might actually spend the rest of his life in prison. Denied "good time" by the prison authorities, he had not completed serving the first of his two life sentences, and it was impossible to estimate when, even hypothetically, he might be released.

John's situation's was infinitely better. He was out of prison but had to report to a probation officer who could send him back to prison for any number of violations. Just keep a low profile, we told him. We would continue to fight to clear him.

On a rainy night in the fall, Leon, Myron, and I drove to Trenton State Prison to meet with Rubin and discuss his options. Leon told Rubin that if he was willing to waive any further state court appeals and forever lose the obvious evidentiary benefits of Caruso's notes, which an appeals court finally ruled we could copy, Rubin could file a writ of habeas corpus.

Rubin decided to do that. He could not tolerate another delay. But John was out. There was no reason for me to waive a state court decision about the notes, I said. They were dynamite. If I kept the issue of the notes alive and you lost your writ, you might benefit from my litigating the notes. I told Rubin I would work on the brief supporting his writ, and join in it. Maybe by the time it was decided, the state courts would have decided the issues raised by the notes, I added.

We filed our writs of habeas corpus on behalf of Rubin and John in February 1985. The judge assigned to our case was H. Lee Sarokin, a scholarly humanist appointed to the federal bench by President Jimmy Carter in 1979. Heartened by our luck, Leon, Myron, and I, with the assistance of our legal team as well as the Canadians and Rubin himself, crafted a 253-page memorandum that we submitted to Judge Sarokin in May. It was long, but the case had gone on for nineteen years, and Sarokin welcomed an exposition that outlined the entire history and culled from all the facts and hearings a well-reasoned theory as to why these convictions could not withstand scrutiny under the prevailing constitutional standards.

On July 22, 1985, Sarokin called the attorneys into his Newark courtroom to participate in a long and searching oral argument. Leon was superb in articulating the constitutional violations that marred our clients' convictions. Following the format of our brief, he concentrated on the lie detector deception that the prosecution had perpetrated on an unwitting polygrapher, Leonard Harrelson, and the prosecutor's appeal to racial prejudice as a ploy because there was no hard evidence connecting Rubin and John to the triple murder at the Lafayette Bar and Grill.

When it was my turn, I followed up on Leon's discussion of the Harrelson deception by pointing to another one—specifically the tape recording on which DeSimone told Bello that the killings were an act of racial revenge. While that tape gave us what we needed to level the charge of racism against DeSimone, as he had no facts on which to base that statement, I argued, it did not open the door to Humphreys's massive leap in logic that the murders could be explained as blacks as a group killing whites to get revenge.

"Well, wait a minute," Sarokin broke in. "The prosecution didn't really say that. That might be inferred, but he didn't actually say that in summation."

"Oh, he did." I startled myself with the force of my reply. "When he started talking about 'Look at what Greeks and Turks and people do in Northern Ireland,' he did say that, Judge."

"By inference," Sarokin carefully maintained.

"He talked about group guilt, and I can't think of anything in American law that we have held in disfavor more than that very concept," I countered. "Are all Germans guilty of the Holocaust, or is there individual guilt in this world?" I asked rhetorically.

Judge Sarokin looked at me impassively.

"And in America." The words hung in the air as I searched for a way to make a point about fairness in our legal system.

"I don't think any, any sense of our community is held more dear than the sense that we're all entitled to be judged as individuals, and the prosecutor's case represented a total breakdown of what we have been struggling and trying to build in this country for centuries."

As I sat down, I was worried that I had not only failed to persuade the judge but that I had hurt our case by being so emotional. I couldn't tell if I had allowed my own inner conflicts about white privilege while blacks as a group suffered to pry me from the rock-hard facts of our case. I also feared that my emotional presentation had detracted from the well-thought-out, more traditional arguments presented by Leon and Myron. As I looked over at Leon, I was relieved to be met by his approving nod.

On November 7, 1985, Judge Sarokin's law clerk notified us that the court's decision would be made public at one that afternoon. Myron and I rushed to Newark, accompanied by Ed Graves. We assured Leon, who was chairing a conference at Hofstra Law School, that we would call him as soon as we had the decision. Hearts pounding, mouths dry, we raced to the judge's chambers at the appointed hour. The judge's law clerk, who labored to verify all the factual assertions in our briefs and research our legal arguments to make sure they were correct, smiled as he handed us our copies.

A quick look at the last page told us what we wanted to know. Our hands flew up into the air as our shouts rang down the corridor. Seven and a half years after Judge Leopizzi passed sentence on Rubin and John, Judge Sarokin let us know that sanity still had a place in the courtroom. The racial revenge theory was, he wrote, "an insidious and repugnant argument."

Supporting that finding, Sarokin wrote: "The evidence does not support the imputation of the racial revenge motive to Carter and Artis. There was no proof that Carter and Artis were black militants with an inclination to kill whites, nor that they had even the slightest hostility toward whites. . . . In fact the only blatantly racial statement placed before the trial court was Bello's testimony that while he was being interviewed by a prosecutor's detective in October 1966, that detective referred to blacks as 'niggers' and 'animals.'"

The next day John Artis and his wife, Dolly, joined Myron and me and our band of lawyers and supporters in Judge Sarokin's ornate, neoclassical courtroom for Rubin's bail hearing. Before the proceedings began, two court officers brought Rubin into the courtroom. Carter waved and sat in the front row, sandwiched between his guards. Opposing bail, Ronald Marmo tried to float the idea that the only safe place for Rubin was in a forensic psychiatric environment, because he was a dangerous man. Myron answered those absurdities, and Sarokin retreated to his chambers to decide Rubin's fate. He returned within ten minutes and told the hushed courtroom it would be a great injustice if Rubin had to stay in prison another day. Marmo jumped to his feet in protest, but the judge held fast. Other attorneys from the Passaic County prosecutor's office rushed out vainly in search of a federal court of appeals judge who could stay the order freeing Rubin immediately. Our supporters cheered and clapped as Sarokin left the bench. For a few exhilarating moments, we turned his courtroom into a place of celebration. My only regret was that Burrell Ives Humphreys was not present to hear Judge Sarokin's stinging words and witness our elation.

In August 1987 the court of appeals accepted Judge Sarokin's ruling that the convictions could not stand, based on the deception and misuse of the lie detector test. There was no mention of the racial revenge theory that Sarokin had assailed. The court held that there was no need to rule on that issue. On January 11, 1988, the U.S. Supreme Court decided not to review the appeals court ruling. The next month a new Passaic County prosecutor, under pressure from the New Jersey attorney general's office, agreed not to seek a third trial. A week after that, a Passaic County judge, occupying a bench in a courtroom next to Judge Leopizzi's, formally dismissed the indictments against Rubin and John, barely managing a nod in the direction of Myron and me.

Myron and I joked about our popularity in Passaic County as we high-fived each other on our way out the swinging doors.

Walking next door, we dropped in on Judge Leopizzi, who had ducked the humiliation of having to dismiss our case by having another judge fill in for him, but on this day of days, there was no way he was not going to see our smiling faces. Looking older and grayer, Leopizzi pretended that we had not invaded his sanctuary, as we sat and watched him move along a handful of criminal cases. Invariably, as was his way when I had observed him handling other cases during breaks in our trial, he accorded the defendants standing before him more dignity than many judges do, and after listening to them or their lawyers, tried to be even-handed and fair, and sometimes even to save them from themselves. With Artis as well, after sentencing him, Leopizzi had later persuaded the corrections authorities to move John to a prison near Newark so he could receive treatment from a specialist for a blood disease that was causing gangrene in his fingers and toes.

Perhaps because he had helped John get expert medical attention when he did not have to, I experienced no pleasure seeing him there after we had finally beaten him. There was only a faint sadness. Had it not been for his racial blindness, Bruno Leopizzi was a man I could have liked. How that was possible I did not comprehend. He had become the face of racism at its worst, and here I was looking at him as if he were a benign old man. I could almost understand the parishioners of the Charleston,

South Carolina, Emanuel AME Church in June 2015 saying that they forgave that racist terrorist who killed nine of their members, including the pastor, at a Bible study session. Leopizzi, however, represented the state. Not only had he covered up for Humphreys and his henchmen, he had misled all those other state court judges who had justified his conduct or covered up for him.

Bob Carter, I knew, would never have experienced a moment of sadness for Leopizzi. Bob would have seen him as one more bigoted white man using his authority to keep black men down, just like so many other white men he had faced in both his personal and professional life. In my brief flash of sadness, however, perhaps I saw Leopizzi in terms of a domineering father figure who wanted me to live by his rules rather than to allow me to find my own way and to lead my own life. My dad, of course, was not in the least like Leopizzi. That said, my moment of sadness quickly dissipated, replaced by feelings of loathing for how Leopizzi had turned Rubin and John's trial into a racial nightmare and viciously attacked anyone he saw as trying to undo his handiwork.

20

The 1970s and 1980s

The work was different in the 1970s and 1980s. The tumult of the civil rights movement in its heyday had dissipated into a new status quo. In the South, despite white resistance, the worst of Jim Crow was dying out. Below the surface, however, little had changed. Whites had virtually all the good jobs. The public schools were still segregated, as were the cities and towns. In the North the new and old status quo looked essentially the same. When I felt optimistic, I thought of the slowly emerging black middle class and the Supreme Court finally pressing to eliminate or at least reduce Southern school segregation. In my darker moments, I saw the staggering increase of the black prison population, the Supreme Court's dire limitations placed upon the Fourteenth Amendment's equal protection clause, and its turning that essential amendment for black freedom into a vehicle used almost exclusively for the inevitable white counterattack to destroy affirmative action.

The reasons for my darker moments were many, but they boiled down to something that began to emerge as I battled through the decades that followed my termination at the NAACP doing criminal work, including high-voltage murder cases of blacks accused of killing whites. That "something" was that the Movement actually began to disband. The NAACP, CORE, SCLC, and SNCC either ceased to function or lost the ability to create or push for a national agenda, and new organizations did not take their place. Civil rights leaders entered politics, and they were not replaced.

The big advances of the 1950s and 1960s were incontrovertible. *Brown v. Board of Education*, the Civil Rights Act of 1964, the Voting Rights Act a year later, and the Fair Housing Act of 1968 were giant achievements, and in the South at least they had a big impact. In the North those laws were often toothless, mostly effective only against easy targets.

When it came to whole industries, however, like the banks, which redlined black neighborhoods; and the real estate interests, which fostered housing segregation; and the unions, which asserted seniority rights, and the employers, who hid behind employment agencies and created hard-to-meet employment qualifications; and school boards, which hid behind neighborhood-school plans; and townships that used zoning to keep blacks and all but the solidly middle class and the wealthy at bay—enforcement became an elusive if not a virtually impossible goal. Even so, it was as if the passage of these laws had drained the passion out of the Movement and left only the anger of the millions trapped in their unchanged environment.

You could say blacks could go wherever they wanted, but racism was woven into the way people moved through the country. There were black and white neighborhoods. There was the undercurrent of malice of whites toward blacks, which was often returned, and the constant pressure of white-controlled police departments, which amplified existing racial tension. Restaurants, businesses, and other public spaces generally still divided along race lines—whether those were formed by real estate practices, economics, word of mouth, a traffic intersection, or a river. Children lived in neighborhoods that remained intractably segregated. Property values became a market expression of racism. Blockbusting was epidemic and white flight a constant. As long as whites resisted blacks moving into their neighborhoods, and fled at the first sign of blacks coming in, ghettos would persist. Blacks couldn't even try to move into white areas without the jobs they couldn't get without a solid education. With an anemic tax base, schools in predominantly black areas remained seriously underfunded. And so the vicious circle went around and around.

Some of my criminal defense work during that period, however, gave me a sense of accomplishment. For example, I defended a black woman charged with murdering her john when she wanted to stay the night after they finished their business because it was cold and rainy outside. When the two had a confrontation at the door, she stabbed him. She fled but called for help. He was taken to Harlem Hospital, and she visited him there. He said to forget it. He'd be okay, but his kidneys gave out both from the stab wound and alcohol abuse, and he died a week later. No doubt I was a soft touch, but I saw what occurred from her perspective, and did not want her to do years in prison. After the judge declared a mistrial because in summation the assistant district attorney commented on her failure to testify, I persuaded the homicide bureau chief to allow her to plead to a lesser crime and go free. Perhaps he did that because he thought I might win an acquittal, based on a self-defense claim, at her retrial. But I thought it certainly helped that this was a black-on-black homicide and therefore not in the public eye. By comparison, I represented a black college graduate who had killed an Israeli restaurateur after he had insulted my client and thrown him and his white girlfriend out. Enraged, my client ran home, grabbed a knife, returned, and stabbed the man to death. That killing made the papers. To the district attorney's office it was murder. I found a forensic psychiatrist who interviewed my client and wrote a report stating that he had reacted without conscious thought due to the racial insult. Eventually, after threatening to take the case to trial, I worked the plea down to a zero-to-ten-year sentence. My client started an inmate newspaper in prison, and from time to time I would receive upbeat letters from him. A model prisoner, he was released after six years. Still, that was a lot more time than the woman who killed her john served. But in both cases I had saved black people from serving many more years of unnecessary prison time.

I was also lucky enough to get another opportunity to argue before the U.S. Supreme Court during these years. The case came about because my first cousin, Joanne Schneider, worked for an American subsidiary of a huge Japanese trading company called Sumitomo Shoji America (Sumitomo). Joanne, the flower girl at the "official" Muldoon-Steel wedding in Miami Beach, was the daughter of my mother's brother and his wife, Harriet, whom my father and I had visited in Jacksonville many years earlier. She had been living with her husband in New York, working for Sumitomo. One day she called up and said in her lovely Southern accent, "Cousin Lewis, can Sumitomo keep all the girls"—yes, she used girls—"no matter that many of us are college educated, as secretaries for young Japanese men to come over here, knowing nothing about America, and have us do most of their work with the company's customers, never promote us, and make us serve them tea?"

"No," I replied, before even checking the law, "that's sex discrimination, and maybe race discrimination as well, and your company is an American corporation and must obey our laws."

Shortly after doing some research, I filed a class-action charge of sex discrimination with the Equal Employment Opportunity Commission and followed that up with a complaint in federal court. Three years later, after initial skirmishes in the district and circuit courts, I had myself a Supreme Court case, with the issue being, Can Sumitomo ignore American civil rights laws because there is a treaty of friendship, commerce, and navigation between Japan and the United States that gives both nations the right to hire employees of their own choice in the host country. While Dick Bellman and I worked on our brief, the Supreme Court asked the U.S. solicitor general to state the government's view. As the State Department Office of the Legal Adviser swung back and forth in response to the lobbying efforts of both sides, I worried until the government finally decided to take our side. Argument day was April 26, 1982. Kitty and I took our children to Washington on my forty-fifth birthday, the day before the argument, and Joanne joined us. The argument, I felt, went splendidly. We celebrated that evening and celebrated again in June after we won, nine to zero. It took another two years before our district-court judge ruled that we were entitled to represent past and present Sumitomo women all over the country. In fighting our request for class-action status, Sumitomo's lawyers accused me of being a racist. I got a laugh out of that, given Japan's well-known reputation for xenophobia. Then another three years went by before Sumitomo decided to settle and, rather than risk a trial, began training and promoting women, paying into a fund to compensate all our class members for having been kept in secretarial positions, and pay our attorneys' fees and costs. It was a great victory that opened up untold numbers of jobs in the American subsidiaries of foreign companies.

While the *Carter* case wended its way through the New Jersey state court system, I continued working with Dick Bellman on his housing cases. What Dick was doing seemed like the most logical way to expand critical parts of the Civil Rights Act that didn't work in real life, and since the causes of segregation were interconnected, the solution required work on all aspects of the laws. Schools would not become less segregated until neighborhoods were more integrated. Market forces predicated that "a good neighborhood" was a place that would remain forever closed to all but a small handful of blacks. The reasons were deep rooted. It was worse than the closed-shop unions Bob Carter and our small staff of NAACP lawyers and I had assailed, because the way neighborhoods were closed relied on systemic racial divides at all levels of society, assuring that—by the sheer weight of economic facts—blacks would live in crowded substandard housing in underserved areas where they would receive a subpar education, which meant they would only qualify for jobs that didn't pay a lot, which meant needing to move to a "better" neighborhood, which would remain out of reach.

Much of my work supporting Dick in his efforts to help blacks break out of the urban ghettos got squeezed into the available time between my criminal cases. During the early di Suvero Myers Oberman & Steel period, a few cases stand out. In 1971, after SASSO in California, Dick Bellman and I sued New York City mayor John V. Lindsay to require the city's Housing and Development Agency (HDA) to approve plans for the construction of a modest subsidized middle-income and 20 percent lower-income housing development in a 99.7 percent white middle- and upper-middle-class neighborhood of Riverdale, near the outer limits of the city. The development had been planned as part of a scatter-site program proposed by Lindsay in 1966 to achieve some racial integration in virtually all-white residential areas. Like a similar proposed development in Forest Hills, an affluent section of Queens, the development, called Faraday Wood, had been scaled back and the number of subsidized units reduced in the face of massive community opposition. While the Forest Hills project went forward in a substantially modified form, the Faraday Wood project was killed. Without a doubt the prospect of some non-whites moving into the neighborhood played a large role motivating those opposing the development. After the district-court judge, Robert Ward, ruled against us, we argued our appeal before the circuit court in 1974. By then Lindsay was no longer mayor, and Faraday Wood had been sold to the Soviet Union to create a housing complex for its New York City consular staff. Fighting only for the return of the builder's development money, we lost by a vote of two to one. The dissenter was a Vermonter, James Oakes, whose long opinion can be boiled down to one sentence: If they can't win this one, what can they ever win? The Supreme Court was not interested; it declined to review the decision.

As Judge Oakes's dissent illustrates, judges matter at all levels of the judiciary. Often they determine both facts and the law. Even when the parties are entitled to a jury trial, judges have the last say about what the facts do or do not prove. Judges also control how fast or slowly a case moves forward. The classic example is a housing case Dick and I started in 1981.

Invoking the 1968 Fair Housing Act, we represented a local NAACP branch that sued the Long Island town of Huntington, New York, for using zoning regulations to block the construction of low- and moderate-income subsidized housing—in the form of garden apartments—in a white neighborhood outside the railroad station area, where virtually all the town's black residents lived in low-income apartment buildings. We trudged through five years of foot-dragging and back-and-forth wrangling before the case was tried in front of district-court judge I. Leo Glasser in the spring of 1985. After trial the judge ignored our phone calls asking him to decide the case. We waited twenty-seven months before he ruled against us.

Dick and I appealed to the U.S. appellate court, arguing that Huntington's zoning restriction to single-family houses in that area violated the Fair Housing Act because it was both an intentional act of discrimination and it had an adverse racial impact on the African Americans who lived in the town's small black section. In order to win we knew we would have to buck the conservative trend that required proof of intentional discrimination rather than just discriminatory impact.

Five days before the argument we learned that Judges Irving Kaufman, James Oakes, and Jon Newman were assigned to hear our appeal. Kaufman was the judge who tried and sentenced Julius and Ethel Rosenberg to death. On civil rights cases, however, Kaufman consistently supported a broad interpretation of existing civil rights laws, as did Judge Oakes. Judge Newman was the least predictable of the three, but we felt we had a fair chance to win his vote as well. A cheer went up in our office when we told everybody which judges we had drawn.

Five weeks later that feeling was confirmed. The circuit court agreed that the Fair Housing Act, in contrast to the Constitution, did not require us to prove that the zoning board intended to discriminate. The discriminatory impact of its policy or practice was sufficient.

The following year the U.S. Supreme Court narrowly upheld the Huntington decision. We were overjoyed, even though the long delay had severely undermined the project's prospects since the property owner claimed that our option to purchase the land had expired. After we won that battle, however, a Republican administration had taken over in Washington, and federal public subsidiaries for financing the project were no longer available. As a result the project sponsors had to start all over again at the New York State level to seek subsidies. Moreover, by ruling on technical grounds and not deciding whether the appeals court's use of the discriminatory-impact standard was statutorily and constitutionally correct, the Supreme Court had discouraged other developers of low- and moderate-income integrated housing projects from risking their start-up capital on plans that would most likely require litigation. On another day, in another case, the Supreme Court could rule the other way, requiring proof of intentional discrimination.

In fact the Fair Housing Act remained in a state of limbo until June 2014, when the Supreme Court by a five-to-four vote upheld the racial-impact standard in a case involving a subsidized housing complex in Dallas, Texas. Only the swing vote of Justice Anthony Kennedy saved that interpretation from the angry dissent of Justice Samuel Alito, Jr., who was joined by Chief Justice John Roberts, Jr., Antonin Scalia, and Clarence Thomas.

Meanwhile, out in Huntington, Long Island, the garden apartments Dick and I were trying to breathe life into still have not been built. In May 2012, shortly after Dick died, the housing sponsor, Housing Help, Inc. (HHI), asked me to join in its efforts to persuade the local sewer authority to reject the continuing local opposition to the project. We won that little skirmish. But by the fall of 2015, ground had not been broken on the project. I asked HHI's executive director, Susan Lagville, when that would happen. She told me she could not give me a date but that it would happen. Even the smallest victories in the fight to defeat segregation come hard.

Dick and I became very adept at suing individual landlords, condos, cooperative apartment buildings, and real estate brokers for violating the fair housing laws either by refusing to rent or sell to blacks or Latinos, or simply steering them away from properties in white areas. The problem, of course, from the point of view of civil rights enforcement, was that only individual remedies involving payments to the plaintiffs were available, as most of the time the properties had been rented or sold to someone else.

My favorite housing case, however, was one of these. One reason was that my daughter, Janine, assisted me at trial. During the summer of 1982 the Federal Aviation Administration transferred two black female air traffic controllers to a center at MacArthur Airport in Ronkonkoma, Long Island, which controlled the flights coming in and out of Kennedy Airport. Jacqueline Grayson and Altheia Futtrell didn't know each other before their transfers, and it was merely by chance that they both looked for an apartment within a month of each other at a Patchogue apartment complex. Both got an all-too-familiar whiff of discrimination when the on-site rental agent told them there was nothing available. While such scenarios go unreported constantly, both Grayson and Futtrell complained about the incident to a local fair housing organization, Suffolk Housing Services (SHS).

Luckily SHS was on the lookout for such cases, calling Dick whenever it thought it had a good one. Its executive director, Janet Hanson, sent out white and black testers to the complex. The result convinced us that the experiences of Grayson and Futtrell were no anomaly.

In my first meeting with Grayson and Futtrell, I could sense that just underneath their repressed anger was much hurt. "What's beneath that anger you're hiding?" I asked them. "Don't hold back from me because I'm white. I need to hear the hurt you're trying to hide."

Slowly Jacqueline and Altheia responded to my prodding. When the trial started, just as I thought, we managed to get only one black on the otherwise all-white suburban jury. As a result Jacqueline and Altheia started tightening up again.

"Just tell your story," I told them gently, "and trust the jury to feel your pain."

And that's exactly what they did.

Altheia said her rejection brought back painful memories of being spit on in West Virginia while looking for an apartment in a white residential area there. Sitting in the witness chair, she was emotionally raw, her lips quivering, as she told the jury about her feelings when the complex representative told her there was nothing available.

Jacqueline also testified about her rejection, and described the pain a mother experiences when explaining to her child that some people might treat her badly just because of the color of her skin.

After Jacqueline, SHS's Janet Hanson and our testers testified about how they conducted a spot-check with white and black "applicants," the black testers all being told there was no availability, and the whites all being told there were apartments for rent.

Then I surprised Paul Rotundi by calling him in our case. Rotundi was the president of a very successful family real estate corporation that owned and operated the apartments. I wanted the jury to see that it was Rotundi who had rejected Futtrell and Grayson, as without testimony that an owner or high-level manager had established a policy or practice of discrimination, the jury could not punish the owners for outrageous or malicious conduct by assessing what lawyers call punitive damages.

Sometimes character is fate, which was fortunate for our case. Proud of his authority, Rotundi readily claimed responsibility for every rental decision made in connection with his family's holdings. But, he said, there had been no discrimination. During a pretrial deposition, however, Dick had already extracted from Rotundi an admission that there were no black people in his complex, except for a person who married someone who already had a lease.

Rotundi also told the jury that only Futtrell had come to see his apartments, and all were occupied at the time. To prove that there were available apartments, I used Rotundi's own records to establish that apartments were for rent at the time Jacqueline and Altheia visited the on-site agent.

By the time I sat down Rotundi was in deep trouble.

Now I had one more thing to accomplish. I needed to pin down that the on-site rental agent was acting on Rotundi's instructions. As the trial was now all about monetary damages, because both Althea and Jacqueline had already found apartments elsewhere, it was crucial for the jury to award them punitive damages, which is a penalty that may make the owners think twice before engaging in such conduct again. But the agent was nowhere to be found. Fortunately I was entitled to read to the jury the testimony we had preserved when Dick took the agent's deposition. To do that effectively I needed someone to play the part of the agent while I asked the questions.

So I asked my daughter, Janine, who had just graduated Vassar, to read the agent's answers. With the judge's permission, Janine joined me. As we stood in front of the jury, and I handed her the marked-up deposition booklet to read from, I could sense her nervousness. So I put my arm around her to steady her, and started to read the questions. When she answered, I peered up at the jury. Some had frowns of disapproval spread over their faces.

I was aghast. They didn't know who Janine was, and saw me with this beautiful dark-haired girl. And here I was, they thought, hitting on her: Oh, my God, I thought, this is trouble. If they don't like me, they won't like my case.

Then I thought, I have another deposition section to read. I'll correct this later in the trial.

When I requested permission to read from the transcript again, I asked: "Your honor, may I have my daughter, Janine Steel, join me in reading from the deposition?"

This time I got big smiles: I was a good dad instead of some lowlife.

Later, in my summation, I appealed to the jurors' sense of fairness: "Are blacks who work hard and struggle and go to college and improve themselves and perform a job which is essential to hundreds of thousands of people who are up there in those airplanes every day—are they entitled to at least be shown an apartment?"

Looking each juror in the eyes, one by one, I stood there with my hands resting on the long rail that separated us. Feeling them open up to me, I pushed harder:

"Look inside your hearts," I charged them. "What are we? What do we think of ourselves? What do we want as a people? This must stop. The fabric of our society depends on it."

Pointing to Rotundi, I told the jury how destructive he and his agents were: "They divide us, turn us against each other."

Then, making room for Rotundi's attorney, who would now get his turn to respond to my arguments before I got a quick last word, I pulled back a little to give the jurors the sense that they need not rush to judgment: "Think about the seriousness of this case," I said, and returned to my seat.

Rotundi's defense attorney, Stanley Somer, harped on all the themes he had hoped would see his client safely through this trial. He attacked Grayson and Futtrell, questioned the integrity of the testers, tried to paint SHS as an evil organization that was interested in stirring up lawsuits rather than getting black people apartments, and then scapegoated the agent, suggesting that if anyone had done anything wrong, it was he and not Rotundi. That said, Somer argued in a rhetorical flourish that, even if the agent had discriminated against Grayson and Futtrell, what was that discrimination worth in terms of dollars? "A verdict of one dollar," he suggested.

Somer also told the jury that if it imposed punitive damages it would be punishing Rotundi's mother and his brother, which was unfair since they had done nothing at all.

Watching the jurors, I sensed that some of them were a little confused by Somer's defense. But not one of them appeared hostile to me when I rose to approach them for my last remarks. Using my first few minutes to clarify some of the events that Somer had spoken about, I saw a few of the jurors nodding their heads in agreement. A good sign. Knowing that jurors often feel ambivalent or hostile to fair housing organizations for what they deem to be unfair "spying" on real estate brokers and homeowners, and are worried about their own property values, I defended SHS.

Then I returned to Rotundi's rejection of Altheia and Jacqueline: "What's humiliation worth, what's your pride worth, what's everything you live for worth—a dollar? What's it worth to have to fight to be treated just like everyone else, not to be treated special—a dollar?"

I felt the words tumbling out.

"We had a Constitution in this country which once said blacks were to be treated as three-fifths of a man. Three-fifths of a man. We fought a Civil War over that. We passed laws to stop that, and one hundred years after the Civil War we are still here in this courtroom right now, and we are still facing it.

"For how many years are juries going to have to sit in a box like you're sitting and listen to this case or cases like it? Can't we get our history behind us? Can't we say blacks are five-fifths of a man, and can't we stop companies like S. Rotundi Realty Co. from saying, 'No, no, they are not? We have got to stop it, ladies and gentlemen of the jury. We have got to stop it here. We have got to stop it now. I ask you to stop it."

Drained, I thanked the jury and slowly turned away. I could see some of the jurors looking at me intently as they filed out of the courtroom. I turned to meet their gazes, wanting them to see how deeply I believed what I had said.

The jury was out for less than an hour after the judge charged them on the law. The foreperson, responding to specific questions formulated by the judge and reading from his sheet, reported that we had won the case on every issue. The jury awarded $40,000 in compensatory damages and $250,000 in punitive damages to Altheia Futtrell, and Jacqueline Grayson got $25,000 in compensatory damages and $250,000 in punitive damages. At Somer's request the judge asked each of the jurors if they joined in the verdict. In solemn voices befitting the occasion they all replied, "Yes."

Judge Jacob Mishler told them he believed that the evidence supported their verdicts. Thanking them for their service, he dismissed them. As they filed out of the jury box, most of the jurors looked over at Altheia, Jacqueline, and me and smiled. They had done the right thing, and they knew it. For at least that day, each of them had put racism behind them, and they felt good about it. Tears welled up in Altheia's and Jacqueline's eyes.

Paul Rotundi and his lawyer fled the courtroom, and our little cheering section broke into applause. This verdict was more than twice as large as any previous housing discrimination award anywhere in America. Altheia, Jacqueline, Janet Hanson, and I hugged one another. There were tears. A *Newsday* photographer captured our smiles. It was truly a great day.

A month after we left the courtroom, Judge Mishler denied a motion filed by Rotundi's lawyer to set aside the verdict as excessive. Mishler wrote that the publicity generated by the decision and award would go a long way toward convincing other landlords that it was not in their economic interest to discriminate. Housing discrimination, however, continues unabated. Six months later—to avoid an appeal and the possible resistance of appellate judges to upholding that large a verdict—Altheia and Jacqueline agreed to accept their share of $360,000 rather than the $565,000 the jury had awarded them. That meant they had the funds to become homeowners rather than renters.

Years later I read what I regarded as a wrongheaded federal appeals court decision that ruled that testimony about the painful memories from prior acts of prejudice was not proper in a housing discrimination case. If Grayson and Futtrell's appeal had gone forward, as I had feared, the appellate court could well have had a problem with Altheia's spitting-incident testimony, as well as Jacqueline's talking about bringing up her child in a racist society, and the jury's verdict might well have been overturned. Like our SASSO precedent, which was undermined by a later Supreme Court decision, I knew it would be hard to win a large verdict in a similar case again.

21

Life Among White Liberals

In contrast to what I saw as the stagnation of the civil rights movement in the 1970s, my personal life was a work in progress. Although I continued to question who I was and what I stood for, my little world was changing around me. I had three children, and while I had fought to desegregate public schools in the North, all three attended private schools. We lived well. Still, the American credo of living at a higher level beckoned. More space for our growing children was the goal. With the Warner largesse in hand and the real estate market at rock bottom, we started looking. When Kitty first showed me the place where we live now, I had a Bridgehampton-Gwathmey-house flashback: "It's too big," I said, "and the building is even more upper class than the one we're in now. I'm a civil rights lawyer."

Kitty had heard that one before, and she wanted the apartment. I resisted until a therapist I was seeing got tired of my whining: "Buy it in Kitty's name," he said, "and walk around in jeans all the time, and if anyone says, 'But you're a civil rights lawyer,' tell them you're just visiting; it's hers."

I took half of his advice. We purchased the apartment in both our names, and have happily lived in it ever since. However, my initial protest was not entirely misplaced. When Rosa Parks came for an event we were hosting, she asked for a tour and spotted the back room.

"Is this where the maid stays?" she asked.

I caught the innuendo. "No," I replied nervously. "This is one of our son's rooms."

While I continued to worry about the divide between my personal life and work life, my law firm was experiencing its own growing pains. A few years after we opened up in our cramped little suite, Dan Meyers's father, Sam, the president of the local United Auto Workers (UAW) union, moved it across the street into a small four-story 1840s warehouse building. The UAW rented the second floor. The floors above were set back and about half the size. Henry, Dan, Gretchen, and I pronounced the third floor perfect for a lefty law firm like ours. Long and narrow, it had windows only in the front and rear, and was wide enough for two offices at each end, a reception area in the front behind the offices there, a small library-conference room in the middle, a file room, and even an associate's office for the law student we had hired. Access was by a creaky freight elevator or stairs. The rent was dirt cheap, so we took a long-term lease.

For almost twenty years I occupied that space. It was a second home. But my law partnerships were short lived. First Gretchen dropped out of the partnership. Then Henry moved to Los Angeles and started a progressive law school called the People's College of Law. Dan moved out next, and two labor lawyers, Gene Eisner and Richard Levy, rented the front offices.

Gene and Richard represented progressive unions, including District 65 of the Distributive Workers of America and the local Store Workers Union. I joined them in the seventies and got my feet wet representing their organization drives and arbitrations. I also continued working with Dick Bellman, who moved into our office and joined the firm a year later.

Eisner Levy Steel & Bellman broke up in 1981, and Dick and I took over the entire floor, eventually expanding our firm by bringing in Susan Ritz and then Miriam Clark.

In the 1990s Miriam and I represented black corrections officers in a class action against the New Jersey Department of Corrections for condoning and sometimes participating in a pattern of racial harassment. It was a long way from twenty years earlier and the catastrophe at Attica. But now there were black guards who were treated with contempt. They routinely received the worst assignments no matter their seniority. The prison parking lots were full of cars belonging to white guards emblazoned with Ku Klux Klan emblems.

Initially the department's equal employment opportunity officer, Frank Budd, a black man who had been an Olympic track star and a Philadelphia Eagles football player, had recommended discipline for the most outrageous among the offending white guards, but when he saw that enforcement was not in the cards, he became a much-despised cover-up artist. We had warned our plaintiffs that they should expect retaliation, and they had assured us they could handle whatever was thrown at them. Sadly the pressure got to our lead plaintiff, who committed suicide. Fortunately our guards didn't blink. After many months, working with a skilled mediator, we entered into a settlement designed to ensure appropriate discipline for racist guards, fair treatment for black guards, and a compensation package for our class as well as our attorneys' fees for the many long hours we devoted to the case.

Another significant case came to us from Marty Needleman, who ran a federally funded legal office called the Brooklyn Legal Services Corporation. A Hispanic nonprofit organization called the Southside Fair Housing Committee (SFHC) needed representation to fight the takeover of a huge parcel of cleared land in the Williamsburg section of Brooklyn by the Hasidic congregation Yetev Lev Satmar, whose adherents were known locally as Satmars. The history of that land takeover stretched back many years. In 1967 New York City designated a huge area of Williamsburg for urban renewal. People of many different nationalities and ethnicities were all squeezed together there in what urban-renewal officials designated as substandard housing, including a large Puerto Rican community and a Hasidic population. The land was condemned and cleared. Then the city began to sell off the parcels. The buyers were all Hasidic groups, including the Satmars, which built yeshivas, or schools, that enrolled only Orthodox Jewish children.

SFHC protested the city's sale of the last urban-renewal parcel, on which the Satmars planned to build the largest synagogue in the country, another yeshiva for male Orthodox children only, as well as housing for Orthodox yeshiva teachers. Already on that central square were the house and headquarters of the Satmar grand rabbi. The Puerto Rican community, whose children had played on that land until the Satmars fenced it in, said the square was going to become the Hasidic Vatican.

Needleman wanted us to roll back that last city land sale. The job fell to me, with assists from Susan Ritz; a lawyer from Marty's office; and an attorney from the Puerto Rican Defense and Education Fund. We attacked the land transfer as a violation of the Constitution's First Amendment clause, which prohibited the government from aiding in the establishment of religion, and under the Fourteenth Amendment, because the enclave would be for an entirely white Jewish group. Our federal judge was Eugene Nickerson. As a young man, he had written an amicus brief submitted to the Supreme Court in *Brown v. Board of Education*.

"What luck," I said to Marty.

"Don't be too sure," he replied. "Nickerson was the chief executive in Nassau County before becoming a judge and used urban renewal all the time to move out blacks and Puerto Ricans from county land. He is no friend of ours."

Worried, I called up Mayor David Dinkins's corporation counsel, Victor Kovner, whom I knew from my Eugene McCarthy days. Kovner held a meeting in his office for Marty and me and his staff, who were defending the sale to the Satmars. I made the pitch, but Kovner put me off.

"The land has been sold," he said, and the deal was closed. "If a playground will help the Puerto Rican community to the north of the site, we can arrange that."

We rejected the offer, thanked him for meeting with us, and left.

"I'm not surprised," Marty whispered as we walked out. "I didn't think he would help us any more than Nickerson will."

Marty was right. Nickerson gave us a quick trial. To him the key facts were that the Puerto Rican community didn't have the money to buy land, the Satmars did, and the sale had taken place. Knowing how strongly the Puerto Rican community felt about the loss of at least a share of the land, we appealed. Once again, however, property rights won out over constitutional rights.

Two of our most disturbing losses resulted from Dick Bellman's attempts to incorporate into the New York zoning laws a concept that he and a few like-minded New Jersey lawyers had persuaded the New Jersey Supreme Court to accept: that under the state's due process and equal protection constitutional mandates, local zoning authorities had to consider the need for low- and moderate-income housing throughout the state, and to ensure that a "fair share" of available land in their jurisdictions was zoned for that purpose. Underlying the New Jersey rulings on a series of cases involving the township of Mount Laurel was the concept that exclusionary zoning that blocked housing for low-income people—and inevitably people of color—was contrary to the overriding purpose of zoning, which was to provide for the public good, not just for the more prosperous classes of the public. Later the New Jersey legislature watered down the state supreme court's ruling, but at least the final result paid lip service to the "fair share" concept.

To test New York's zoning laws, Dick teamed up again with Suffolk Housing Services to challenge the town of Brookhaven's zoning. The town kept all its available land in parcels designated for agricultural use. Any building permit on purchased land required the local zoning authorities to rezone it into the appropriate category. SHS wanted the law changed so that builders would know in advance that they could construct low- and medium-income multifamily housing. Brookhaven had never made any provisions for such housing, so this was a good test case. After Dick lost in the state's trial court and at the appellate level, I helped him write his brief to the state's highest court and went to Albany with him for his argument one spring day in 1987. We knew the case was a long shot, as many of New York's suburban towns practiced economic segregation through zoning and had filed briefs asking the court to reject our arguments. But we thought some judges would ask tough questions, and at least some would have open minds. We were mistaken. The chief judge lectured Dick before he opened his mouth about how wrong our theory was, and the other judges listened in silence when Dick tried to explain. Soon afterward all the judges voted against us, with the one black judge declining to join the majority opinion but writing a narrow concurrence.

One of the court's main justifications for its ruling was that SHS did not own specific parcels of land it wanted rezoned. So Dick tried again. He represented a group called the Interreligious Coalition on Housing that did have an option on two Brookhaven parcels it wanted rezoned for subsidized garden apartments. The local trial court judge ruled for Dick on one parcel and against him on the other. Dick thought he had a sure winner when both sides appealed to the intermediate appellate court. The appellate division did not agree, and he lost on both parcels.

In the meantime I had become tired of legal commentators opining that the New York Court of Appeals was a liberal court. When it came to civil rights enforcement, it had impeded public school desegregation, blocked substantial damage awards to victims of racial discrimination, ruled against Dick in his fair-share case, and against peaceful demonstrators seeking to picket in shopping malls. To my mind this was not a liberal court. Out came my pen and paper, and on May 12, 1990, the *New York Times* published my op-ed, "N.Y.'s Backward High Court." The piece was a New York State–focused short version of the "Nine Men in Black" article that had gotten me fired from the NAACP. Again the reaction was swift. My neighbor and friend Judith Kaye, who was a judge on the court of appeals, snubbed me. The few letters following up on my article said that I didn't understand the legal process. Dick worried that my op-ed might reduce our chances of having his latest loss in the appellate division reviewed by the court of appeals.

The court of appeals did refuse to review our second Brookhaven case. But I was convinced that my article was not the reason. Again money and privilege had won out. The judges were not about to challenge America's class structure any more than I was about to give up my house in Sag Harbor or my apartment overlooking Central Park. Years later, after Judge Kaye had written some fine opinions herself and had been appointed the court's chief judge, we exchanged letters and resumed our friendship. Both of us, of course, continue to live in our high-class apartment building in our virtually all-white neighborhood. And both are happy to be here, a stone's throw from the opera house we both love.

In 1999 our firm moved to new digs at 225 Broadway across the street from Trinity Church, with its ancient graveyard, a block away from the World Trade Center. Our suite was up on the twenty-fifth floor and was large for our four partners, one or two associates—depending on the month—one legal secretary, and a paralegal-receptionist, so we became landlords and rented out some space. Looking out of the large old-fashioned windows of my corner office, I could see City Hall and its small adjacent park. Lower Broadway stretched right below us. Behind my desk rose the Woolworth Building with its elaborate facing and griffins and gargoyles. To my left I could see three bridges spanning the East River. The view was breathtaking. The river shimmered in the sunlight.

Tugs, barges, small freighters, sightseeing boats, and, in the summer, sail-boats and yachts plied the waters up and down as helicopters darted around. At night the skyscrapers lit up, and the strings of lights on the bridges sparkled. I had my doubts about this new luxury. After all, as I had protested years ago, "I'm a civil rights lawyer."

While all of us belonged to the National Lawyers Guild and sup-ported the most progressive Democratic Party candidates, there was nothing resembling a progressive, much less a radical, movement in the country for a firm like ours to support. We were all married and had children, and my partners needed to work hard to support their families in an increasingly expensive city, and that would be easier to accomplish in a space that looked like a real law firm. Also, our practice had grown. In the race, sex, and age discrimination matters we handled, our clients rarely had any interest in expanding the law. They just wanted money or the resolution of whatever issue they faced—or both. Additionally, we were trying to expand our negligence practice and represent tenants in conflict with their landlords. I hadn't worked on a criminal case since the last days of representing John Artis, and I had no interest in ever show-ing my face in a criminal court again. Dick kept us focused on meaning-ful civil rights work, as he was still handling housing discrimination cases. Together we were still struggling to get the Huntington garden apart-ments built. But much of our work was routine.

That left me with a feeling of deep unease. My career, with its origins in my relationship with Bill and Lorraina, had always been defined by a sense of mission, and that only deepened as Bob Carter and Kitty and I drew ever closer over the years. Now my "home away from home" was like my Central Park West apartment. Also, I had long since banned Tony Maynard from coming around because he would appear without calling, looking like the street person he was, sometimes wet and soggy, driving our receptionist and my partners nuts. Wondering what Tony was up to and how he was surviving grated on my mind. But at least I had some peace, and I assumed he could take care of himself.

Fortunately Myron Beldock had asked me if I wanted to join his firm in a class-action racial discrimination case against the New York City Department of Parks and Recreation. It was a strong case. White workers with lesser qualifications and education were being promoted over blacks and Latinos. The parks commissioner, Henry Stern, had instituted a program he called "Class Of." It recruited new employees at elite colleges— twenty or thirty graduates each year—with the promise that they would be doing public service work, occupy positions of responsibility, and receive a five-thousand-dollar raise after the first year. Yet our black and Latino clients had to train these entry-level employees, virtually all of them white, to fill the middle-level positions that they themselves had been trying to get for years.

You would think such a case would be a slam dunk, but it wasn't. Henry Stern had been a powerful New York City councilman and was a key figure in the state's Liberal Party, which at times held the balance of power between the Democratic and Republican Parties. Stern was close with the city's power brokers, including former mayor Ed Koch, and he was a favorite of the mayor at that time, Rudy Giuliani. As a result, even when we broke the story to the *New York Times* and made the front page, the city decided on massive resistance. Nor did it matter that the Justice Department later joined our lawsuit. The city's Office of the Corporation Counsel even recruited volunteer lawyers from the city's major firms to aid its already large staff on a pro bono basis.

We were up to the challenge, however, with Myron's firm doing most of the financing, and assigning two fine lawyers, Cynthia Rollings and Jody Yetzer, to the case, and along with some needed help from the Justice Department lawyers, we bulled our way forward.

Taking deposition after deposition of the parks department's key higher-ups, including Henry Stern and his deputies, I became obsessed with the case. After a few years of steady progress, however, the financial and manpower drain on our firms became a major problem. Fortunately the NAACP Legal Defense Fund saw the case's merit and joined our team. It helped with our finances and supplied us with one of its best lawyers, Robert Stroup.

Our position strengthened after we persuaded Judge Denny Chin to grant us class-action status and later to deny the city's attempt to have our case dismissed without a trial. In a long and detailed opinion, the judge ruled that we had presented significant evidence of racial discrimination, including statements I had pried from Stern at a deposition. The judge also rejected the city's attack on our three experts—a statistician to testify about the racial impact of the parks department's policies, as well as an organizational psychologist and a sociologist. At the judge's urging the city finally entered into a mediation process that lasted a year before it threw in the towel.

Even then, however, after paying out twenty million dollars and agreeing to injunctive provisions designed to open up promotions to blacks and Latinos, and monitoring provisions designed to ensure enforcement, the mayor under whom the case was finally settled, Michael Bloomberg, issued a press release stating that the city had long ago mended its ways and had no further racial discrimination class actions against it.

That blatant misstatement galled me, so I called the *New York Times* reporter covering the case and set him straight. The resulting story noted that the city was engaged in an even more bitter struggle with blacks who were trying to integrate the fire department. Having fought Mayors Wagner, Lindsay, Giuliani, and Bloomberg, and even Mayor Dinkins, over issues of discrimination for more than thirty years, I was left with few illusions about how liberal New York City was when it came to racial matters. Like virtually all politicians, they would twist the facts to fit their political needs.

Equally frustrating to me in our parks department case, Judge Chin had ruled against us on a major issue that remains an open sore in the city to this day. We had claimed that an additional reason that blacks and Latinos received so few promotions was the result of their assignments to parks in the most impoverished and segregated sections of the city, which were allocated the least funds for their upkeep. Worse, those are the very areas of the city that need the parks most to allow their residents some respite from their crowded housing and clogged streets. Perhaps Mayor Bill De Blasio, who was elected on the backs of black and Latino voters, will attempt to ameliorate this situation, which Judge Chin left untouched. Living next to beautifully manicured Central Park—which is supported by millions of dollars of private funding from its affluent residential neighborhoods and the city's real estate interests—and knowing the value of such a great open space, I can only hope that will happen.

22

Navigating Racial Lines

On April 18, 1986, less than six months after Judge H. Lee Sarokin issued his ruling, and long before the endless appeal process was finished and the charges against Rubin and John were dismissed, my receptionist buzzed to see if I wanted to talk to a reporter who had followed the case.

"Have you heard that John Artis has been arrested on a drug charge?" the reporter asked. My heart sank.

"Oh Lord," I said.

The reporter was considerate.

"The news must be very upsetting to you," he said.

I didn't want to be quoted in the story, especially not about my feelings, so I mumbled something and asked him to tell me what he knew.

The police had been tapping the phone of a small-time drug operation run out of a woman's house in Passaic County, New Jersey. Purely by chance the cops picked up John talking on that line. He had received instructions about where to drop off and pick up small quantities of cocaine. When the police had what they needed, they obtained search warrants and started making arrests. A gun was found in John and Dolly's apartment, but no drugs. They were both arrested. Dolly was released almost immediately, but John was being held in the Passaic County jail.

It was a quick phone call. I slumped in my chair and stared out of the window. The news didn't come as a complete surprise. A few months earlier John had called me to borrow five hundred dollars. He said he had been stopped by the Paterson police while driving Dolly's car, and needed the money to pay the fine. He was out of work and too embarrassed to ask Dolly for the money.

I knew that John wasn't working. He had gotten two or three jobs since his release, and had held one for a relatively long period of time, but when his vasculitis, the disease he got in prison, flared again he had another finger-joint amputation, so he had to quit his job. I had stayed in touch with him, and it was hard not to notice that he seemed worn out, and more depressed each time we talked. So I was worried even before I got the call for money.

John's request brought with it additional baggage. Tony Maynard was still hitting me up for cash infusions. I felt like an illustration of the saying about how you become responsible for a man after you save his life. It wasn't only about the money. It was about the shared indignity of being the giver and the taker in a world that made that necessary, and the way it underscored the contradictions of my life's work.

While I did not discuss my feelings with the reporter, I could not push away my irritation. Myron and I had been telling John to get out of Paterson with Dolly.

"Why haven't you left that damn city?" I asked John before responding to his request for cash.

"Because of Dolly's job, and also my family are here," he answered.

"But why take chances?" I persisted. "They're dying to get you back behind bars. They're never going to let up."

"I know," John answered, "but can you help me out?"

John had never asked me for a cent, and had always dealt with me as an equal. It felt as if he'd turned a corner with that phone call, and we were on the road to changing that relationship.

Like Myron, who was a soft touch for clients he had rescued, I hated the trap of being the white man with money. Worse, I knew that the best part of the relationship could die.

I called Myron, who thought the world of John. Since his release, they had met from time to time to play jazz together. Myron and I were both worried. We decided to go fifty-fifty on the money. We could hope all we wanted that there was nothing more to it than what John had said, but we both had a hunch that something was very wrong.

When John came to New York the next day, I was afraid to press him about his story. Perhaps "hesitant" is a better word. I realized that the more I learned about the particulars of his situation, the more I would be sucked into his life, and I knew from prior experiences that was a slippery slope.

Please let him be okay, I said to myself when John left, money in hand. Months passed. And now this. Myron and I agreed that John would be better off with a New Jersey attorney who had no connections to the murder case. William Perkins, Jr., and Robert Utsey, Jr., two well-respected black criminal lawyers, agreed to take on the job. If the prosecutors treated the case like a run-of-the-mill first offender's low-level drug offense, John would have a good chance of getting probation.

"We'll have to see what happens at court," Perkins said.

"They owe him," I pointed out.

"That's not the way they see it," Perkins replied.

A few days later John was released on bail on the condition that he enter a drug program. When we talked, he was mortified. He told me the part of the story that Myron and I had wondered about. At first he had started taking drugs to escape the pain in his hands and feet. As a result he developed a habit. To get the money he needed to pay the woman who supplied him, he became her runner. She called him to make pickups and drops, and that was it.

As for the gun, John had been visiting relatives in Virginia, and they had taken the gun to shoot targets in the woods. When he drove back to New Jersey, he saw the gun in the trunk of his car and brought it into his apartment. "I let Dolly down, and you," he said. "I'll never let something like this happen again. I'll die first."

I believed him.

Almost fifteen months after he was arrested, John pleaded guilty to being involved in a drug conspiracy, and to the possession of the gun. The prosecutor did not challenge his statements as to his role in the drug conspiracy, or the small amounts of drugs and money that were involved, nor was his explanation of how he obtained the gun disputed.

Superior Court Judge Frank M. Donato held John's sentencing hearing on August 7, 1987, two weeks before the federal court of appeals upheld Judge Sarokin's decision that had thrown out the Lafayette bar convictions.

Before passing sentence on John, Donato had to apply a New Jersey statute that instructed judges how to determine if either aggravating or mitigating factors should affect the sentence.

Donato agreed that John's medical condition was a mitigating factor, as he was seeking drugs to alleviate his pain. Instead of focusing on John's clean record as another mitigating factor, however, he did just the opposite. Despite Sarokin's ruling wiping out the Lafayette bar convictions, Donato ignored that John was once again presumed innocent of the 1966 murders. There were going to be appeals, and there could be another trial, the judge noted, as if that speculation had anything to do with the presumption of innocence. Worse, Donato opined that John "was not likely to respond to probation because even his past has not been a deterrent to new criminal activity." It was like a Kafka novel—completely surreal. Rather than give John the benefit of fifteen years of wrongful imprisonment to reduce his sentence, the Judge pointed to the time John had spent in prison as evidence that he could not be rehabilitated. Yet John's parole officer stated that he had adjusted positively since entering the drug rehabilitation program. Sentencing John to six years in state prison, Donato also refused to allow him to remain free while he appealed. This was Passaic County justice at its finest, a real tribute to Judge Leopizzi, whose courtroom was down the hall.

When Perkins and Utsey called me to tell me the news, I was aghast. We would appeal, and Leon and I would write the brief, with Utsey handling the argument.

On a dreary winter day in early 1988, I accompanied Utsey to Trenton. He emphasized the injustice of using the Lafayette bar murders against John as well as the fact that one of the other coconspirators with three prior drug convictions was given probation. Afterward, Utsey was optimistic. Knowing the appellate division from prior experience, I thought he was living in a fantasy world.

On April 4, 1988, as I suspected, the judges upheld the sentence.

Once again Leon and I appealed to the New Jersey Supreme Court. We filed our brief on May 2, 1988. A little more than a month later Chief Justice Wilentz signed an order remanding the issue of Artis's sentence to Donato, and instructed him to conduct a "reassessment of defendant's prior record or lack thereof." Utsey and I returned to the

Paterson courthouse. For the last time I witnessed John brought into a courtroom with a guard gripping him firmly above the elbow. Filled with indignation, Donato lectured the local press that the prosecutors and judges of Passaic County who handled the Carter-Artis case were honorable men and outstanding public servants. They constituted a who's who of the state bar, and he would never agree that John had no history of prior criminal activity. But Donato understood his marching orders. Sullenly he vacated Artis' six-year sentence, and placed him on probation.

"You don't do well up here," Donato told John. "Maybe you should consider a change of climate."

As I was leaving the courtroom, a reporter asked me for my reaction. "This is Paterson." I shrugged. "I'm just glad John is free."

Shortly after his release, John and Dolly moved to Portsmouth, Virginia, where he got a job teaching at-risk youth about the perils of getting caught up into the criminal justice system. Dolly continued to work for the Social Security Administration. Then one day John came to see me. We had gone through so much together that it was difficult for us to make small talk, so there was very little of it before he produced an envelope from his pocket and handed it to me.

"I want you to have this," he said as I opened it.

There were five hundred dollars inside. I looked at John speechless.

"Taking that money was one of the worst things I have done in my life," he said. "I could not leave until I paid you back."

"This is one of the nicest things that has happened to me," I told him.

We held each other by the forearms.

"You take care," I said.

"You too," he responded, giving me his open John Artis smile.

I cried after he left.

There are many little rays of light I see as I survey the five decades I've spent doing this work. There have been powerful black CEOs—including Time Warner's Richard Parsons and American Express's Kenneth Chenault. Oprah Winfrey became a phenomenon unto herself.

We've seen black chiefs of police and a black United States attorney general followed by a black female United States attorney general. Black mayors have come and gone, and of course a black family resides in the White House.

Over the years I discussed these milestones of racial progress with Bob Carter. He had moved to the same neighborhood as us, also on the park. We became very close, going to the theater and the opera together, talking about cases that interested us, and keeping up with each other's families. In the winter Kitty and I would stay for a week at a villa Bob rented in Jamaica.

In 1972, many years before we started vacationing with Bob, Richard Nixon had appointed him to a U.S. district-court judgeship on the recommendation of New York's liberal Republican senator Jacob Javits. Bob had wanted to be a judge since leaving the NAACP, and gave up a lucrative partnership in a midsize management-oriented firm to take the appointment. I remember Bob telling me that some of the high-powered attorneys who practiced in the federal courts tried to push him around, and there seemed to be an attitude among certain lawyers that a black judge could know nothing about the mysteries of complex litigation. Whether Bob's belief as to what white lawyers thought was right or wrong, he had no time for anyone who failed to accord him the respect he deserved. Bob ruled his courtroom with an iron hand. No one was exempt from his ire, and even civil rights attorneys complained that he could be harsh. I appeared before him only once. As usual, I had my say. After that, he told me, never again. It was a wise decision.

Over the years Bob wrote some groundbreaking civil rights decisions and suffered his share of reversals from the far more conservative judges on the court of appeals. He has been hard on those accused of certain crimes, especially when the charges involved conduct that had a serious impact on black communities. He has also had a light touch when he thought he could save certain defendants by keeping them out of prison. Always Bob tried to do what he felt was the right thing, caring little for public opinion. The young law clerks who worked for him often tried to follow in his footsteps.

Our relationship was hard to categorize. He started as a mentor, but our connection over time became more like a family relationship. I saw him as a great man capable of warmth, kindness, and humor, but also through the lens of a son—critically—and he was indulgent of that dynamic between us. That we were not father and son, however, made it easier, as did the deep affection Kitty and Bob had for each other.

Our fellow houseguests in Jamaica varied from trip to trip. Sometimes we were with Bob's sons, David and John, and the latter's son, Christopher. Law professor and author Derrick Bell and his wife, Janet Dewart Bell, then the communications and public relations director of New York City's public employees union, District Council 37, were regulars, as was Kenneth Clark, the social psychologist whose studies helped the Supreme Court understand the effects of segregation in *Brown v. Board of Education*. Shirley Williams, whose brother was the *New York Times* literary critic, Anatole Broyard, also visited as did her husband, Franklin, who was a former ambassador to Ghana and a close friend of Bob's from their early NAACP days. Rhoda Karpatkin, who was the executive director of *Consumer Reports* and Bob's dear friend since her late husband worked with him at the NAACP, also visited sporadically, as did Dick Bellman and his artist wife, Bobbie Beck. There were also friends from Bob's bridge club and Rose Ryder, his former neighbor, close friend, and traveling companion.

Whatever the combination, conversations about books, politics, theater, opera, family, and the pleasures of eating and travel were our staple. Humor and poking fun alternated with seriousness.

One year Bob and I walked down the rocky little road from his villa to the nearby Caribbean-hugging tourist hotel. I was wearing my threadbare "Reverse the Arms Race" T-shirt and bathing trunks, and Bob wore a designer shirt and Bermuda shorts. Our destination was the hotel shop, which carried the *New York Times*. The doorman had allowed me unchallenged access the day before; today he intercepted Bob and questioned him about his destination. The guy was black himself, but he had his orders. Faced with Bob's show of authority, the doorman backed off and waved us through.

"Even in Jamaica." Bob shook his head ruefully.

"He just recognized the well-dressed man," I wisecracked.

"I guess that's it." Bob scowled, chuckled, and added, "But just you remember we have a dress code for dinner. And there's no fooling around about that."

Another time we were having a discussion about opera singers, when I made the mistake of mentioning my friend who wrote opera reviews for the *New York Times* and *New York* magazine. Bob frowned, saying, "I don't know about him and his put-downs of Jessye Norman, and for writing all that stuff about Kathleen Battle being difficult to work with." Bob was friends with Norman and thought she was the greatest. Kitty and I thought she was superb, too.

"He's said wonderful things about both of them," I replied. "He just gets a little critical when the prima donnas start thinking too much of themselves. He said cruel things about Beverly Sills when she sang certain roles well past her prime."

"Sills used to call him up and leave irate messages on his answering machine," Kitty added.

"Just because he's your friend," Bob teased, keeping the conversation playful and serious at the same time, "you come to his defense, but you know as well as I do that he sees black singers as being in a different category."

I didn't think Bob was right, but I knew that discussion would go nowhere. I understood Bob's concern, however. It's rare that black people reach the pinnacle of their profession. Once they get there they are all too often shot down or accused of things that whites are suspected of doing all the time. So of course Bob got his back up.

I remember the time in Jamaica we talked about the Republican "Contract with America" rhetoric coming out of Washington, and the O. J. Simpson trial, which had polarized the country. On the former issue we all agreed that America was headed in a frightening direction, and that the Democrats were too spineless to stop it. The OJ trial was more controversial. We got Court TV down there. I remember when the trial was at a standstill because Judge Lance Ito was holding one of his endless hearings. It was all a sideshow. The defense revolved around an allegation of planting evidence by a racist cop, while the prosecution had everything but a videotape of the crime. The whole thing hinged on a predominantly black working-class jury.

After working on the Carter-Artis case, I knew only too well about juror predispositions. We had a tape recording of the detective in charge telling a hesitant key witness that he should finger Rubin and John because "colored people are only out for themselves," and not one of the white working-class jurors thought twice about registering a guilty vote. They didn't seem to care whether the police had planted key evidence.

As it became clear that OJ stood a good chance of getting off because his jury might buy the very true charges of police racism, white Americans became apprehensive. Poll after poll showed that a large majority of blacks believed that OJ was innocent, while a large majority of whites, including me and Bob's other white houseguests, thought he was guilty. Bob was more judicious, wanting to watch the trial unfold.

I hoped the jury verdict would reflect the evidence, but I was guessing Simpson would be acquitted and that whites would ask the same questions Myron and I asked about the Carter-Artis jury: How could they do that? I could hear whites complain about how blacks protected their own. But I wasn't going to be upset. What goes around, comes around, was pretty much how I saw it.

We talked a lot about Johnnie Cochran. I was pretty sure he told the jury "facts" for which he had no proof, all the while daring the judge to stop him. A good criminal defense lawyer has to push hard and attack, but there are limits. A judge can embarrass a lawyer in front of the jury and severely damage the defense. Cochran, however, crossed the line over and over and got away with it. Often that annoyed me, but I had trouble articulating the reason. He was getting away with things I couldn't do. Big-time lawyers with outsize reputations invariably got deference from judges. But black attorneys, no matter how good, rarely got that respect. And civil rights lawyers almost never. I was envious.

Bob was loving every minute. He got a kick out of seeing a powerful black lawyer take control of that courtroom, even if the trial's lethargic pace drove him batty.

Bob liked what Cochran stood for: He was an African American getting major recognition for being handsome, self-assured, highly skilled, and fearless. He was giving his client the strongest possible defense, and he was standing his ground in a white world. He and his office of black attorneys took over the lead role from a big-name white attorney. It was something all African Americans could cheer about in an otherwise fairly bleak landscape.

One evening, during a lull in the dinner conversation, Bob, his voice heavy with resignation, started one of the more serious conversations of that visit: "Whites seem to hate us so much, I don't see how it is ever going to get better," he said.

I remember thinking that Bob didn't feel that way about all whites—not me, Kitty, or Rose, for instance. As he presided at the head of the table, with Kitty next to him in her regular seat, he had to be deeply aware that he shared love and affection with some of the white people breaking bread with him. It was the world of white people he was talking about, who would never let up. For a black person, "they" were always coming at you. For the first time since I'd known him, I wondered if Bob was getting tired of the fight.

I wanted to say it wasn't so, but all I could think of was Derrick Bell's two books *And We Are Not Saved* and *Faces at the Bottom of the Well*. I wondered what Derrick would have said if he had been there. His work presaged Bob's lament. Derrick's argument in a nutshell was that whites will do everything in their power to keep blacks down, and that every possible mainstream solution to racial inequality is doomed to failure because of white resistance. Keep fighting, however, he urged.

Breaking with Bob, Derrick had long ago turned away from integration, at least in the setting of public schools, as a solution to educational inequality. To Derrick blacks would have been better off if *Brown v. Board of Education* had not been decided. Then they would have turned inward to develop and strengthen their communities and create the power to control their own destinies.

As I think about Bob and Derrick, who remained the best of friends, the conversation brings to mind the wider debate in the black community between those who continue to favor integration as the main road to equality, and those who believe blacks should turn inward and strengthen their own institutions. The logic of both sides is clear. In a racist society, the nationalists argue, white America will always keep blacks at bay and leave them with the crumbs, so blacks should go their own way and develop their own communities. To this the integrationists respond that it is in whites' interests to let blacks in the front door. We share the same country, and they cannot be healthy unless we are healthy too. Whites control everything, the integrationists add, and blacks need access. Like Bob, I straddle both sides of the argument, looking for any approaches that may ameliorate the country's racial wounds and their terrible effects on millions of blacks. I also think it's possible that America's racial divide can tear us apart, but not today—and if we are lucky, not tomorrow either.

Looking at Bob in the deepening silence, however, I was acutely aware that the color of my skin protected me from such pain. On both a physical and psychological level, the racism that swirls around me does not threaten my survival. I am motivated by my need for atonement, my empathy for friends like Bob, and my perception that unmitigated, un-evolved tribalism as the driving force of the human condition impels us all toward disaster. I see much of the chaos threatening the world as an ugly extension of the racial grief that scars our lives at home. Time does not seem to heal old enmities. Different groups, no matter the nature of their differences and no matter how long they may live in apparent harmony, in reality are only a split second away from being at one another's throats. You see that in countries all over the world. I think it is the job of gatherings like the one at Bob's table to fight that and try to educate people to think and act differently.

I said as much to Bob when I finally managed to break the silence, concerned that our thoughts might be very far apart—he perhaps believing that the black experience is unique and very different from other forms of oppression, and that I had generalized too much. But Bob acknowledged that I might be right.

"Maybe intermarriage is the solution," I offered.

"It may be," Bob answered without much enthusiasm. Neither of us pursued the thought, perhaps because we both knew that the children of blacks marrying whites would have to adjust to the reality of being forced to work hard to gain acceptance in either world.

A few months later Kitty and I were watching the OJ summations on television at home. The prosecution appeared to have overwhelming evidence of OJ's guilt. To counter the accumulation of incriminating details, the defense had no traditional response—no alibi, no memory problems on the part of witnesses, and no alternate suspect. Instead Cochran went on the attack, alleging that Los Angeles police department (LAPD) investigators intentionally overlooked exculpatory evidence, contaminated other evidence, and that once detectives locked in on a suspect, they would do anything to make their case—whether that entailed planting evidence or lying under oath.

Usually, however, jurors heavily discount claims that police planted evidence or engaged in conspiracies to get a conviction. Even where the police work is shoddy, jurors routinely overlook the defects rather than allow someone they think is a killer to go free.

In the defense of O. J. Simpson, the way to reach the predominantly African American jury was to argue that the LAPD was riddled with racist cops who targeted black people—Detective Mark Fuhrman, who in a tape recording sounded a lot like Vincent DeSimone, being the prime example. "Save us from this racism," Johnnie Cochran preached. "Tell America we will have none of this," he bade the jurors. And in a stretch that made no sense, Cochran compared Detective Fuhrman to Adolf Hitler.

I frowned at Cochran's hyperbole. The Fuhrmans and DeSimones of the world were dangerous, especially to the races and the ethnic groups that they despised, but they needed the power and capacity of willing prosecutors to back them up. As both a Jew and a civil rights lawyer, I had given statements like Cochran's, and Rubin Carter's at his sentencing, a lot of thought. To many Jews it was anathema to liken what blacks face in the United States to what Jews faced in Nazi Germany. I also knew that there were many black intellectuals who heard that as a denial of the reality still faced by the majority of African Americans: choked off by color lines and doomed to lead shortened lives. I also thought of the way Bill Rutherford died at the bottom of the Hampshire House service stairs, and of the more than one million black men "missing" from their communities. Still, in my view, Cochran had done more than enough to raise the consciousness of the black jurors about the police department's racism without opening that wound.

During and after the trial, I also found myself thinking a lot about Christopher Darden, the black assistant district attorney who famously asked OJ to try on the bloody gloves. While that was a stupid move, I was more interested in Darden's decision to join the prosecution. Fuhrman's reputation as a racist must have been well known in police and prosecution circles, and Darden had to know that lead prosecutor Marcia Clark was going to present Fuhrman as a latter-day choirboy.

Ever since my NAACP days I had been angered when African American attorneys joined what had always been all-white defense teams in race cases. In the few prior times where that had happened, the black attorneys had said nothing: Their very presence was the point. They were there for show. Darden, however, had taken an active role in the OJ prosecution. Also, in all my cases in which a black lawyer had appeared, I had no doubt that our side was in the right. Here Darden was prosecuting a man whom I considered guilty. If not for Clark's portrayal of Fuhrman, I could have accepted Darden's presence. But I saw his being there as serving little other purpose than supporting Clark's spin on Fuhrman. It was brave of Darden to defy black sentiment by seeking to convict OJ, and I could see the value of his participation if the prosecution had clean hands. It didn't, though. Exposing police racism to me had a higher value than seeking the conviction of another black man whose life would be wrecked no matter what the jury verdict. On the other hand, who was I, a white man, to lecture a black man on how he should conduct his professional life? Since the settlement of the American colonies, white men had controlled how black men could lead their lives. It was long past time for white men like me to butt out.

It was October 3. In our office lawyers and nonlawyers alike huddled around a tiny television set waiting for the verdict. The phones had stopped ringing. Our whispered antsy comments covered our anxiety as Judge Ito dragged out the final moments. Like white Americans everywhere, we were disappointed at the not guilty verdicts, but most of us had anticipated the outcome, so there was little emotion in the room.

Instead of thinking about OJ I thought about Rubin Carter and John Artis. They were just as innocent as OJ was guilty. Yet a white-dominated jury found Rubin and John guilty beyond a reasonable doubt, while a black-dominated jury found OJ not guilty. The white jury had accepted a bogus racial revenge theory to overcome what should have been obvious reasonable-doubt evidence. By contrast the OJ jury had allowed racial prejudice among police investigators to overcome evidence that should have answered any reasonable-doubt questions. To blacks the Carter-Artis verdicts were business as usual, and the OJ verdict was something to cheer about, as Howard law students did on camera for the evening news. Whites, on the other hand, assumed the correctness of the Carter-Artis verdicts and were frightened by the OJ acquittal. For blacks the OJ acquittal offered the illusion of justice. To whites, blacks were out for their own kind. To me, with few exceptions, everyone favored their own kind, and until we as a nation could even things out, there would be chaos in our hearts and on our streets.

How would I have voted if I had been a black man sitting on the OJ jury? Not guilty.

Don't talk to me about guilt when there's all that blood on the hands of your police, I would have said. Don't ask me to accept that you have treated this or that black man justly when your police and courts treat my people so badly. When your hands are clean, I'll listen to your calls for justice.

As a white man fantasizing about saying these things as a black man, I had to shake my head in sadness. If my fantasy bore any relationship to reality, it meant that we had allowed the chasm between black and white in America to grow so wide that even with our common culture and language, we had come to the point where we processed information in entirely different ways. The saving grace for me, however, was that I started to rethink my disappointment with the verdict as a white man. Why not go all the way? I said to myself. Why not see the not guilty verdict as a righteous vote? Indeed, why not? I asked myself. It is a thought I still have.

On November 6 Kitty and I attended a lecture celebrating Derrick Bell's sixty-fifth birthday. Derrick had become an icon among progressive law students and lawyers. A visiting professor at New York University Law School, he had given up his lofty tenured position at Harvard

Law School a few years earlier over its failure to recruit and grant tenure to a single black female legal academic.

The lecture was at the Schomburg Center for Research in Black Culture on Malcolm X Boulevard in Harlem. Bob Carter was talking to Kitty and a group of friends when Dick Bellman and I joined them. Immediately Bob was on me about a music review written by my friend. The review had treated a newcomer to the Metropolitan Opera, a black soprano, unkindly. With Bob Carter, Kitty and I had seen and liked the soprano, and we had disagreed with the review, as we often did with theatrical reviews. My friend thought her characterization was superficial. When I read the review, I knew it would bother Bob. He would see it as another example of how contemptuously opinion makers treated blacks, whatever their accomplishments. And he would be especially irate because I had touted my friend as being very astute about opera.

Long before going to the lecture, I was tempted to call my friend, but he knew a thousand times more about opera than I, and writing reviews was his job. I was also worried he would hear an accusation that might threaten our relationship. It had happened before when I was representing Tony Maynard. Through Tony's case, I'd become friendly with William Styron. Antiracist to the core, Styron had written *The Confessions of Nat Turner*, a historical novel about the slave insurrection led by Turner three decades before the Civil War. It won a Pulitzer Prize, but some highly regarded black intellectuals were extremely critical of the way Styron described Turner's sexual fantasies about a white woman.

Styron was deeply hurt by the criticism. He asked me to read the book and let him know what I thought. For months I avoided the assignment, hoping his more literary friends would reassure him while I procrastinated. But he kept pressing me to read it, so I finally did. The story and character Bill had developed were terrific, and I was astounded by his ability to write such great dialect for his characters. Had I not read the criticisms, I would never have questioned the motivations Styron assigned to his intelligent, sympathetic Turner. But once alerted, I understood the attack. Styron had created a Turner whose innermost driving forces corresponded to the worst fears of white Southern males. Still I hesitated. It was possible that I was all too ready to accept criticisms from blacks waving their flags of liberation in the face of a white writer. And I was worried about upsetting Styron. It seemed like a sure way to damage a budding friendship. As Bill's prodding continued, I hesitantly sketched out my feelings, trying to be as gentle as I could, and mailed them. To my dismay, Bill wrote me off as a friend. Years later I read and fell in love with *Sophie's Choice*. Though it dealt with anti-Semitism, I found it to be one of the most deeply moving and searching antiracist books I had ever read. By turning to Europe and the Holocaust, Styron seemed to liberate himself from his Southern roots. I meant to write telling him that. But fearing a second rejection, I never took the letter further than the confines of my mind. When Jimmy Baldwin died in 1987, Bill delivered a poignant and insightful eulogy at his funeral. Touched, I wrote him the letter I should have written years earlier, and received a warm response. But time had passed, and our friendship had been irretrievably lost.

Right or wrong, that was the reason I hadn't called my friend about his review. I also hoped Bob would somehow miss it. If I kept on challenging everybody about issues of race, he would be one of my few friends.

By the time I saw Bob at the Schomburg Center, I'd forgotten about the review, so his attack caught me by surprise. I stood sheepishly as he lambasted me. When he was finished, I wandered off to recover. Getting myself together, I went back and told Bob that I disagreed with the review too, but that he should not have taken me to task for something my friend had written. He looked shocked and told me that was not his intent.

But the underlying issue did not go away. I thought of Derrick Bell's books, which contain instructional fable after fable about whites abandoning blacks to their fate when the going gets tough. The most graphic is a story called "The Space Traders," about extraterrestrial visitors that appear in huge ships and demand all the country's blacks in return for desperately needed gold. The political leadership initially resists because blacks are citizens just like whites. After listening to public opinion, however, they agree to the space traders' terms. Derrick's fable makes me think about Germans who died opposing the Holocaust, and about others who remained silent. How does a person make such decisions? I asked myself, and what would I do in similar circumstances? Is life so precious that I would become a passive bystander? I had no answer.

I finally did speak to my friend about his review. The conversation was difficult. He told me that for him it was all about the music, and that he often reviewed black performers in a very positive light. When the call ended, I felt that familiar ache of having caused pain to someone I cared about deeply, and who was no more a racist than I was.

But I also worried about what Bob might feel when I told him that I respected my friend and believed him to be a sensitive, highly intelligent person who was deeply distressed that anything he had written might have been taken to demean African Americans. I trusted, however, that the love Bob and I felt for each other would enable us to bridge the divide of the separate racial worlds that have shaped our lives. I also hoped that my relationship with my friend had not been damaged. No matter what Bob thought, I believed my friend to be caring and egalitarian. If I could not maintain a meaningful relationship with him, I might find myself adrift, uncomprehending as to what it is that I should be asking myself, and isolated in a sea of equally uncomprehending humanity.

23

Black Lives Matter

Curbing police brutality has always been a top priority of the Movement. Back when I first became an NAACP lawyer, the sheriffs and cops in the South were often linked to the Klan. In the North the police were a constant danger faced by African Americans. Whenever blacks ventured out of their ghetto neighborhoods, cops were quick to question their presence. If they talked back, beatings and arrests usually followed. Parents like Bob Carter constantly warned their sons to watch out, be respectful, and never talk back. In the 1960s black anger boiled over, often leading to deaths at the hands of the police as well as mass incarcerations.

In New York City the NAACP advocated a civilian review board that could discipline brutal cops. To that end Bob Carter, with me assisting him, met with then–police commissioner Vincent Broderick in the 1960s to see if they could agree on an appropriate program. Broderick, however, was all talk and no give. Years later the city experimented with a civilian review board, but it had no teeth, as it does not to this day. The police department also had an internal affairs division that could recommend departmental hearings, but police abuse of citizens hardly ever led to discipline.

Over my years in private practice I have handled a few relatively low-level police abuse cases and settled them all without going to trial. On a few occasions I unsuccessfully tried to impress on the attorneys who defended the city and paid my clients out of the municipal budget that their office should work out a protocol with the police department for disciplinary follow-up. Then, in the year 2000, a serious police brutality case came my way.

On February 4, 1999, police officers in a so-called street crimes unit shot down an unarmed African immigrant, Amadou Diallo, as he was about to enter his apartment building in the Bronx. The cops claimed that they thought Diallo was about to draw a gun. Robert Johnson, New York's first black district attorney, indicted the cops for second-degree murder, but the case was transferred to Albany for trial, and the cops were acquitted. That led to angry protests much like those that have recently rocked America in Ferguson, Staten Island, and Baltimore. While the wording on the placards the demonstrators carried then may have been different from the current "Black Lives Matter" banners, they expressed similar sentiments. A day of many disparaging remarks about the police and demonstrations that ranged up and down Manhattan, blocking traffic but causing little or no property damage, ended up at nightfall in a square near New York University, where our soon-to-be client Stacey Patton was an undergraduate. Angered by the taunts, the cops took their revenge. A police commander yelled out a warning to disperse, and the cops immediately attacked. A young black woman, Stacey was not only an excellent student but a mainstay on the NYU women's basketball team, and she was participating in her first demonstration. After she was knocked down, a cop stomped on her leg and crushed it, then charged her with resisting arrest and assault. She was held for hours before being taken to a hospital. Fortunately there were witnesses. I got the charges dismissed and sued the city in federal court.

While I was preparing Stacey's case for trial, disaster struck. On 9/11 two hijacked planes crashed into the Twin Towers, and the city shut down. When the courts reopened weeks later, a few blocks from our closed offices, which were just around the corner from where the World Trade Center had stood, federal marshals in battle gear, with automatic weapons pointed downward, stood guard. With the police considered as heroes—and some certainly were—for their rescue efforts, I viewed a trial as risky business. Luckily the federal judge assigned to the case saw the facts the way we did and prevailed upon the city attorneys to do the right thing. As a result Stacey received a substantial financial settlement to cover her follow-up medical care and have significant funds to carry her through the academic program she envisioned. Today Stacey has her Ph.D. in history, is a published author, and has taught at the university level. But the city attorneys were no more interested in seeing that a brutal police officer was at least subjected to disciplinary proceedings than they had been in lesser cases. My arguments that cops like the one who injured Stacey endangered the entire city, and that their conduct could set off riots leading to untold deaths and destruction of property, were to no avail. The city attorneys and the corporation counsel to whom I addressed a letter were apparently more afraid of the police reaction than some possible uprising.

So here we are, still watching the videos of a Staten Island black man being killed by the police, moaning, "I can't breathe." Other cities exist on the brink of disaster as well, with African Americans fed up with police violence and cops resisting reforms. Yes, police work can be dangerous, like the work of others—our firefighters, construction workers, miners, and many more who face serious injury or death when they ply their trades and jobs. And yes, like all workingmen and -women, they are entitled to respect. But the police have a duty to the citizens. It is their job to protect us, and we as citizens have a duty to see that they perform their duties properly. As James Baldwin warned many years ago, unless we police our police there will be a fire next time.

24

Going Forward

The glue that held my law firm together came apart in 2004. Dick Bell-man had Parkinson's disease, and it was beginning to limit his ability to attract clients. The parks department case began to take up most of my time, affecting the revenue I could generate, so our firm's survival ability was reaching the end of the line.

Needing a new home away from home, I accepted Wayne Outten's offer to join his firm in the capacity of what lawyers call "of counsel," a catchall category that would enable me to devote myself to the parks department case while allowing me to work on firm cases as my time opened up. Dick moved a few blocks away from our office to work at a newly formed organization, called the Anti-Discrimination Center. Later he decamped to the Puerto Rican Legal Defense and Educational Fund. Susan and Miriam planned to continue practicing together.

I was grateful for Wayne's offer. Outten & Golden was a well-respected, growing liberal firm, whose cards read, "Advocates for Working Fairness." Dedicated to employee cases against employers, it was my kind of firm. Moving, however, was something else entirely. I had occupied a spacious corner office. At O&G there were no empty offices, so I spent the better part of two years squeezed into a small windowless former library space next to the pantry. When my desk arrived, it took up almost half the room, leaving space only for my files and two chairs.

At my old firm I had close and caring relationships with Dick, Susan, and Miriam. Dick and I often ate lunch downstairs together, sometimes with Susan and Miriam, sometimes just the two of us. Hardly knowing a soul at O&G, I quickly realized that the environment was different. Most attorneys ate at their desks in order to get their work done and put in the time expected of them. That's not to say that the firm required the humongous hours of the gigantic corporate firms, but it was run on a more highly scheduled basis than my much-freer-form firm. So there I was, after thirty-five years in private practice, camping out in cramped quarters, reminiscent of my early di Suvero days, when there were the four of us in two rooms. Although I did have a reputation among progressive lawyers, I felt I had to prove myself all over again to a whole new crew.

All that history at my old firm slowly became just that—history—and except for my regular lunches with Dick, the camaraderie that had been a staple of my life began to dissolve. For those early O&G years, my lawyer comrades in arms became Jody Yetzer and Cynthia Rollings at the Beldock firm, who, along with Bob Stroup, formed the core of our parks department team. But lunches were rare, and work was always on the agenda.

Cramped or not, I had no complaints. I had my fine family and wonderful Central Park views to make up for being an office shut-in. Every Thanksgiving we celebrated the Macy's parade with friends and family jamming the apartment and packs of children crowding every window or scurrying around as the bands, floats, and the enormous cartoon balloons passed by. Comrades from old cases would come and chat away, and I invited O&G folks as well.

Getting into the swing of things at O&G was made easier because one of the O&G attorneys, Kathleen Peratis, and I had a passing acquaintance. She had been a partner at former U.S. attorney general Ramsey Clark's short-lived firm and was later the top litigator at the ACLU's women's rights project. Kathleen and I had some of the same friendships. We also shared the same intensity. She swore as much as I did, and we quickly became friends. Another soon-to-be O&G partner, Justin Swartz, and I also clicked. A former Chicago ACLU lawyer, he and I had the same hard-knuckled attitude.

Once the parks department case was settled, there was plenty for me at O&G. Except for some individual cases the firm handled on a pro bono basis, our work rarely involved racial discrimination, but O&G aggressively went after the bad guys in many different contexts. Often the defendant was some corporation like Gristede's (Red Apple), where my mother used to buy her groceries, which failed to pay its many low-income black and Latino workers, as well as its white employees, overtime. In another case a restaurant chain's management had siphoned off some of the serving staff's tips. After we settled, forcing management to take its hand out of the cookie jar and pay back what it had taken, Kitty and I frequented one of the chain's fine Italian restaurants, Cafe Fiorello, right across the street from Lincoln Center. Financial firms also caught O&G's attention, as both women and African Americans often received less pay for the same work.

At the NAACP and during most of my prior O&G years, at least until the bills piled up in the parks department case, we could litigate and win major cases with modest expenditures. These days, however, large employment class actions cost hundreds of thousands if not millions of dollars to litigate. In the old days many experts saw participating in civil rights cases as a public service and either volunteered their time or substantially reduced their fees. Nowadays experts want big bucks. So, while the NAACP had no choice but to throw me into the fire as a novice, law firms like O&G—there are only a small handful like it in the entire country—have to be careful in choosing their cases and how they litigate them. For an experienced hand like me, that means a lot of showing, teaching, and reviewing the written work of young associates before it goes out the firm door. That's real enjoyment, transferring skills to a new generation of attorneys who continue the work of progressive lawyering, especially in O&G's supportive and sometimes fun-loving environment.

Luckier still, I have been working for the past five years on what is certainly one of the most important racial discrimination class actions in the entire country, the brainchild of an extraordinarily creative O&G partner, Adam Kline. Our clients are suing the U.S. Department of Commerce for how one of its key constituent units, the Census Bureau, hired approximately one million temporary employees, mainly as enumerators, to conduct short data-collection interviews for the 2010 decennial census. In its hiring process, the bureau had the FBI do a criminal-background check on all the applicants. Census personnel then decided the types of crimes and arrests that would disqualify applicants. The flaws in its system, however, were many. In the first place the FBI records were in terrible shape, as the FBI obtained most of its records from states that often did not update them after an arrest or add the actual disposition of the charge. Second, the Census Bureau developed its own completely arbitrary criteria for whom it should eliminate from the pool of acceptable applicants. To do so it conducted no studies and employed no qualified personnel to decide what crimes were job related, or how much time an applicant should be crime-free before becoming eligible for hire. The results were grim. Beside eliminating some applicants for arrests only as well as for convictions having nothing to do with the enumerator's job, the bureau rejected candidates who had been crime-free for many years after being released from custody. To make matters infinitely worse for the applicants, the bureau sent out about one million letters to the approximately four million applicants with a "hit" on the FBI database, instructing them that they had thirty days to return a certified copy of the final dispositions of whatever crimes were on the database, even though the letter did not list those crimes. For more than 90 percent of the applicants the "thirty-day letter" killed the application.

To Adam, looking at that "system," the outcome was obvious. Blacks and Latinos are arrested at much higher rates than whites. As a result they were disqualified at much higher rates than were whites. Therefore that "system" had a racially disparate impact on blacks and Latinos, in violation of a key section of the 1964 Civil Rights Act and its 1991 amendment. The U.S. Justice Department, however, did not see it that way. With Adam, another O&G partner, Ossai Miazad, and I taking or defending a seemingly endless number of depositions in Washington and New York, writing innumerable briefs, and with each side employing experts to bolster its arguments, we have beaten back the Justice Department's attempts to dismiss our case, but the battle goes on. If we prevail, that could be "the next big thing" in racial discrimination litigation, as legions of private employers apply equally arbitrary and discriminatory means to screen their job applicants. That means we may be able to begin the process of opening up hundreds of thousands of jobs to people of color as well as to whites who also find themselves rejected for work, perhaps for life, based upon something they did, or maybe even didn't do, in their younger years.

It is probably fairly common for people still working in their late seventies to live in the present but think often about the past. Bill Rutherford, of course, is a fixture in my mind, a reminder of what set me on this journey. Bob Carter is also a constant presence, as are attorneys and clients who have been with me in my courtroom battles.

Many years after we lost the Cincinnati school desegregation case, I attended an NAACP LDF celebration honoring Bob. There, I ran into Nathaniel Jones, who had replaced Bob as the NAACP general counsel, before becoming a U.S. Sixth Circuit Court of Appeals judge. He said he had become friendly with Judge Peck, who had been elevated to his court. Judge Jones said that Peck had told him that in all his years as a district-court judge, the only decision that he regretted was the one he rendered in the *Deal v. Cincinnati Board of Education* case.

"You should tell Judge Peck he should go public. It might have some impact," I replied.

I have no idea whether Judge Jones did that, but I do know that Peck never went public. So his one big mistake died with him, and another generation of children has paid the price. If Peck had come clean, in all probability that would have changed nothing. But change, if it is to come, must start somewhere, and Peck's silence was a lost opportunity to start the conversation.

Years later, in 2004, when returning to Indiana for my fiftieth reunion at Culver Military Academy, I called the president of the local Kokomo NAACP branch to find out what had happened to that city's schools. They were all integrated, I was told, all the way from the elementary grades right up through high school, and I received a confirming photo and article in the local newspaper. There, in the front seats of the bus, a black and a white kid were riding next to each other.

The situation in South Bend, only forty miles from Culver, was not so positive. Kitty and I drove to a NAACP education committee meeting chaired by the branch president. While South Bend's schools had been integrated as a result of the Justice Department suit, the NAACP committee members said a Hispanic population was moving into South Bend, and that the school board was calling their children white so that they could put them into schools that, when combined with the black children already there, might make them tip and bring about white flight. I told the assembled group that I would bring their situation to the attention of the Legal Defense Fund. Back at Culver the next day, I tried to persuade the administration to start a tutoring program for the South Bend schools to meet their students' public service requirements. South Bend is too far away, I was told.

I was not surprised. The elite private schools, including Culver, with their patina of integration, and multi-million-dollar fund drives, inhabit a separate world and keep their distance from the problems of educating public school kids, especially the ones that need their help the most. Back in New York City, an LDF colleague told me that recent U.S. Supreme Court decisions foreclosed new school segregation cases.

With the Supreme Court now blocking even voluntary integration, Bob Carter's concern that over time the North and the South, at least when it comes to school segregation, would mirror each other, has become a reality. So it will be up to a new generation of activists to tackle the horrendous problems unequal educational opportunities inflict on African American children and the communities in which they live. But one thing seems obvious to me from the events in both Kokomo and South Bend—that at least in small- and medium-size cities, school integration is both possible and beneficial. And that is reflected in my personal family history as well. My granddaughters in Raleigh, North Carolina, go to well-functioning magnet public schools that offer high-level elementary and secondary education.

As the present century rolled in, I would read from time to time about how longtime prisoners, many on death row, were exonerated. Some of the best work to unravel wrongful convictions has been done by two friends, Peter Neufeld and Barry Scheck, who made their names in the O. J. Simpson case when they cast doubt on the prosecution's DNA evidence. There is, however, plenty of unfinished business involving wrongfully convicted prisoners.

I was in Raleigh when the local newspaper ran an article about a man there who had spent many years in prison for a crime he did not commit. Most people view that as a rare exception. From my experiences, however, I knew the innocent could be convicted even when they had dedicated lawyers. When the defendants were poor, and especially when they were people of color with inexperienced, uncaring lawyers, or those with little or no resources to mount a defense, prevailing in an often prejudiced jurisprudence system was a crapshoot. Although I had not practiced criminal law for many years, I wrote an article for the *Raleigh News and Observer* outlining a way the authorities might try to exonerate some innocent persons prior to trial and avoid them suffering long years of imprisonment or execution. Years later, a former homicide prosecutor, Tim Bakken, wrote a similar article. With both articles in hand, I met with New York Law School's dean, Richard Matasar. We agreed it would be a great idea for the school to hold a symposium on the issue of exonerating the innocent prior to trial, and turn the papers into a law-review issue.

Despite an article by a distinguished law professor estimating that there are thirty thousand innocent persons in prison today, and other articles, including ours, as to what could be done to ameliorate that massive injustice, we have gotten no traction for a demonstration project to test any of the ideas. To me that remains unfinished business.

Equally unfinished is another idea triggered by my many years of work. In America today thousands of attorneys work for federal, state, or local governments, and many are prosecutors. All are public lawyers. But in my practice few have consistently represented the public interest as I would define it. Certainly the public should want to see the innocent exonerated, and just as certainly the public should not want its public agencies, like the New York City Department of Parks and Recreation and the New Jersey Department of Corrections, engaging in systematic racial discrimination. Just as certainly, police departments should discipline cops who treat brutally the citizens they are supposed to protect. Otherwise we will see many more confrontations like those we have recently seen in American cities, and polarizing racial attitudes. Similarly, when a city's corporation counsel settles police brutality cases, invariably they do nothing to see that the offending cop is brought before a disciplinary board. Yet brutal cops threaten the peace of entire cities. And for sure, governments should be helping former convicts to get work rather than creating insurmountable barriers to their employment, as the Census Bureau has done.

To study the problem and teach a law school seminar with me, I enlisted my good friend the law professor Larry Grosberg. Larry thought he could go on the Internet and come up with courses like I was talking about to lighten our workload. Unfortunately he found very little. Larry also researched the profession's legal precepts and cases interpreting those principles, and found very little to distinguish public from private law practice. It goes without saying that private attorneys have a duty of loyalty to their clients that is very firm and very clear. But with regard to the public lawyer, the question arises: Who is the client? For example, when the city's corporation counsel defends a massive racial discrimination case against the parks department, do the public attorneys involved have a duty to the parks commissioner, or the mayor, or to the citizens of the city who pay their salaries when they pay their taxes? Essentially that question is rarely discussed, let alone answered. Instead the public attorneys defend public agencies and do whatever they can to get the case dismissed, no matter how overt the discriminatory conduct. To say the least, new ethical standards for public lawyers are necessary.

The Huntington case Dick and I began thirty-five years ago is also unfinished business. According to Bob Ralph, a mainstay at Housing Help, the nonprofit sponsor of the project's 140 garden apartments and community center, groundbreaking is just around the corner. To get the project this far, Dick and I had to litigate a second federal case against the town of Huntington and New York State's Division of Housing and Community Renewal to secure the project's funding. And Bob Ralph, who is now ninety-one years old, tells me there is still resistance from local residents. Now the fight is over who will live there, with the old guard doing whatever it can to ensure that the applicant pool will include as many whites as possible. As Alabama's former governor in the 1960s, George Wallace, used to say, "Segregation, now and forever." But you only have to look at the Crimson Tide, the University of Alabama's football team, to realize that some things actually do change. My bet is that that will happen in Huntington too. The town may not need football players, but it sure does need low- and middle-income housing for the teachers, firefighters, and service workers who keep it functioning.

Until we die, of course, there will always be unfinished business. Those close to me made it through the first decade of the twenty-first century, but the second has not been so kind. Derrick Bell died in 2011. He was eighty years old.

Although Derrick and I broke bread together from time to time, through no fault of his own he triggered my racial insecurities. I wanted Derrick to see me as an equal but was never confident that he did. I always wanted to close the distance, but I didn't know how. Time and contact helped, but Derrick's death ended the possibility. But there, I've said it. I felt badly for myself as well as for Janet and their family. There is good news, however. Kitty and Janet Bell, who are both extraordinary women, are now bonding and pulling me along. And Janet, who is a civil rights activist herself and received her doctorate last year, was with Derrick every step of the way.

Bob Carter passed away in January 2012 at the ripe old age of ninety-four. Along with his sons, close friends, and Kitty, I regularly visited with him as he slowly declined. We had so many memories together and so much to talk about that race slowly fell away. The memory I treasured most was formed only a few years earlier.

In November 2008, we had an election-night party at his apartment. When the votes were counted and the first network announced that Barack Obama had been elected president of the United States, tears welled up in Bob's eyes.

"I never thought I would live to see this day," he said.

Sitting next to him, I teared up too.

Bob's sons, John and David, did me the honor of asking me to deliver the eulogy at the Riverside Church memorial. Jessye Norman flew from Europe to sing farewell to her dear old friend. It was a grand occasion. I miss Bob, but our relationship was complete.

Dick Bellman passed away on April 18, 2012. He died on the way to work. He was seventy-four. Kitty called to tell me. I choked up when

I heard the news. Dick was like a brother to me. From our first days to-gether at the NAACP, we had worked together seamlessly. I was hon-ored to be one of the speakers at Dick's funeral. I told the gathering what a great civil rights lawyer and what a caring, kind, and principled man he was, and what a force of nature he was in court. I keep a picture of the two of us together in my office and miss him every day.

Speaking of brothers, my relationship with John, the "golden boy" of my childhood, has much improved from the times recounted earlier when the women from the Weather Underground invaded his Bridge-hampton house and I "machine-gunned" his guests. Now married to Bunny Freidus, he has become politically very progressive. John and Bunny have lived for many years in Telluride, Colorado, where he was the mayor and successfully opposed both the local mining and real estate interests. He is involved with the Institute for Policies Studies (IPS), a progressive think tank, whose longtime general counsel I have been. As an expert in tax law, John suggests to the IPS ways to shift the tax bur-den to the financial markets and the rich, and writes op-eds that it dis-tributes to local newspapers.

When I think of John, I often think of Bill Rutherford and how I saw him as my protector. My children did not have a Bill, but for four years they did have a Joyce McKenzie, who fortunately has lived in a better time than Bill did. Best of all, my children don't have to search their memories to conjure up her image. Joyce became a practical nurse and a homeowner. Kitty, Joyce, and I remain close friends, and Janine and Joyce, who lives in Atlanta, talk regularly. Joyce's children live productive lives. Her daughter Pauline's three children have all graduated from elite colleges, and one, Alexis, earned her Ph.D. at Duke and is a noted poet, activist, and scholar.

Rubin Carter was seventy-six when he died in 2014. After his release from prison he moved to Canada and married (and later divorced) Lisa Peters, the leader of the commune that came to his aid. He became a spokesperson for two organizations seeking the release of the wrongfully convicted. Even though President Bill Clinton hailed him as a survivor of a flawed criminal justice system, the president signed antiterrorism legislation including an attached provision that significantly limited the authority of the federal courts, under what has been called the "great writ" of habeas corpus, to review factual findings in state court criminal matters. Under that law Judge Sarokin would not have been able independently to evaluate the facts of Rubin's case, and he would have died in prison. Someday I hope Congress will restore the great writ to its rightful place as a safeguard of liberty. As for John Artis, he moved to Toronto to take care of Rubin as his cancer worsened. John is a stand-up, no-nonsense man, and he has my respect.

Thinking of long-term relationships, I inevitably return to Tony. Half street person, half gentleman dreamer, always wanting to be free but never quite able to free himself from the restraints that this world places on everyone, he presents multiple images to everyone around him and I am sure to himself as well.

Tony and I resumed our relationship shortly after a team of National Lawyers Guild attorneys, led by the indomitable Liz Fink, and including my old partner and friend Dan Meyers, settled a twenty-five-year struggle in the federal courts to get some compensation for the killed and wounded "brothers" who were shot and beaten on that September day in the Attica yard. Tony testified about the wounds and beating he received and was awarded thirty thousand dollars out of the eight-million-dollar fund. Along with what Tony received from the Baldwin book deal and his wrongful conviction case, that money soon evaporated and Tony was again in need of financial help. Why I have continued to help support him remains an unresolved question of this memoir. I can trace my doing so back to Bill Rutherford and my inability to come to his rescue. But there must be something more to it than that.

Tony's travails have never stopped. He has been arrested for driving while black in Maryland. (Cops stop black drivers constantly, search their cars, and arrest them, for whatever they find.) He has been evicted from a Bay of Biscayne beach in Florida where he had wintered in the open air. He has tried to enter Honduras in his jeep without paying whatever fees, taxes, and bribes the local authorities demanded, prompting me to rescue him after receiving a call from an assistant United States consul assigned to that region. Innumerable times repair shops have called seeking money to fix his jeep. A Pennsylvania cop called to tell me he would have to evict Tony from a Walmart parking lot, where his jeep had been towed after breaking down. Most recently he had been arrested for criminal trespass for shopping while black at an auto parts shop. (Storekeepers are quick to accuse black customers of trying to steal.) Those charges have been dismissed, but Tony spent the night in jail before going to court.

Recently, when Tony visited me in my office, still rail straight and strong at seventy-nine, he gave me his business card listing himself as "Djata Samod, Holistic Healer and Spiritual Advisor." Perhaps that may be part of the answer: Tony, by his very presence, may have been healing me. I told him he would turn eighty next year and could not continue to live outside forever, especially up here in the North. I suggested he talk to his sister. But Tony said, "I'm a Maynard, and the Maynards come from Nevis, and I will go there and be welcome." "Good idea," I said.

Then we entered into one of our few conversations about our lives. Tony said, "My passion before that happened to me was to be an actor. After I was released my passion was to always be free, to live free without any restraints, and that is what I have done." Then he said, "And your passion has been to set people free. We have both lived our passion."

Perhaps there was some truth to that. My privileged lifestyle locks me in just as Tony believes that our forty-five-year relationship, with all its twists and turns, places an obligation on me to come to his aid so that he may escape from the reality that living places on all but a privileged few and live out his life just as he wants, complete with the hardships and beauty of forever being a wanderer.

But, despite the brutal winter of 2014–2015, Tony was not ready to retreat to Nevis. Instead he wintered in Florida again and returned to New York in the spring, taking up his old "residence" under the Verrazano Bridge connecting Staten Island to Brooklyn. He had just come from Baltimore, where he had spent a week with his sister, Valerie. Tony told me she had just finished renovating her studio. "It's magnificent," he said. "She has five houses. Her artwork is all over the city. You must come down to Baltimore to see her." I told Tony I would do that, as he left my office after having almost hugged the breath out of me.

Thinking about Tony after he left, my irritation at the role he assigned to me in our mutual lives melted away. His passion about Valarie's accomplishments was real. And perhaps there was a hidden message there. If he could care about her, he could care about me. Sure, he is vain and self-absorbed. But so are all of us, and the little help I have given him was paltry compared to what my white world had taken away. White guilt, lingering there in the corner of my mind? Perhaps. But so what. A little white guilt never hurt anyone. As for what Tony had said my passion was when we were last together, I had never defined it. There are way too many parts.

Would I never have changed a day in my life, as Kitty likes to say? Not if that meant changing how I lived my life. But I sure could have done without the Tony Maynard and Hurricane Carter–John Artis verdicts, suffering the losses of some of my other cases, and being fired for writing "Nine Men in Black Who Think White." Then again, Kitty would certainly have wished away her little brother's tragic death. But that is not what she meant. As Kitty puts it, "I would not have changed a day of my life if that meant being other than *who* I am now." I agree.

Never changing a day of my life means having been born into the Warner family. Having drifted away from those roots, I decided while visiting the Muldoon-Duffy family in West Covina, California, not too long ago to take up an offer from John Rogovin, a good friend of my son Patrick. John, who had just become the general counsel of Warner Bros., invited Kitty and me to visit the studio in Burbank. We drove there one chilly day. The place was just as I remembered it more than sixty-five years ago. The water tower with the company's logo, the low-slung executives' offices along a well-manicured driveway, the imposing sound studios, the back lots with Western towns, New York City brownstones, and even a little jungle—it was all there. Kitty and I also visited the Warner museum, filled with costumes and photographs. There was Doris Day. I have a picture of us together when I was eleven years old.

"What a great thing to do for a day," I said to Kitty.

Thinking now of my reaction to visiting the Burbank studios, I detect a little of that "look at me" satisfaction in the choices I have made. Then my mind swivels to other Warner grandchildren. There is my brother, of course, who also went his own way but maintained some connection to the Warner family, as he was Major's lawyer and trustee for some of the other Warner children. Then there was Warner LeRoy, who became one of New York City's most illustrious restaurateurs. Finally I think of Warner's sister, Linda LeRoy Janklow. Two years ago Kitty and I attended a benefit dinner for Arts Connection, an organization Linda established, whose moving force she has been for many years. Reading the program describing Arts Connection, listening to Linda make her presentation, as well as the students and teachers who accompanied her, I knew that her efforts were critical to the survival of art education in New York City's public schools. Going home, I thought there was more than one way for a Warner grandchild to contribute to the well-being of our society. That made me feel better about my roots.

Bob Carter had no problem with my Warner connection, nor did he have any problem with class privileges. Years ago, shortly before he became a judge, his wife, Gloria, died, struck down by a rare neurological disease. Gloria had once said about Bob during a political discussion, "He's just a race man. That's all he is." Bob had replied, "That's right. I'm just a race man." Obviously, however, he was much more. While he focused on issues that denied equality to African Americans and marginalized their lives and had a well-tuned ear for racial insults, Bob was a strong advocate of equal opportunity for all people, whatever their race, nationality, or gender. That said, Bob liked the good life. He moved down to my Central Park neighborhood. He traveled the world, loved fine restaurants, the opera, and the theater. He abandoned Brooks Brothers for a finer men's clothing store. And of course he enjoyed a fine villa in the Caribbean. Sure, he was a liberal Democrat, but so were FDR, the Kennedys, and untold liberal millionaires. Bob was certainly entitled to that good life, much more so than I, who rode the wave of family privilege, and stayed afloat to enjoy the pleasures of this life.

I have written in this memoir that I loved Bob and that I am certain I occupied a special place in his heart. Following Bob's example, I have tried to live up to his faith in me as I attempted to honor the memory of Bill Rutherford. Never let the possibility of defeat deter you, was Bob's unspoken motto. Always see racism for what it is, and never ignore it. But Bob would also let me know, with a twinkle in his eyes: By all means enjoy your life.

Acknowledgments

Without Beau Friedlander, I would still be struggling to write this book. A few years ago, I gave Beau what I thought was a viable 650-page manuscript filled with many family- and work-related stories. Beau crafted a framework and a focus to make these stories come alive, have meaning, and present a lifetime's journey. Then the two of us worked, sometimes alone and sometimes together, to create the book you see. Beau is a fine editor, writer, and creative thinker. It was a pleasure working with him.

Along the way, many others offered suggestions and encouragement. The suggestions of New York University professor Pamela Newkirk focused me on the need to use my work to explore my feelings on the deepest possible level. University of South Carolina professor Patricia Sullivan encouraged me to discuss in depth my efforts working first for NAACP general counsel Robert L. Carter and then with my partner Richard Bellman and many others to bring civil rights litigation to the North. Marc Raskin and John Cavanagh of the Institute for Policy Studies also read manuscript drafts and urged me on. My wife, Kitty, spent many long hours reviewing and critiquing drafts, and our children, Janine (and her husband Peder Zane), Brian, and Patrick also helped me shape this book.

I would also like to thank my publisher, Thomas Dunne, for taking a chance on an unknown author and this book, and his excellent staff— especially executive editor Laurie Chittenden, whose fine editorial eye was invaluable, and associate editor Melanie Fried. I would also like to thank Sue Llewellyn for her fine line editing, and Diane Fisher, who fashioned the final manuscript out of the drafts and handwritten corrections I handed her as our deadline stared me in the face.

Finally, the story of waging the struggle in the courts for justice in the North as well as in the South is the story of many committed lawyers working toward a common goal. Some of these attorneys are named in this book and others are not. But all should be remembered, as should the organizations that support and guide their efforts. In my work I would like to thank the National Association for the Advancement of Colored People. Yes, it fired me in 1968 but through my present law firm, Outten & Golden, I am part of a legal team representing the NAACP in New York City, the NAACP Legal Defense and Education Fund, the National Lawyers Guild, the New York City chapter of the American Civil Liberties Union, the Center for Constitutional Rights, Latino Justice and the Puerto Rican Legal Defense and Education Fund, and the Lawyers Committee for Civil Rights Under Law. All will be needed in the future as well as a new generation of civil rights lawyers.

Index